SCOTTISH CLANS & TARTANS

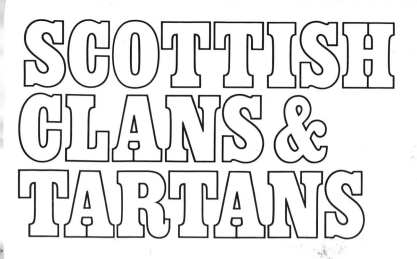

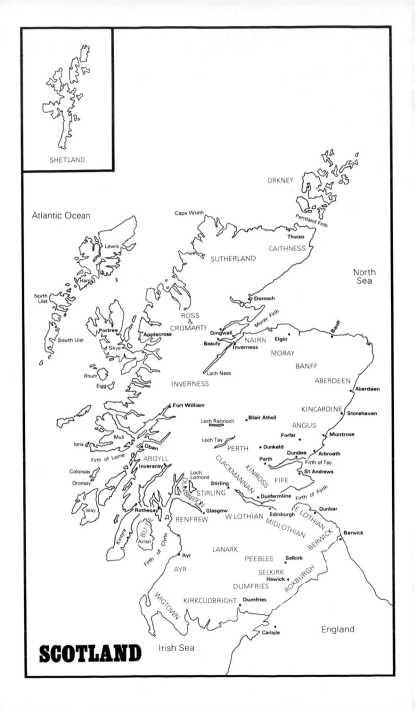

SHETLAND

ORKNEY

Atlantic Ocean

Cape Wrath

Pentland Firth

Thurso

CAITHNESS

North Sea

Lewis

SUTHERLAND

Harris

North Uist

Dornoch

ROSS & CROMARTY

Moray Firth

Banff

South Uist

Portree

Applecross

Dingwall

Skye

Beauly

NAIRN

Elgin

Inverness

MORAY

Rhum

BANFF

Eigg

INVERNESS

Loch Ness

ABERDEEN

Aberdeen

Fort William

KINCARDINE

Stonehaven

Loch Rannoch

Blair Atholl

Mull

Loch Tay

ANGUS

Forfar

Montrose

Iona

Oban

PERTH

Dunkeld

Dundee

Arbroath

Firth of Lorne

ARGYLL

Perth

Firth of Tay

Colonsay

Inveraray

CLACKMANNAN

St Andrews

Oronsay

Loch Lomond

KINROSS

FIFE

DUNBARTON

Stirling

STIRLING

Dunfermline

Firth of Forth

Islay

Rothesay

Glasgow

Edinburgh

Dunbar

BUTE

RENFREW

W LOTHIAN

E LOTHIAN

Kintyre

Arran

MIDLOTHIAN

Berwick

Firth of Clyde

Ayr

LANARK

PEEBLES

Selkirk

BERWICK

AYR

SELKIRK

Hawick

ROXBURGH

WIGTOWN

DUMFRIES

KIRKCUDBRIGHT

Dumfries

England

SCOTLAND

Carlisle

Irish Sea

SCOTTISH CLANS & TARTANS

Ian Grimble Ph.D., F.R.Hist.S.

LOMOND BOOKS

In memory of
Geordie Hamish
1894 – 1966

George, son of Donald son of George son of James Mackay, all of
whom lived at Invernaver in Sutherland, where he died. his deep
wisdom, his wit, his princely manners and his philosophy of life
will never be forgotten.

First published in 1973 by Hamlyn, a division of
Octopus Publishing Group Ltd.

This edition published in 1993 for Lomond Books
by Bounty Books, a division of
Octopus Publishing Group Ltd.,
2–4 Heron Quays, London E14 4JP

Reprinted 1993, 1995, 1997, 1999, 2002, 2004

This edition published exclusively for Lomond Books

ISBN 0 947782 28 1

A CIP catalogue record for this book is available at the
British Library

Printed in Hong kong

Contents

Introduction

The origins of Scotland's clans and of their distinctive dress are wrapped in controversy. Yet their story can be traced back with certainty to the middle of the 5th century, and to Ireland where the Scots then lived. Here the earliest historical High King was known as Niall *Noígiallach* (of the Nine Hostages), whose descendants of the O'Neill dynasty expanded northwards into Ulster. As a result Fergus *Mór* of the little kingdom of Dalriada moved his seat of government from northern Ireland, and crossed the sea to found a new Dalriada for his Scots in the land that now bears their name. In 563 a prince of the house of O'Neill called *Colum Cille* (Dove of the Church) joined them there, and is remembered today as Saint Columba. A century later the Scots were organised in three principal kindreds from Ardnamurchan in the north to Kintyre in the south: the kindreds of Lorne, Angus and Gabrán.

In the course of time these kindreds, and the dynasties of the Celtic church, proliferated into the clans of mediaeval record. To the north and west of them lived the Picts, to the west and south the Britons, while their first serious encounter with Germanic peoples occurred early in the 9th century when the Viking long-ships appeared. The Scots held their own against all these peoples. Their Gaelic tongue replaced Pictish throughout the Highlands; it replaced the Welsh tongue in large areas of south-western Scotland; it drove the Norse language from every island in the Hebrides. And when the Gaels were in the death-throes of their final struggle against another Germanic people, the English-speakers of the south, they gained their last and most spectacular victory. After every attempt had been made to destroy their ancient clan organisation and their distinctive dress, these were adopted as the proper emblems of all Scots throughout the world.

The most distinctive garment which the Scots brought with them from Ireland, and which had probably been worn in the reign of Niall, is called in Gaelic *Léine*. It was a form of shirt which men wore of a length that ended a little above the knee. Probably it was generally made of linen, and although the earliest references describe it simply as light-coloured, it was probably of the yellow shade which led to the English description of it as a saffron shirt. There are ample descriptions of this garment throughout the 16th century, of which that of a French visitor in 1556 is typical: 'They wear no clothes except their dyed shirts and light woollen coverings of several colours, *'certaines couvertures légères faites de laine de plusieurs couleurs.'* It was at about the same time that a cleric in the north of Scotland commented on this spartan attire in a letter to Henry VIII. 'We of all people can tolerate, suffer and away best with cold, for both summer and winter (except when the frost is most vehement), going always bare-legged and bare-footed.'

There is no evidence that the Scottish Gaels continued the Irish

6

practice of marking the *léine* with stripes to indicate the rank of the wearer. A High King wore seven stripes, one of them purple. The *Ollamh* (chief man of learning) wore six, a striking reminder of the importance attached to scholarship. But in the 17th century the shirt gradually went out of use in Scotland, while the 'coverings of several colours' grew in size and significance. At the battle of Kilsyth in 1645 Montrose instructed his soldiers to put away their plaids and knot the ends of their shirts between their legs. But many of his men actually came from Ireland, while others from the west had perhaps not been affected by the ruin of the Irish linen export trade that resulted from the Elizabethan conquest.

Meanwhile wool, a commodity that had been rare in the Highlands, was now becoming available to all. And so the rug grew into the ample plaid which a Highlander could pleat round his waist in many folds, draw over his head when it rained, and roll himself up in to sleep at night. It expanded in fact into a garment measuring five feet in width, and between twelve and fifteen feet in length. The belted plaid took the place of the *léine* as a covering for the lower half of the body. This had been long enough for the men of Montrose to be able to knot the ends between their legs for the sake of decency in 1645. The earliest portraits of men wearing the belted plaid show its apron reaching to about the same length — almost to the knee. Yet there is evidence that it by no means always did so. When William Sacheverell was appointed in 1688 to recover stores from the sunken Armada ship in Tobermory bay, he observed that a minimum of the plaid was being worn below the belt. 'It is loose and flowing, like the mantles our painters give their heroes. Their thighs are bare, with brawny muscles. Nature has drawn all her strokes bold and masterly; what is covered is only adapted to necessity . . . What should be concealed is hid with a large shot-pouch.' This helps to explain why the logical French called the *sporan*, which is simply the Gaelic for a purse, a *cache-sexe*.

In about 1730 another Englishman, an official of the Forfeited Estates Commission of the name of Burt, wrote comments on the way this dress was worn which confirm and amplify those of Sacheverell. 'A small part of the plaid, which is not so large as the former, is set in folds and girt round the waist to make of it a short petticoat that reaches half way down the thigh, and the rest is brought over the shoulders, and then fastened before, below the neck.' He adds later: 'The stocking rises no higher than the thick of the calf, and from the middle of the thigh to the middle of the leg is a naked space . . . and for the most part they wear the petticoat so very short, that in a windy day, going up a hill, or stooping, the indecency of it is plainly discovered.'

By this time the patterns woven into the plaids had already become elaborated into what are today called tartans. The original French word *tartaine* had no reference to design or colour, but defined a type of material. But it was already acquiring its new association by 1538, when it was used in the Lord High Treasurer's accounts. James IV had abolished the Lordship of the Isles, and his son James V was continuing his aggressive policy towards Gaelic Scotland in an attempt to bring it at last within the effective jurisdiction of the Crown. James IV had learnt the Gaelic language: and the accounts show that James V adopted a form of Highland dress, a short Highland jacket of velvet, tartan trews, and the long shirt. 'Heland tertane to be hoiss' evidently refers to the kind of tight trousers or hose of which one actual example survives from before the Forty-Five, besides numerous portraits in which they are depicted.

By 1730 Burt noticed: 'Few besides gentlemen wear the *trowze*, that is, the breeches and stockings all of one piece and drawn on together; over this habit they wear a plaid, which is usually three yards long and two breadths wide, and the whole garb is made of chequered tartain.' But there is no mention of a plaid in the 1538 accounts when James V adopted the dress of a Highland gentleman.

There is increasing reference during this century, however, to the coloured mantle noted by Beaugué the Frenchman in 1556. In his Latin history published in Rome in 1578 Bishop Lesley wrote: 'All, both nobles and common people, wore mantles of one sort (except that the nobles preferred those of several colours)'. Writing in his own incomparable Latin, George Buchanan, who possessed a Highlander's knowledge, commented in 1581: 'They delight in variegated garments, especially stripes, and their favourite colours are purple and blue. Their ancestors wore plaids of many colours, and numbers still retain this custom but the majority now in their dress prefer a dark brown.' It is a pity that the use of the word plaid depends upon James Aikman's translation of 1827, rather than the direct testimony of Buchanan.

The learned Robert Gordon of Straloch described the dress of Highlanders in 1594. They were still wearing the saffron linen shirt, but he described it as short. 'In the sharp winter the Highland men wear close trowzes which cover the thighs, legs and feet.' The summer saw the emergence of Highland dress as we know it today. 'Their uppermost garment is a loose cloak of several ells, striped and party-coloured, which they gird breadth-wise with a leather belt, so as it scarce covers the knees.' The proto-kilt and the proto-tartan appear to have evolved at roughly the same moment.

They had done so at about the time when most of the clans had assumed their final identifications and alignments. The bagpipe and the Gaelic language were about to give unprecedented expression to clan loyalties, triumphs and disasters. What part, if any, did those stripes and party-colours play as symbols of a clan spirit? If they had signified anything in 1411, Lachlann *Mór* Mac Mhuirich would have exploited the fact in his incitement to battle at Harlaw. Yet between that date and this the actual sett of a tartan has developed something of the mystique of the Colour of a regiment, and the question is, just when and how it did so.

Pride in the dress itself is an entirely different matter. A mediaeval knight was doubtless proud of his horse and arms. But his precise coat-of-arms was in the first place a form of military identification, as the tartan had not yet become by the time of the last, decisive clan conflict, the battle of Culloden. By 1594, indeed, Lughaidh O'Clery distinguished Hebrideans even from their nearest kinsmen the Irish by their dress. 'They were recognised among the Irish soldiers by the distinction of their arms and clothing, their habits and language, for their exterior dress was mottled cloaks of many colours.' The distinction was lost upon foreigners when Mackay's regiment fought in the Thirty Years' War. Five soldiers were depicted in 1631, wearing identical tartan, though they carry the belted plaid in various ways and one has adopted tartan pantaloons. The news-sheet calls them Irish, as English-speakers called them likewise in their own country by this time. If they felt any loyalty to their uniform tartan, Gaelic literature is silent on the subject, and so is the unique record of their services which was published in 1637.

John Taylor the 'water poet' paid a visit to Braemar in 1618 and described the Highlanders 'with a plaid about their shoulders, which is a mantle of divers colours.' But it was the dress itself, rather than these colours, that was the object of pride. 'As for their attire, any man of whatsoever degree that comes among them must not disdain to wear it; for if they do then they will disdain to hunt.' A hundred years later Burt remarked the same. 'The whole people are fond and tenacious of the Highland clothing, as you may believe by what is here to follow.' He then describes a woman who reprimanded a Highlander for wearing Lowland costume.

By this time there is evidence of the standardisation of setts. But it appears that a particular pattern had become common to a particular locality, and was only associated with a clan because different clans predominated in each district. Martin Martin testified in 1703 to the development of the weaver's skill. 'The *Plad* wore only by the men, is made of fine wool, the thread as fine as can be made of that kind; it consists of divers colours, and there is a great deal of ingenuity required in sorting the colours, so as to be agreeable to the nicest fancy. For this reason the women are at great pains, first to give an exact pattern of the *Plade* upon a piece of wood, having the number of every thread of the stripe on it.' Alas, not a single sett stick has survived the proscription of Highland dress after the Forty-Five. 'Every isle differs from each other in their fancy of making *Plaids*, as to the stripes in breadth and colours. This humour is as different through the mainland of the Highlands in so far that they who have seen those places is able, at the first view of a man's *Plaid*, to guess the place of his residence.'

Although nobody remarked on this before Martin in 1703, it could by then have been true for a very long time. This highly developed weaving craft of the women of the Highlands could not have been introduced suddenly in a thousand scattered homes. It might have been true when O'Clery wrote his observations in Irish Gaelic in 1594, although he did not allude to it. From 1587 the annual rent to the Crown from Islay consisted of sixty ells of black, white and green cloth. The lands from which this tribute was raised were occupied during almost the entire period in which it was paid by the Macleans, and to this day the tartan now called Hunting Maclean is of precisely those colours.

On the other hand the step taken by Sir Ludovic Grant of Grant, between the date of Martin's account and the 1715 rebellion, appears to offer contrasting evidence. He ordered that all his tenants should provide themselves with Highland dress made of red and green tartan 'set broad-springed'. These colours predominate in the modern Grant tartan, but it was described again as 'red and green dyce', which sounds closer to the sett ordained by Sir Iain Moncreiffe of that Ilk for his name. Anyway, nearly a dozen family portraits of the time of Sir Ludovic Grant's son attest that his attempt at standardisation had not been supported even by his own family.

Before the Forty-Five and the proscription of Highland dress, it had undergone a final transformation. In 1743 a set of six engravings was made of soldiers of the Black Watch, showing how they wore the belted plaid in the traditional manner. But in about 1730 an Englishman called Thomas Rawlinson conducted iron smelting in Glengarry. He wore Highland dress himself, as the water poet had once recommended, and he noticed the inconvenience of being unable to remove the upper half when it had become drenched by rain, without being stripped of the lower half also. He accordingly divided the garment into two halves, which also enabled him to tailor the lower into the permanently pleated kilt. Iain MacDonell, who had succeeded his father as Chief of Glengarry in 1720, adopted the same dress and he was soon followed by others. The proposition that it was an Englishman who invented the kilt has been too much for many Scotsmen to swallow, but the part which Rawlinson played is sufficiently well attested. Anyway, he did not invent the kilt. He merely noticed a convenient improvement that could be made, as foreigners are so apt to do in any society.

It was called the *féileadh beag* (little plaid) to distinguish it from the entire *féileadh bhreacain* (plaid of tartan). *Breacan* is Gaelic for party-coloured cloth, and by the time its use was forbidden it had become the rallying symbol in an outburst of indignation. Alasdair MacDonald, greatest of 18th-century Gaelic bards, composed his famous eulogy on the *Breacan Uallach*, the gallant tartan. He was a Jacobite, but Rob Donn Mackay in the Hanoverian Reay country expressed no less indignation over the abolition of the *Breacan*. The ground was prepared for a wave of enthusiasm once the ban was lifted, which was to give resounding celebrity to the achievement of generations of anonymous Highland women. The intricate designs which they had evolved on simple hand-looms, to give colour as well as warmth to life in a chilly land, were adopted and developed by the Lowland Scots, manufactured by machinery, and raised to the status of their country's most colourful emblems. Whatever doubt there may be about the earlier focus of enthusiasm, it had now shifted decisively from *Féileadh* to *Breacan*. *Féileadh* is Gaelic for Folded, and thus has the same meaning as Kilt, which means Quilted. But *Breacan* stands for the actual setts, which were now recovered where possible from the days before the proscription, and newly designed for surnames that had never been associated with a tartan before.

Sir Walter Scott believed that this enthusiasm had begun in the Lowlands as early as 1707, when hatred for the Union with England expressed itself in the first blush of tartan there. Obviously his own poetry and novels played a powerful part in extending the vogue, and the state visit of George IV in 1822 increased the prestige of a Highland Chiefship in fashionable society. Some exceedingly odd ones have been invented since then, though not odder than the notion that Chiefs are the fount of clan tartans. For this the unsuccessful experiment of the Grant Chief provides little authority. More books like the present one have established clan tartans than any chief: and while Queen Victoria ordained a Johore tartan, such essentially Highland clan names as Currie and MacCrimmon have simply been overlooked. It is the same in the Lowlands, where tartans have been distributed since the 19th century. The Turnbulls were as unruly a border clan as the Armstrongs yet they possess no tartan. The lack of any authority such as that of the Lord Lyon in matters of heraldry has contributed to this.

But this merely helps to emphasize the strength of the emotion which seized upon the symbol of the tartan to express a sense of kinship which has lasted in Scotland ever since the kindreds of the earliest Scots of Dalriada blossomed into clans.

Note on Scottish Names

There is no means of standardising names in a country in which so many were first recorded in a language of such entirely different roots as English and Gaelic possess. Iain and John are interchangeable, and so are Alasdair and Alexander, and many others. There are several examples of a handful of names in bowdlerised English which could derive from several quite different Gaelic originals. It is known, however, that Beaton and MacBeth (and some other English forms) all derive from *Mac Bheatha*. In this case the name Beaton has been selected; and Currie and Thomson have been used in similar circumstances.

After the word *Mac* (Son) a capital letter has generally been used. But *Mac Aoidh* has been anglicised as Mackay, and *Mac an Toisich* as Mackintosh or Macintosh. In such cases it would obviously be ridiculous to make a capital of a letter that ought not to be there at all. Often the anglicised Irish forms are nearer to the Gaelic original than the Scottish ones: such as Magee for Mackay, and Behan for Bain. But the forms predominant in Scotland have naturally been preferred.

Abercromby

Today Abercrombie remains a parish in Fife. William of Abercrombie did homage for his lands there in 1296 and is thus the earliest known progenitor of the Abercrombies of that Ilk, who died out in the senior stem in the 17th century. They are now represented by the Abercrombies of Birkenbog in Banffshire, who became baronets in 1636.

The Abercrombies have a distinctive religious record. Soon after the Catholic Church had been abolished in Scotland by Act of Parliament in 1560, John Abercromby, a Benedictine monk and author, was executed for his attacks upon the heresies of reformed doctrine. He was the contemporary of Robert Abercromby (1534—1613), a Jesuit of the Scottish mission who was alleged to have converted Queen Anne of Denmark, wife of James VI, before her death. He suffered imprisonment once, but when £10,000 was later offered for his capture he succeeded in escaping, to die abroad. David Abercromby followed in the footsteps of these two men when he went to Douai to study, and became a Jesuit. He returned to Scotland to defend his faith against Protestantism, only to become converted to it. His celebrated *volte face* was first published in 1682 and reprinted in 1686 under the title *Protestancy Proved Safer than Popery*. As the Catholic King James VII had just inherited the crown it is evident that Abercromby was concerned exclusively with spiritual safety, and that he was no Vicar of Bray. At the same time lived Patrick Abercromby (1656–?1715) of the house of Birkenbog, who remained a Catholic, wrote historical works, and also became physician to James VII.

But the reformed doctrines had already penetrated Birkenbog itself. Alexander, the 1st Baronet, became a devout Covenanter, so that when Montrose undertook to restore the authority of Charles I in Scotland, he once took the punitive step of quartering his troops on Birkenbog.

In the military field the greatest name is that of Sir Ralph Abercromby (1734–1801), the general under whom Wellington learnt his first lessons in the art of war during the dreadful winter retreat from Europe in 1795, at the outset of the Napoleonic wars. Abercromby was then considered to be his country's greatest general, and he shares with that other Scot, Sir John Moore, the chief credit for reforming the army which won Wellington his victories. In 1797 he was sent to Ireland, where he instantly set out to curb the English and Scottish militia forces which were committing such atrocities against the Irish. But the magnates of Dublin Castle soon secured his removal, and so he returned to active service abroad. He died from wounds received in Egypt in 1801.

He left a remarkable family. His eldest son George became Lord Abercromby; his second son, General Sir John Abercromby (1772–1817), served in India when his compatriot Gilbert Elliot, Earl of Minto, was Governor-General there. Another of his sons was a soldier also, while James became Speaker of the House of Commons and was raised to the peerage as Lord Dunfermline.

Prominent among those who used the alternative spelling of this name was John Abercrombie (1780–1844), son of a clergyman of Aberdeen. By the time he was born, Scottish medicine and medical education led the way in Europe: and to them he contributed his published researches into diseases of the brain, the spinal cord and the abdomen. He had been anticipated by Patrick and David Abercromby, who both practised as physicians in the 17th century. The latter's *Nova Medicinae Praxis* was sufficiently esteemed to be reprinted in Paris in 1740.

Anderson

Anderson and MacAndrew appear to mean simply Son of Andrew, but it is contended that even in its English form it may denote a servant of Scotland's patron saint. This is certainly the meaning of the Gaelic form of the name Gillanders, Servant of Andrew. It seems likely that Andersons are of diverse stock, however their names are spelt. Although arms were granted to an Anderson of that Ilk in the 16th century, there is in fact no place from which the name can derive.

However, it rests on an extremely solid foundation of intellectual achievement, which first received European recognition when Alexander Anderson published his works on geometry and algebra at Paris between 1612 and 1619. He was born in Aberdeen, and his cousin David Anderson of Finshaugh was more locally celebrated for his mathematical skill. He earned the nick-name of Davie-Do-a'-Things, and his most famous achievement was to remove a large rock that had obstructed the entrance to Aberdeen harbour. The family talent passed through a daughter to his grandson James Gregory, the inventor of the reflecting telescope.

Adam Anderson, born in about 1692, was appointed one of the trustees for establishing the colony of Georgia, under the charter granted to General Oglethorpe in 1732. Many Scotsmen emigrated there, to build and hold its fort of St Andrews against Spanish attack. But Anderson's contribution was a scientific study of the *Historical and Chronological Deduction of the Origin of Commerce, from the earliest accounts to the present time; containing a history of the large commercial interests of the British Empire.* It was published in 1765, shortly before his death, and brought up to date in a later edition by David Macpherson. Among Adam's contemporaries was James Anderson (1662–1728), the antiquarian born in Edinburgh to a Calvinist minister. He obtained grants from Parliament for the publication of facsimiles of Scottish charters, seals and coins, and transcribed and edited original historical documents for publication. After his death, his work was continued by Thomas Ruddiman.

A later generation included James Anderson (1739–1808), son of a farmer at Hermiston in Mid-Lothian, a writer on agricultural themes of powerful intelligence. In 1785 appeared his *Account of the Present State of the Hebrides and Western Coasts of Scotland,* while the entry he wrote on 'Monsoon' for the first edition of the *Encyclopedia Britannica* in 1773 accurately predicted discoveries made by Captain Cook before he had returned from his first voyage to announce them. He was well matched by John Anderson (1726–1796), born at Roseneath in Dunbartonshire, who became Professor of Natural Philosophy at Glasgow University. He invented a method of diminishing the recoil in a gun, and when the British government ignored it, he took it to Paris in 1791, where it was accepted with gratitude by the National Convention. So the Professor was present to witness the return from Varennes of the unfortunate King Louis XVI. His *Institutes of Physics* went through five editions during his lifetime and at his death he bequeathed all his possessions to found Anderson's University, where non-academic classes might be held.

Meanwhile, at Carnwath in Lanarkshire, Robert Anderson, the biographer of Smollett and Johnson, was born in 1750: and in 1805, William Anderson, the minor poet and author of *The Scottish Nation.* His name has been given greater distinction since by the Rev. William James Anderson, late editor of *The Innes Review,* Librarian of Blairs College, and scholarly editor of its documents. Among his contemporaries who use different versions of the name are Hector MacAndrew, the finest living exponent of Scots fiddling in the tradition of Neil Gow; and Farquhar Gillanders, who brings this Gaelic form of it from his birth-place of Applecross in Ross-shire, to the department of Economics and Political Science at Glasgow University.

But the most versatile in his abilities was John Anderson (1882–1958), created Viscount Waverley. He was born in Edinburgh and became an outstanding Governor of Bengal during the critical years of 1932-7. He was perhaps the last British statesman to sit in Parliament as an Independent and attain high office. He was a member of Churchill's cabinet, and made his contribution to the preservation of life in the Anderson shelter, which he commissioned his Scottish colleague Sir William Paterson to design before the outbreak of war.

Anstruther

The district of Anstruther lies along the north shore of the Firth of Forth, dotted with the burghs of sea-faring communities—Crail and Pittenweem, St Monance and Largo. In a country with a turbulent history, its parishes enjoyed a relatively untroubled life for centuries until the 20th. The earliest record of the family bearing its name is as early as 1100, when William de Candela was lord of Anstruther. It was then rare for such a man to possess a family name other than that of his property, and William was one of the most considerable barons in Fife. He was still alive in 1153, and the son who bore the same name after him was a benefactor of the abbey of Balmerino and died some time after the accession of William the Lion in 1165. It was the first William's grandson Henry who first assumed the name of Anstruther in a charter of 1221.

He was a benefactor of the monastery of Dryburgh, and his son Henry was a benefactor of both Balmerino and Dryburgh, and a crusader who accompanied St Louis of France. Thereafter their descendants played conventional parts in Scotland's history until Sir James Anstruther of Anstruther became a favourite of that patron of handsome young men, James VI. He was appointed Hereditary Grand Carver, an office that his descendants have continued to hold to this day. His eldest son Sir William became a Gentleman of the Bedchamber to the King and died without an heir in 1649. But his second son Sir Robert, also a Gentleman of the Bedchamber, left the son, Sir Philip, who succeeded as the 15th of Anstruther.

In 1651 Sir Philip was captured, fighting for Charles II at Worcester, and his estates were forfeited until the King's restoration. His son Sir William accepted the Revolution of 1688 and in 1699 became a judge with the courtesy title of Lord Anstruther. It was the judge's son, Sir John (1673–1754), who was created a baronet in 1700. This honour had already been anticipated in a cadet branch, when Sir Robert, third son of Sir Philip of Worcester and founder of the Balcaskie line, was created a baronet in 1694. Both lines are equally noteworthy for their prudent marriages, while that of Balcaskie is also distinguished by its military record. Robert Anstruther (1768–1809), son of the third baronet of Balcaskie, is particularly deserving of notice. He was the Brigadier-General who commanded the rearguard of Sir John Moore's army on its famous retreat to Corunna during the Peninsular war against Napoleon. Like Moore, he died and was buried at Corunna after he had brought his men to safety.

Armstrong

It was not until 1237 that the frontier between Scotland and England was established by treaty where it remains today, and as late as the 16th century parts of it were still debateable. In the west, Cumberland which had been inhabited by Welsh-speaking Britons before the English invasions from Northumbria, lies to the south of it. It is not surprising that so many border names such as Inglis, Scott, Fleming and Wallace denote ethnic origins. To whichever of these groups the Armstrongs belonged, they are first found south of the border. It is a curious fact that the earliest reference to an Armstrong in Liddesdale occurs as late as 1376, especially considering how prolific and powerful the name was to become in this area.

The legend of its origin resembles that of the Turnbulls, another border clan, except that in one essential detail it appears to be more modern. The heroic progenitor of the Armstrongs saves a king, but not from a wild beast. With his strong arm he lifts the king on to his own horse after the king has been dismounted in battle—no mean feat in the case of a man wearing full armour. Both legends are given too late a context, and this is particularly obvious in the case of Armstrong. The name is not likely to have originated in Scotland with the rescue of a mediaeval king when it had for so long been a family name south of the border.

From Liddesdale the Armstrongs expanded into Annandale and Eskdale; and it is here, along one of the most lovely reaches of the river

Esk, that their most romantic memorials are still to be seen. In about 1425 John, brother of Armstrong of Mangerton in Liddesdale, built Hollows Tower near the river bank. The well-preserved ruin is often called Gilnockie today, the title by which Johnnie Armstrong himself is distinguished. In fact Gilnockie stood further along the river bank and only its base now remains.

In the time of Johnnie Armstrong it was said that three thousand of his name, all mounted, were in virtual control of the debateable land. The English Warden of the Border, Lord Dacre, attacked and set fire to Hollows Tower in 1528, but the Armstrongs simply retaliated by burning Netherby. It was the King of Scots himself, James V, who disposed of Johnnie Armstrong. James had a high-handed way of suppressing disorder in his kingdom, and in 1529 he invaded his own borders with an army, imprisoning some of the most powerful men there. According to the contemporary (but imaginative) historian Pitscottie, John of Gilnockie came to meet the King near Hawick with a tail of thirty-six horsemen. James V had them surrounded and hanged from the nearest trees. One of the finest border ballads tells how Gilnockie pleaded for his life, and exclaimed when this was refused:

To seek hot water beneath cold ice,
Surely it is a great folie—
I have asked grace at a graceless face,
But there is none for my men and me!

In Pitscottie's account, Gilnockie told the King: 'I know King Harry would down-weigh my best horse with gold, to know I were condemned to die this day.' When Henry VIII invaded Scotland in 1542 James reaped the whirlwind of his harsh methods. His army was routed at Solway Moss, many preferring to surrender tamely rather than to fight for so unpopular a King. Perhaps this contributed to the posthumous reputation of Johnnie Armstrong as a patriot who might have held the border against the English if James V had not executed him. In fact he was a thief and a blackmailer.

Before the century was out another Armstrong of the Gilnockie branch had provided the plot for another outstanding border ballad. He was William of Kinmont Tower, whom the English ambushed in Liddesdale during a truce and carried off to the castle of Carlisle.

And have they ta'en him, Kinmont Willie,
Against the truce of border tide,
And forgotten that the bold Buccleuch
Is keeper here on the Scottish side?

In 1596 the Scottish warden, Sir Walter Scott of Buccleuch, made a surprise attack on Carlisle Castle and rescued him. A few years later the union of crowns brought peace to the borders. The Armstrongs turned to more peaceful pursuits than reiving. But four centuries have hardly dimmed the glamour of their deeds in the debateable land.

Baird

This is another name to which, like that of Campbell, is attached the legend of the killing of a wild boar. The King whose life was said to have been saved was William the Lion; before the first surviving charter of the 13th century, to Richard Baird of Meikle and Little Kyp in Lanarkshire. Early in the following century King Robert Bruce bestowed the barony of Cambusnethan on Robert Baird, and from there the family spread first to Banffshire, and then to Auchmeddan in Aberdeenshire. Here George Baird married a member of the great Keith family, hereditary Earls Marischal, and a succession of Baird sheriffs of Aberdeenshire testify to the prestige which this alliance brought them.

From Auchmeddan sprouted the branch of Newbyth which gave birth to John Baird. Before his death in 1698 he had become a judge of the post-revolution regime, with the courtesy title of Lord Newbyth, and a baronet. This baronetcy passed to William Baird, whose second son David became one of the leading generals of the Napoleonic wars.

But the world renown of this name was bestowed on it by John Logie Baird (1888–1946), whose ancestry is uncertain. He was born at Helensburgh in Dunbartonshire, son of the Rev. John Baird, and educated at Glasgow University. In 1926 he gave the world's first demonstration of television in an attic. In 1928 took place the first trans-Atlantic transmission. From first to last, Baird was the pioneer of every development associated with television, and few men have done more to alter the habits of the human race throughout the world.

Barclay

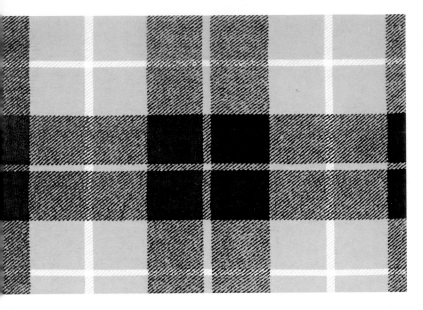

The Barclays, long thought to have come from Berkeley Castle in Gloucestershire, may in fact have originated at Berkley in the county of Somerset. In 1165 Sir Walter de Berkeley, first lord of Gartly, was Chamberlain of Scotland. Until 1456 the chiefship of this name descended through males of the Gartly line, until it expired with Walter Barclay of Gartly, Canon of Moray. It then passed with his sister to the Towie-Barclay branch into which she married, which stemmed from the Chamberlain's brother Alexander. On the death of the late Chief in California in 1967, the title passed to his cousin Peter Barclay of Tollie Barclay and of that Ilk (b. 1924).

Meanwhile, early in the 12th century, a Theobald de Berkeley also settled in Scotland, and his descendant Alexander acquired the estate of Mathers when he married the sister of the Great Marischal of Scotland in 1351. Their son Alexander was the first to adopt the Barclay form of this surname. About a century later, their descendant David was compelled to sell Mathers; and so his son (also named David) joined the many Scots who went to seek their fortune in the Thirty Years' War, and the comparatively few who returned, having found it. He acquired the estate of Urie near Stonehaven in Kincardineshire, but he was not destined to pass his retirement here in peace. In 1648 Colonel Barclay of Urie took up arms for Charles I, and under the rule of Cromwell he was several times sent as a Scottish representative to London. After the Restoration in 1660 he suffered a brief imprisonment in Edinburgh, on suspicion of hostility to the new regime: and this trivial episode was to be the most significant of his life.

Sharing his prison was the laird of Swinton, another Scot who had trafficked with Cromwell's regime. In London, Swinton had become converted to the beliefs of the Society of Friends, and in his Edinburgh prison he converted Colonel Barclay to the Quaker faith.

Barclay's son Robert had been born in 1648 and brought up, as he later wrote, 'amongst the strictest sort of Calvinists'. Later he was sent to the Scots College at Paris, of which his uncle Robert Barclay was Rector, and there became indoctrinated with Catholic teaching. 'In both these sects I had abundant occasion to receive impressions contrary to this principle of *love*: seeing the straitness of several of their doctrines, as well as their practice of persecution.' Thus wrote Robert Barclay after he had returned from Paris in 1664, embraced the Quaker beliefs of his father, and become their most eloquent apologist. In addition to his writings, he paid missionary visits throughout Europe, sometimes in the company of William Penn. Both men did much to increase the respect in which Quakers were held, and probably to lessen the persecution which Christians of all other sects generally inflicted upon them.

The greatest contrast to the Quaker Barclays of Urie is that of the branch of the house of Towie which produced the Russian Field Marshal Michael Andreas, Prince Barclay de Tolly. He commanded the army which defeated Napoleon in 1812, three years before Wellington did the same at Waterloo.

Beaton

In the history of the Scottish Highlands and Islands this name is equalled in distinction only by that of MacMhuirich—and its modern form of Currie. In similar fashion it has been anglicised from the Gaelic *Mac Bheatha*, and also takes the forms Bethune and MacBeth. Its meaning, Son of Life, is appropriate to a family which brought to Scotland the most advanced medical knowledge which reached Europe from Greece and the Arab world.

The Beatons came to Scotland from Ireland in the 13th century, according to tradition, in the wake of Margaret, daughter of *O Catháin*, when she married Angus, Lord of the Isles. They became physicians as well as shenachies in Islay, the seat of the Lordship; and also in Skye, Mull and the outer Hebrides. But the deposition of the Catholic King James VII in favour of the Calvinist King William III (and II of Scotland) in 1688 brought about the downfall of this learned dynasty. The last of its long line of scholars was the Episcopalian clergyman John Beaton, who disappeared from his charge in the island of Mull when all of his profession were required to conform to the Presbyterian establishment. By the end of the century he was in northern Ireland. At the time of the 1715 rising his widow remarried: he had died in the interval in total obscurity. Thereafter the Highlanders were left to salvage what

Macbeth

traditions they could of the medical knowledge of the Beatons, and to search their untended gardens for plants which they believed to possess healing powers. So it might be believed that the Beatons were mere purveyors of primitive magic.

But before the Rev. John Beaton and his great manuscript library vanished, a Welshman called Edward Lhuyd, second Keeper of the Ashmolean Museum at Oxford, traced him to Ireland, visited him there, and drew up a list of part of the contents of his library. Much of the poetry, history and legend was extremely ancient. But in addition to tales of pre-Christian Ireland, Lhuyd found the earliest account of the fall of Troy translated into any European language apart from Latin, a tale of Charlemagne, and another of French origin.

It is the medical treatises which Lhuyd listed, however, that are of the greatest significance. For we know now that it was the Arabs who preserved and built upon Greek medical science; and that the very Crusaders sometimes asked for and were provided with Arab doctors, to save them from the ignorance and superstition that passed for medical knowledge in Christendom. The Gaelic library of the Beatons contained not only the Aphorisms of the Greek Hippocrates, but also 424 leaves in folio of the foremost Arab scientist Averroes. Among European works it included the *Lilium Medicinae*, and a 13th-century treatise which had been published in Padua in 1483. 'Yea, very many other books,' wrote Lhuyd in Welsh at the end of his list.

Black Watch

42nd Regiment, the Black Watch

Between the Jacobite risings of 1715 and 1745, the most able upholder of the Hanoverian interest in the Highlands was George Wade, created a Field Marshal in 1743. It was he who constructed the roads whose bridges are still such an attractive feature of the northern landscape. Wade came to the Highlands in 1724, and in the following year a military police force or 'watch' was formed in six independent companies. Three were commanded by Lord Lovat, Grant of Ballindalloch, and Munro of Culcairn. The other three were commanded by Campbells, and all wore their several tartans. Despite this variety they were known as *Am Freiceadan Dubh* (The Black Watch) to distinguish them from the Red Coats. In 1739 their numbers were increased to ten companies and a thousand men, and they were embodied as the 43rd Regiment. It was now that a uniform tartan was designed for them, known ever since as the Black Watch tartan.

Comparison with the Campbell tartan shows that the two setts are identical, and that it is only the shades of colour that give the two such a different appearance. Yet there is no evidence that this was the Campbell sett before it was adopted by the 43rd Regiment, although it might appear plausible in view of the dominant Campbell influence when the Black Watch was first formed.

In 1749 it became the 42nd Regiment, when the old 42nd was reduced. By 1815 its tartan was being identified as the Sutherland, Campbell, Munro, Grant, Black Watch or Government sett.

Boyd

The Gaelic for Bute, the island next in size to Arran in the Firth of Clyde, is *Bod* and its genitive case is *Boid*. The first in Scottish records to take their name from this island were vassals of the de Morevilles, and may have accompanied them from England. In 1205 Dominus Robertus de Boyd witnessed a contract, and throughout the 13th century the name is found in many parts of south-west Scotland. During the wars of independence Sir Robert de Boyt was taken prisoner in 1306 while Duncan Boyd was hanged in the same year for aiding the Bruce. The royal connection was strengthened in the reign of the Stewarts, when Malcolm de Bute became chaplain to Robert III in 1405, and Thomas Boyd was selected as one of the hostages for the King of Scots in 1425.

In the same century Robert, eldest son of Sir Thomas Boyd of

Kilmarnock, carried out a daring coup d'état, such as occur in the history of all nations. He had been created Lord Boyd in 1454 by James II, who was blown up by a cannon, leaving an infant son to succeed him. In 1460 Lord Boyd became Regent for young James III, and in 1466 the King's instructor in knightly exercises. He then kidnapped his charge and obtained an Act of Parliament and the royal assent appointing him sole governor of the realm. His rule was competent, and his position was cemented in 1467 when he was appointed Great Chamberlain for life. His son married the King's sister Mary and was created Earl of Arran and Lord Kilmarnock. In 1468 Boyd negotiated the royal marriage with Norway which brought the Orkney islands to the Scottish crown.

But the Boyds were now as close to the crown as the Stewarts had been under the last Bruce sovereign, and their rivals struck. Boyd and his brother Alexander of Duncole were sentenced to death by Parliament for treason. Boyd fled to England; his brother was executed. The Earl of Arran fled abroad with his royal wife and there died, after earning the highest praises for his character and abilities from Sir John Paston. The Princess Mary was compelled to marry James, Lord Hamilton, who was created Earl of Arran, and thus placed the Hamiltons next in line to the throne instead of the Boyds. It was to prove a poor exchange.

But Lord Boyd's second son survived, and his title was restored to his grandson in 1536. The 10th Lord Boyd was created Earl of Kilmarnock in 1661 for his family's services to Charles II. The 3rd Earl supported the Union with England in 1707, but the 4th commanded the cavalry of Prince Charles at Culloden and was beheaded on Tower Hill and his earldom forfeited. However, his second son became 15th Earl of Erroll by inheritance from his great-aunt, and adopted the surname of Hay. To this title the barony of Kilmarnock was added in 1831. So when the 22nd Earl of Erroll died in 1941, leaving a daughter as Chief of Clan Hay and Countess of Erroll, his brother resumed the name of Boyd and became 6th Lord Kilmarnock as Chief of Clan Boyd. He was succeeded in 1975 by the 7th Lord Kilmarnock (b. 1927).

Brodie

In 1646 Lord Lewis Gordon captured Brodie Castle near Forres in Moray, and destroyed its muniments. It may be on this account that so little is known for certain of the origins of a family of such evident antiquity. Michael Brodie of Brodie received a charter for his properties from Robert Bruce, but he was not one of the many incomers amongst whom King Robert parcelled out the lands of the defeated Comyns as a reward for their support. The charter states that he held the thanages of Brodie and Dyke as heir to his father Malcolm of Brodie. So he was a survivor of the old aristocratic order of what had once been Macbeth's kingdom, and earlier still, the Pictish realm of the Brude kings. A finely carved Pictish symbol stone still stands close to the castle as a memento of the dynasty which Saint Columba came here to visit, while beyond lies the blasted heath on which Macbeth was reputed to have met the witches. The name of Brodie is almost indistinguishable from the king-name of the dynasty which ruled here before the coming of Kenneth Mac Alpin. None of this adds up to evidence that the Brodies have preserved a male line of the royal family which used a system of matrilinear succession in the remotest period of Scottish history. On the other hand, no alternative explanation for their origins is more probable. It is perhaps significant that the Brodie chiefs regarded their names as that of a family, not of a clan.

From the time of Bruce until the 16th century, the succession of the thanes of Brodie continued in the male line, but remarkably little is known of their activities or of their junior branches. Where their marriages remain on record, their wives possess the principal names of the neighbourhood, Dunbar and Douglas, Sutherland and Hay. As early as Robert Bruce's reign Michael of Brodie was the object of a complaint from the Prior of neighbouring Pluscarden Abbey. The King ordered Brodie to repair the pond which enabled the local mill to operate, as his family had been responsible for doing in Alexander III's reign, 'that it may not behove the Prior and abbey of Pluscarden to have recourse to us with just complaint of your defect in this matter'. The mill upon which Pluscarden depended crops up again in documents of 1466 and 1540: but before long matters of far graver moment were to disturb the peace of that pleasant neighbourhood.

Alexander of Brodie died in 1583 leaving David Brodie his heir by his first marriage. By his second marriage he left five sons and five daughters, and their mother's family attempted to disinherit David in favour of her own eldest son. The plot failed, and so it was David's son Alexander (1617–1680) who succeeded as Brodie of Brodie. He was a fanatical Presbyterian, and in 1640 he led the party which descended upon Elgin Cathedral to mutilate its carvings in stone and wood and to destroy its paintings of the Crucifixion and the Last Judgment. Ten years later he was sent by the General Assembly to persuade Charles II to sign the National Covenant and to invite him to Scotland as King.

After Charles' defeat at Worcester, Brodie 'resolved in the strength of the Lord to eschew and avoid employment under Cromwell'. But he was still fined at the Restoration, for Charles II found it hard to forgive the men who had tried to force their Calvinist beliefs upon him as the price of their allegiance. Alexander had filled the office of a Lord of Session during this troubled period, and his diary, which has been published, contains much valuable political information as well as formidable piety.

In 1727 his namesake Alexander (1697–1754) became Lyon King of Arms, but the family has continued to maintain its tradition of avoiding any part in public affairs corresponding to its social consequence. It has watched other families rise and fall while, since time immemorial, it has continued to occupy the same home. Here in 1972 Mrs Helena Brodie of Brodie made a remarkable discovery in a loft in which pigeons nested. Beneath a complete set of Bleau atlases, their bindings disfigured by bird-droppings, lay a vellum pontifical which has been dated to about the year 1000, and which shows evidence of associations with Durham. The Brodie Pontifical (now in the British Museum) is therefore earlier than the reign of Saint Margaret and the advent of Turgot of Durham, older than Elgin Cathedral itself. Mysterious as its origins are, it bears an appropriate name.

In 1979 Ninian Brodie of Brodie conveyed Brodie Castle to the National Trust for Scotland, in whose care it is now open to the public.

Bruce

At Brix, in Normandy the ruins of Adam de Brus's 11th-century castle are still to be seen. In 1066 Robert de Brus crossed to England with William the Conqueror, and when David I, hitherto the greatest baron in England, went to Scotland in 1124 to become King there, the 2nd Robert Bruce accompanied him. He was granted the lands of Annandale, which he renounced to his second son Robert before the battle of the Standard in 1138. This battle was fought against the English, and the 2nd Robert objected to the King of Scots: 'When, I ask you, have you ever found such fidelity in the Scots that you can so rashly renounce the counsel of the English and the aid of the Normans? . . . You are turning your arms against the very men to whose support you owe your kingdom.' David I was the youngest son of Queen Margaret, and the double usurpation of his line had been secured by Anglo-Norman arms as Bruce pointed out. But his words are scarcely those of a Scottish patriot.

The 5th Robert Bruce married into the royal house, and in 1238 his son the 6th Robert was named heir to the Scottish crown. But this right was extinguished for ever, first by the birth of an heir to the King, and next by the birth of a son to the daughter of his wife's elder sister, who had married John Balliol. When the royal line ended in 1286 with the succession of the baby Maid of Norway, the 6th Robert Bruce attempted to seize the crown, and the Scots appealed to Edward of

England, whose subject he was. The Maid of Norway died, the Scottish crown passed legitimately to John Balliol, and Bruce became Chief Justice of England.

While Edward of England bullied King John Balliol, then invaded the country and deposed him, embarked on direct rule and defeated the independence movement of William Wallace, the Bruces remained loyal English subjects. The removal of the Balliols left the Comyn (Cumming) family the most powerful in Scotland, and the only one with a claim to the crown senior to that of the Bruces. In 1306 the 8th Robert Bruce invited John Comyn into a church and there slew him. A few weeks later he was crowned King, and began the long struggle to make himself effective ruler of an independent Scotland which ended in 1314 at Bannockburn. His task was made infinitely harder by the weakness of his claim, by his family's past record, and by the sacrilege of the Comyn murder, for which he remained excommunicated throughout his reign. But this only increases the measure of his achievement, both as a military leader of outstanding courage and resource, and as an administrator who had shouldered the responsibility of rebuilding a nation.

King Robert I's line expired with his son David II in 1371, whose reign was bedevilled by the presence of the legitimate King of Scots, Edward Balliol. Thomas Bruce, whose kinship with David II is uncertain, organised a rising against Balliol's English supporters in 1334, and was rewarded with crown lands in Clackmannan.

One of his descendants was Sir George Bruce of Carnock in Fife, who established the coal-works at Culross. His 16th-century house there, known as the palace, is Scotland's finest example of the home of a merchant prince of the period. Sir George's elder brother Edward (1548–1610) accompanied James VI to London when he inherited the English crown in 1603 and was created 1st Lord Kinloss. Thomas, the 3rd Lord (1599–1663), was raised to the earldom of Elgin, but the 4th Earl died without heirs. His title was revived in the line of the merchant prince. His grandson had already been created Earl of Kincardine in 1647, and so these two titles became united in the senior family of the name of Bruce.

James Bruce of Kinnaird (1730–1794), the explorer in Ethiopia who wrote the supreme epic of African travel, took an excessive pride in his royal Bruce descent. In fact his grandfather was David Hay, a cadet of the equally distinguished family of Erroll. He married Helen Bruce, the heiress of Kinnaird, and so their son became David Bruce of Kinnaird. It was at about the time of his death that coal was discovered beneath this estate, once again making a Bruce fortune, and enabling the traveller to make his journeys in regal style.

Barely contemporary was Thomas Bruce, 7th Earl of Elgin and 11th of Kincardine (1766–1841). A General and diplomat, he spent his fortune in rescuing the marbles of the Parthenon at a time when they were in grave danger of destruction. He disposed of them to the British Museum in 1816 for far less than this operation had cost him, and was branded as a vandal for his pains.

Buchan

The district of Buchan in Aberdeenshire became a form of identification for inhabitants who had no connection with the successive families that became possessed of the Earldom of Buchan. Church records preserve many instances of this. Richard of Buchan was a clerk of the bishopric of Aberdeen in 1207-8. Others carried the name to the extreme north. Andrew of Buchan, who died in about 1309, became Bishop of Caithness, while Walter of Buchan was Canon of St Magnus Cathedral at Kirkwall in Orkney in 1369, and had moved to Shetland as Archdeacon by 1391. In the secular field, William of Buchan held land in Aberdeen in 1281, while another William of Buchan was a burgess in 1436. At an early date the name was carried south to Edinburgh, and to the barony of Morton.

One of the principal families to emerge in Aberdeenshire was that of the Buchans of Auchmacoy, which produced an early Jacobite general. Thomas was the third son of James Buchan of Auchmacoy, and he claimed that his family descended from the earls of Buchan. After the death of Bonnie Dundee at the battle of Killiecrankie in 1689, General Thomas Buchan became the leader of James VII's forces in Scotland in their opposition to William's usurpation. But he was defeated in 1690 and went to the exiled court at St Germains in 1692.

Since then the name has acquired increasing celebrity in the literary field, culminating in that of John Buchan (1875–1940), the novelist.

Buchanan

Buth Chanain is Gaelic for Canon's House, and the lands which received this designation border Loch Lomond. The Earl of Lennox, to whom the first MacMhuirich bard to come to Scotland addressed a poem early in the 13th century, referred to Sir Absalon of Buchanan as *'clericus meus.'* The Buchanans thus appear equally early in the ranks of the Scottish intelligentsia.

Two men above all built upon this tradition. George Buchanan (1506–1582) was born at Killearn in Stirlingshire, of which the Chiefs of his name were successive parish clerks during his lifetime. George was sent to study in Paris during the intellectual ferment of the Reformation. He became an outstanding scholar, wrote plays and poetry in Latin, and returned to Scotland a convert to Calvinism at the time when Mary, Queen of Scots returned from France to begin her personal reign. In her remarkable tolerance she extended her patronage to Buchanan until her downfall. He then sold his pen to her enemies.

His mendacious and obscene libels against his late benefactress, composed in Latin of the greatest distinction, were circulated throughout Europe and continued to be mistaken for historical fact for centuries to come. It was one of Queen Mary's greatest griefs that Buchanan was ever appointed tutor to her son, and thus enabled to poison the child's mind against her. The erudition of James VI and I must be credited in large measure to Buchanan, and it may be possible to account for his perverted character also in so evil an influence.

Dugald Buchanan (1716—1768) committed his more conventional sins at an earlier age, and repented them in the most inspired religious poetry his country has ever produced. He was born, the son of a miller and farmer, at Strathyre beneath Ben Lomond, and became in 1753 the teacher at Kinloch Rannoch. Here, by his personal influence, the poetry he published and the Confessions he left behind him, he made himself the Milton and the Bunyon of Gaelic Scotland. The Highland militia troops—whose successors were to earn such a reputation for piety in the Napoleonic wars—would go on pilgrimage to Kinloch Rannoch to attend Buchanan's fellowship meetings.

The chiefs of this period reckoned their descent from Walter Buchanan of Spittal, who was infeft in 1519. His son and grandson were the parish clerks of Killearn, and each married a Galbraith. The chiefs of the next two generations married Buchanan wives, and recorded their contracts at Drymen in Stirlingshire, the new parish centre of the reformed religion. But although the Buchanans escaped the consequences of being either Catholics or Jacobites, they contrived to part with their lands, and it was another country that reared their most illustrious clansman of modern times.

James Buchanan (1791—1868) was the son of a Scottish Calvinist of the same name whose family had settled in Donegal. He emigrated in 1783, so that the 15th President of the United States was born in the country he was to rule. It was Buchanan's misfortune to preside over the outbreak of the Civil War. Today, while his clansmen no longer possess their ancient territories around Ben Lomond, Buchanan County in Missouri commemorates their name and their President.

Burns

This very ordinary Lowland name, possessing no clan history, has been raised by the genius of a single brief life above every other in Scotland. The father of Robert Burns (1759—1796) emigrated from Kincardineshire in eastern Scotland to Ayrshire in the south-west, in search of more fruitful farming prospects. There he leased two successive farms, and died bankrupt in 1784 after a lifetime of appalling drudgery. He could not know, as the father of Mozart did, that he had reared one of the outstanding geniuses of his race. The collection of *Poems, Chiefly in the Scottish Dialect*, which raised his son to instant celebrity, was not published until two years after his death.

Their author's early death has been attributed directly to the over-work to which he had been subjected in his youth on his father's farm. But he was also given as good an education as was possible in his father's circumstances. He was taught some French and Latin, and introduced to a great deal of English literature. He was by no means reared as an unlettered peasant, and in fact it required his own peculiar creative genius to turn from his schooling in polite letters to a study of the Scottish folk tradition.

In his first publication he was careful to omit his greatest satires, so as

Burns Check

not to shock the genteel reading public; neither did the collection include the songs that were to give the most resounding expression to his thoughts and feelings. But during the unsettling years that followed, while he was being lionised in Edinburgh, he met the collectors of Scottish songs, and this led to his collaboration in the great collections in which his own were given to the world. Often he rescued and re-worked fragments of old verse without claiming authorship. As often, he found the perfect words for a traditional air which no longer possessed any. Thus he played a part without parallel in the history of literature, in recreating the entire corpus of his country's Lowland folk poetry and song at a time when it was on the verge of disintegration. He was also an outstanding letter-writer, a sound literary critic and a hilarious and penetrating satirist. One enthusiast said his conversation was even more impressive than his poetry.

One of his Edinburgh patrons settled him on the farm of Ellisland in Dumfries-shire, and here he remained until 1789, when he joined the Excise service and moved to Dumfries itself. This was where he died, of the rheumatic heart complaint caused by the over-exertion of his youth. Ever since his death, his birthday, 25 January, has been celebrated with rites such as have never been accorded to the memory of any other man of letters in the world. And those fortunate enough to have inherited his name need neither pedigree nor clan history to enhance it. Certainly, the Burns check would gild no lily.

Cameron

Although the Camerons are reputed to be one of the most ancient of Highland clans, the clan historian Sir Iain Moncreiffe of that Ilk has traced their name and origins back to the kingdom of Fife, and suggested that they stem from the royal line of Macduff. Certainly theirs is a Fife place-name, *Cam brun*, Gaelic for Crooked Hill. Although now it is more naturally rendered *Cam shron*, which means Crooked Nose or Headland, Moncreiffe has noted the persistence of the letter B when the name appears in mediaeval documents. He has also pointed out the similarity between the heraldry of the Camerons and the Earls of Fife. A charter in favour of a brother of the Earl of Fife was witnessed by Adam of Kamerum in the 13th century, and in the same era Robert of Cambrun was granted the lands of Ballegarno by William the Lion.

It was not until 1296 that Sir Robert Cambron appeared in the office of Sheriff of Atholl in the neighbourhood of Lochaber. It was probably he who owned Ballegarno Castle when Edward I of England occupied it in that year. In 1320 Sir John of Cambrun was among the signatories of the Declaration of Arbroath. By 1388 Ballegarno and its properties had passed with heiresses to other families, and before the century ended the Camerons had become established in Lochaber.

Here, on the east side of the loch and river Lochy, lived the Mac-Gillonies, of whom the MacMartins of Letterfinlay were a sept. Donald, reckoned the 11th Cameron Chief, married an heiress of Letterfinlay and left two sons: Allan, Constable of Strone Castle and succeeding Chief, and Ewen, progenitor of the Camerons of Strone. Strone is once again the Gaelic name *Sron*, a Headland. Ewen the 13th Chief adopted the title of Lochiel when his estates were erected into a barony of that name in 1528.

It has given its name to one of the three Cameron tartans worn today, the second being that of Erracht. The general Cameron tartan was not widely adopted until the late 19th century.

The name of Cameron itself has been bestowed, through the fanaticism of one man, on an object that may appear somewhat surprising, considering that it is generally a Highland and a Catholic name. But a certain Richard Cameron, son of a small shop-keeper in Fife, was converted by the extreme Calvinists while he was a school-master and an Episcopalian. This was at a time when the Covenanters had lost political power in Scotland, and were being treated with a comparatively mild form of the intolerance with which they had bludgeoned the country in the days of their supremecy. Cameron joined the exiled Calvinist ministers in Holland, but returned in 1680 to indulge in field-preaching. In July he was surprised by a body of horse in the moors between Nithsdale and Ayrshire, and urged his followers to fight it out. Richard Cameron himself was among the slain, and so did not live to see the Calvinist triumph of 1688. But the regiment which was raised then in support of William of Orange was named the Cameronian regiment in his memory.

(*Above*) Cameron; (*below*) Hunting Cameron

Cameron of Lochiel

Donald Cameron, who married the Letterfinlay heiress, led a contingent from Lochaber to fight for the Lord of the Isles at Harlaw in 1411. Its territories belonged to the Isles, and after the abolition of the Lordship, Lochaber suffered from the power vacuum and those who sought to fill it. Inverness-shire lay between the spheres of influence of the Campbells of Argyll and the Gordons of Huntly, armed with vice-regal powers by the Stewart Kings. In 1547 an Earl of Huntly beheaded Ewen Cameron of Lochiel.

Nevertheless the Camerons remained staunch supporters of the royal Stewarts in adversity, notably Sir Ewen Cameron of Lochiel, the last Highland Chief to hold out for Charles II against Cromwell. He had been born in the Campbell castle of Kilchurn in 1629, and brought up by the Calvinist Marquess of Argyll, who held him hostage for the peaceable behaviour of the Camerons at a time when he was in open rebellion himself. But at the age of eighteen he became free of Argyll's tutelage, and after Charles I had been executed and his son Charles II defeated at Worcester, Lochiel supported Glencairn's uprising in 1652.

After Glencairn's defeat, Lochiel continued his resistance as a guerrilla leader, despite the generous offers which the Cromwellian General Monk made to him. He had made peace in time to accompany Monk to London when the General marched south from Scotland after Cromwell's death, to restore Charles II to his throne. Although Lochiel received no compensation for all he had suffered save a knighthood, he still retained his loyalty when James VII lost his throne in 1688. In spite of his age he fought for the Stewart sovereign at Killiecrankie, and his clan was one that Dalrymple of Stair was particularly anxious to exterminate, as he tried to exterminate the MacDonalds of Glencoe. But finally Lochiel took the oath of allegiance to William and Mary, and so remained undisturbed until his death in 1719, at the age of ninety.

But it is his grandson Donald, remembered as 'The Gentle Lochiel', who is held to be the noblest of all Highland chiefs. His father had been obliged to escape to France after the failure of the 1715 rebellion, where the family were at last rewarded by a Jacobite peerage. So Donald succeeded his grandfather, while the Pretender at St Germains invested him with full powers to negotiate in Scotland for a Stewart restoration. But when Prince Charles arrived without any military provision for an uprising, Lochiel sent him advice to return. Charles responded by inviting Lochiel to his presence, and so won his support as he had gained that of MacDonald of Clanranald. To Glenfinnan Lochiel brought 700 of his clansmen—more even than the MacDonalds mustered on that day—and to him, more than to any other, it was due that Prince Charles was enabled to pursue the fatal road to Culloden, with all its terrible consequences for the Scottish Highlands.

His brother, Dr Archibald Cameron, who had carried his first message to the Prince, and another brother who had become a priest, both lost their lives in his cause. His clansmen shared in every Jacobite victory, and charged with suicidal courage at Culloden. Lochiel was carried from the field, wounded in both legs, and hidden in the mountains while he recovered. Here he encountered Prince Charles on his return from his adventure in the Hebrides, and embarked with him for France. He was given the command of a French regiment, but in 1748 he died. A few years later his brother Dr Archibald was apprehended, and was the last Jacobite to suffer the torment of being hanged, drawn and quartered.

Like the Jacobite leader MacDonald of Clanranald, the Gentle Lochiel left unworthy descendants who scourged his clansmen in the era of the Highland clearances. Achnacarry, seat of the chiefs, had been destroyed by Hanoverian troops, and the castle that was built to replace it early in the 19th century was one of the expenses that was met by evicting clansmen and letting their lands to the highest bidder. As Allan Cameron wrote in 1803, when the process was just beginning: 'Lochiel's lands are in the papers to be let at Whitsuntide first, nothing but spurring and hauling, and, I am afraid, the tenantry have no chance . . . The grand castle at Achnacarry is going on with great speed.' In it still lives the present Chief, Sir Donald Cameron of Lochiel (b. 1910), a former Balliol scholar and Colonel of the Lovat Scouts during the Second World War, with a long record of public service after it.

Cameron of Erracht

Sliochd Eòghain 'ic Eòghain, the offspring of Ewen son of Ewen, descend from Ewen Cameron of Lochiel of the early 16th century, who married as his second wife Marjory Mackintosh. Their son Ewen was the first of the cadet branch of Erracht.

Sir Alan (1750 – 1828), the eldest son of Ewen (d. 1780), gave the name of his clan to a regiment of the British Army.

Alan was a Loyalist prisoner of the American rebels from 1775 – 78, and survived, though crippled by his first attempt to escape. In 1793 he raised the 79th Regiment, *Reismeid an Earrachd*, officially the Cameron Highlanders from 1804. It served in Flanders and the West Indies, where it was drafted in June 1797. Alan raised it again in September 1797, and in 1804 he raised a second battalion. He was Colonel of the Regiment until his death in 1828. His grandson, William Cameron of Erracht, died in 1903, when this family became extinct in the male line.

From the beginning, the Erracht family had been intermittently at variance with their Lochiel cousins. Sometimes they married each other, sometimes they murdered each other, and it was probably for this reason that when Alan raised his regiment he asked his mother to design its tartan. She was Marsali Maclean, whose father, Charles of Drimnin, was killed at the head of the Macleans at Culloden. The basic sett of the tartan was a local one, such as could easily have been woven in Lochaber, using local dyes.

Campbell of Argyll

This name appears to derive from the Gaelic *Cam Beul*, meaning Crooked Mouth; while those who bear it are called Clan Diarmaid as the supposed descendants of the handsome Ossianic hero with whom the wife of Fingal fell in love. In revenge, Fingal challenged Diarmaid to slay the wild boar that harried the neighbourhood, and then to measure its carcass, against the lie of its bristles, with his bare feet. A bristle pierced Diarmaid's Achilles heel, and Fingal refused him a draught of his healing cup as Diarmaid lay dying. Scotland's supreme interpreter of Gaelic song, J. C. M. Campbell (1896–1979), is among those who have left a recording of this ballad.

Such are the legendary origins of a clan that was already of considerable consequence in the lands of the earliest Scottish kingdom of Dalriada by the time these had evolved into Lorne and Argyll. The support which their chief Sir Colin Campbell of Loch Awe and his two sons gave to Robert Bruce was rewarded by a marriage with King Robert's sister, and the Campbells began their rise to supremacy in the Highlands by assisting in the downfall of Bruce's opponents. From this time their chiefs were named as the descendants of Sir Colin of Loch Awe, *Mac Chailein Mór*, Great Son of Colin.

At this time their stronghold was a castle occupying almost the whole of one of the little islands in the loch, called Innis Chonaill. Its ruins still stand under the peaks of *Cruachan Beann*, the Haunch of Hills that provided the Campbells with their war-cry. But Colin

Campbell, 1st Earl of Argyll, moved his headquarters to the burgh of Inveraray on Loch Fyne which he founded in 1474. He was created Master of the Royal Household and Lord Chancellor, and he played a leading part in destroying the rival power of the Lordship of the Isles: which did not prevent him from lending his support also to the rebels who hounded the King of Scots, James III, to his death. But the 2nd Earl died with James IV on the field of Flodden.

The 7th Earl (c.1576–1638) was involved with Campbell of Cawdor in overthrowing the MacDonalds of Islay, but after his second marriage he became a Catholic and ended his days in exile. It was in these circumstances that his son was placed in a position of such responsibility before he inherited the earldom, and reacted so strongly against Catholics himself. The 8th Earl (1598–1661) was created 1st Marquess of Argyll and raised his name and clan to its highest pinnacle of power as leader of the Covenanters who defended Calvinism in Scotland against the attempts which Charles I made to introduce Episcopalian forms of worship—and to recover Church property from the hands of the aristocracy. The power of the 8th Earl was frequently invoked by the Synod of Argyll against the Highland Catholics, and when the Covenanters had made themselves the most powerful force in any of Charles I's three rebellious kingdoms, they even tried to impose their creed upon the English.

Then Montrose arrived in Scotland in 1644 with nothing except the King's commission to retrieve the broken royalist cause. The victims of the Campbells rallied behind him, Catholics, Macleans and Mac-Donalds. Under the brilliant leadership of Montrose they routed Calvinist and Campbell, ravaged Argyll as far as Inveraray, and left a thousand killed or drowned at Inverlochy, while *Mac Chailein Mór* fled by sea to his castle. Iain *Lom* MacDonald was present at Inverlochy, and celebrated the victory in one of his fiercest poems. And although Argyll brought Montrose to the gallows in the end, his own power never recovered. At the Restoration he was executed in his turn by Charles II, and his son, the 9th Earl, was forfeited and executed in 1685 for his treason against James VII. But fortune returned to his family in 1688 when the Catholic King James VII lost his throne to Charles I's Calvinist grandson William of Orange. The 10th Earl was raised to a dukedom and the family estates were restored to him.

Archibald, 3rd Duke of Argyll (1682–1761) played so large a part in public affairs, particularly during the Jacobite uprising of 1745, that he was known as 'King of Scotland'. It was he who built the new castle of Inveraray. The design by Roger Morris was based on a plan sketched by Vanbrugh, while the classical interiors were the achievement of Robert Mylne. The dormers and turret roofs were added in the 19th century. The castle was seriously damaged by fire in 1976 but has been restored by Ian, 11th Duke and 25th *Mac Chailein Mór* (b. 1937), by whom it has been reopened to the public.

Campbell of Breadalbane

The east end of Loch Awe faces three valleys: Glenoe of the Macintyres, which winds behind *Cruachan Beann* to the north; Glenstrae of the MacGregors in the centre; and Glenorchy to the south, which the Campbells claimed to have obtained with a MacGregor heiress at the auspicious time when they supported Robert Bruce. Glenorchy, that early prize of Campbell greed, was bestowed by Sir Duncan Campbell of Loch Awe on his second son Colin. Meanwhile, the lordship of Lorne, which the MacDougalls had lost through their loyalty to the true heirs to the Scottish crown, in opposition to Robert Bruce, had passed to co-heiresses of the Stewart family. Sir Colin of Glenorchy married Margaret Stewart, one of these co-heiresses, and thus obtained the properties that enabled him to build the castle of Kilchurn in about 1440 and to found the cadet branch of the Campbells of Breadalbane. Its chiefs are named after him *Mac Cailein Mhic Dhonnachaidh,* Son of Colin Son of Duncan.

It was a later Sir Colin of Glenorchy who, by high-handedness and trickery, engineered the proscription of the MacGregors in 1603, thus clearing Glenstrae opposite the entrance to Kilchurn. In 1625 Black Duncan, the 7th of Glenorchy, was created a baronet. There followed the upheavals in church and state which occasioned such vicissitudes in the parent house of Argyll. Of these the 4th baronet attempted to take advantage by marrying a widow of the Earl of Caithness and buying up the estates of the earldom when the Gordon Earl of Sutherland, whose family had been attempting for decades to obtain it for themselves, found himself under a cloud at the Restoration of Charles II. Such a move was rare in Highland history. Although the Gordons and the Campbells sometimes clashed in the political field, they generally confined themselves to their own ample spheres of influence in their more private enterprises. Neither did Sir John of Glenorchy now succeed in obtaining the Sinclair earldom in the far north. But in 1681 he was created instead Earl of Breadalbane.

When William and Mary became joint sovereigns by the Revolution of 1688, commissioners travelled to London to offer them the Scottish crown. Argyll administered the oath; when he reached the final clause William objected, until he was persuaded that he might take it with a good conscience. He then swore 'to root out all heretics and enemies to the true worship of God that shall be convicted by the true Kirk of God of the foresaid crimes, out of the lands and empire of Scotland.' The Campbells had already planned the assault on their Catholic neighbours which produced such little profit and widespread obloquy in the massacre of Glencoe.

It was Dalrymple of Stair who persuaded King William to take the oath, and Dalrymple's friend, the 1st Earl of Breadalbane, who was entrusted with a fund of public money with which to buy the allegiance of Highland chiefs. But a man who was not trusted by his friends could not secure the confidence of his enemies. A policy of coercion was consequently adopted instead, which led to the massacre. The military expedition to Glencoe was entrusted to a drunken cadet of Glenorchy, Robert Campbell of Glenlyon. The wily Breadalbane was careful to conceal his own part in the murder of his old enemy MacIan of Glencoe; and this stood him in good stead when he was arrested on a charge of complicity in the massacre.

The line of Breadalbane has suffered misfortune since then. It has failed three times and been revived again: Kilchurn is a ruin: the more modern seat of Taymouth Castle has been sold.

Campbell of Cawdor

At the very time when the Gordons were conspiring to seize the earldom of Sutherland in the far north, the Campbells scored their most dramatic success in the Gordon sphere of influence. John of Calder died in 1494, leaving a daughter Muriel as his posthumous heir. The baby's maternal grandfather, Rose of Kilravock, faced a criminal prosecution at the time for robbery, and the Justice-General was Archibald, 2nd Earl of Argyll. By 1495 he had eased Kilravock's difficulties and obtained the wardship of the baby heiress of Calder from James IV. A force of Campbells then seized her by force and carried her away to Inveraray in 1499.

Legend tells that her mother had time to brand her with a red-hot key, and her nurse to bite off the joint of a little finger, lest the Campbells should put a spurious heiress in her place. It would have been a wise precaution. The Campbells lost many of their men as they beat off their pursuers, and someone suggested that if the child were to die, much blood would have been spilt in vain. To this the leader of the Campbell gang replied that the heiress could never die so long as there was a red-haired lass on the banks of Loch Fyne. Supposedly it was the genuine heiress Muriel who was married in 1510 to Sir John Campbell, third son of Argyll, and returned with him to live at Calder in the country of Nairn, now known as Cawdor.

Their castle stands in the fertile lands south of the Moray Firth which enjoy an exceptionally fine climate for their latitude, and it is said that the lord of Cawdor had selected this pleasant location in 1454 by letting loose a donkey laden with gold, and observing the spot where it stopped to rest. The hawthorn tree beneath which the donkey halted still stands in the vaults of the castle.

Here the heiress Muriel outlived her husband by several decades and was succeeded by her grandson when she died in 1573. But instead of resting content with his delightful patrimony, he sold many of his lands in order to finance the conquest of Islay, still the possession of Sir James MacDonald after the abolition of the Lordship. In this operation Sir John of Cawdor was assisted by the 7th Earl of Argyll, who became a Catholic and ended his days in exile. In 1624 Cawdor too was converted to the Catholic faith, by the Irish Franciscan Father Cornelius Ward. Thus these two Campbells demonstrated in the end that their convictions meant more to them than material gain. But Islay fell under the remote dominion of the Campbells of Cawdor until 1726, when it was purchased by another member of the same clan.

Fine additions were made to the castle by Sir Hugh Campbell (1642–1716), who married Henrietta Stuart, daughter of the Earl of Moray. But after their son Sir Alexander married the heiress of Stackpole in Pembrokeshire the family gravitated increasingly to Wales. John Campbell the heir married another Welsh heiress, and it was their grandson John who in 1796 was created Baron Cawdor of Castlemartin in Pembrokeshire. The second Baron was created Earl of Cawdor after George IV's visit to Stackpole in 1827.

Subsequently his kinsfolk have earned one of the most impressive collections of gallantry awards on record in a single family, including three Victoria Crosses. The 5th Earl, a Lieut. Colonel in the Cameron Highlanders during the Second World War, returned to make Cawdor his family's principal home once more. He was also Chairman of the Scottish Historic Buildings Council and a Trustee of the National Museum of Antiquities. Since his death in 1970 his son Hugh, the 6th Earl (b. 1932), has dismantled the gigantic mansion of Stackpole and opened that gem of Scots baronial architecture, Cawdor Castle, to the public.

Campbell

Campbell, Old Colours

The supremacy of the Campbells of Argyll by the time printing was invented assured their patronage of the first books to be published in Gaelic, while their support of the reformed religion helped to make Argyll a centre of the dissemination of Calvinist literature. So it was that, a thousand years after the mission of Saint Columba, the very parts of Scotland to which he had brought the Christian message first issued it in print in Columba's own tongue. The Liturgy of John Knox was published in 1567 in Bishop Carswell's translation, and was followed in 1631 by a Gaelic version of Calvin's Catechism. Its authorship is uncertain, but the very fact that the translator may have been the family bard of the Earl of Argyll is significant.

It was the Synod of Argyll which authorised the Gaelic Shorter Catechism which it distributed in print in 1653: Dugald Campbell, minister of Knapdale, was one of the translators. The Synod next commissioned Gaelic verse translations of the psalms, and Dugald Campbell undertook to provide numbers twenty to forty. His son Duncan, minister of Glenorchy, was given the responsibility for the last fifty. Political upheavals endangered the enterprise, but the entire collection found safety among the papers of the Earl of Argyll, and was published in 1694.

This religious affiliation separated the Campbells from the rich and ancient literary tradition preserved by the Beatons and the Mac-Mhuirichs. Even the evidence of Clan Diarmaid's links with its ancient cultural heritage was allowed to become scanty. The MacEwens were bards to the Campbells of Argyll, yet only one of their poems survives. It was a MacGregor who preserved a solitary Gaelic poem composed by Sir Duncan Campbell of Glenorchy who, at the age of seventy, gave his life in 1513 on the field of Flodden. The strictures which Carswell published in 1567, in his Gaelic introduction to the Liturgy of Knox, are suggestive. They roundly condemn the profane and Catholic literature, with its roots in Ireland. Yet at the end of the day Campbells, even in the Calvinist ministry, have been pre-eminent among those who have preserved this heritage. John Gregorson Campbell, minister of the island of Tiree, is especially noteworthy. In 1891 was published his Ossianic collection, called *The Fians*. It was followed by *Clan Traditions and Popular Tales* in 1895, by *Superstitions of the Highlands and Islands of Scotland* in 1900, and two years later by his work on *Witchcraft and Second Sight.*

But it was in the great houses of the Campbells that their achievement is without parallel. It includes the *Records of Argyll* published in 1885 by Lord Archibald Campbell, and the help which his father the 8th Duke gave to John Francis Campbell of Islay in his lifelong study of Gaelic tradition. Campbell of Islay did on his private initiative what no Scottish institution has succeeded in doing: he organised the collection of folk-tales all over the Highlands and Islands. The successive volumes of his *Popular Tales of the West Highlands* were issued between 1860 and 1862, and two further volumes of his material have been published since 1940. In 1872 he produced *Leabhar na Féinne*, the first volume of Scotland's incomparable Gaelic ballads to be published in the country.

The successor to these devoted men belongs to the military family of Inverneil, and descends from the elder brother of its most distinguished soldier Sir Archibald Campbell (1739–1791). Dr John Lorne Campbell exchanged Inverneil for the low fertile island of Canna, which lies south-west of the Cuillin mountains of Skye. He published his *Highland Songs of the Forty-Five* in 1933, and since then no Scottish university has equalled the productions of his mind and pen during the same period. His lifelong collection of songs and stories has given us English and Gaelic texts of the *Tales of Barra told by the Coddy* (1961), showing how a bilingual storyteller manipulates two such different languages.

The Furrow Behind Me preserves the autobiography of a Gaelic monoglot Hebridean crofter, as well as giving it to the world in English translation. Campbell has searched out and edited neglected manuscripts, as in *Edward Lhuyd in the Scottish Highlands 1699–1700* (1963) and *A School in South Uist* (1964). He has published the poetry of Father Allan Macdonald of Eriskay in *Bardachd Mhgr Ailein* (1965), and exposed the fraudulent use that Ada Goodrich Freer made of his papers in *Strange Things* (1968) – a fascinating detective story. In 1981 Dr Campbell published the third and final volume of his great work *Hebridean Folksongs,* and conveyed the isle of Canna with his library and folklore collection to the National Trust for Scotland.

Carnegie

The name derives from the barony of this name in the parish of Carmyllie, Angus. The Carnegies of Southesk were previously designated by the Gaelic township-name of Balinhard, also in Angus. It first appears in records in about 1230, in connection with the abbeys of Arbroath and Balmerino. In 1358 the lands and barony of Carnegie were granted to John of Balinhard, great-grandson of John who had died in about 1275. John the 1st of Carnegie died in 1370 and was succeeded by John Carnegie of that Ilk, whose line ended in 1530.

Meanwhile Duthac of Carnegie, presumed to be a younger son or nephew of the founder, obtained part of the lands of Kinnaird in 1409. From him descended John of Kinnaird who was killed at Flodden in 1513, and whose son Robert became a judge in 1547, was captured at the battle of Pinkie and knighted on his release, and was appointed ambassador to France. He died in 1565, before the downfall of Mary, Queen of Scots, to whom his son Sir John remained faithful until her death. Having no heirs he was succeeded by his brother David, father of David (1575—1658), created 1st Earl of Southesk. The family's loyalty to the house of Stewart led to the forfeiture of the 5th Earl after the 1715 rising, but the attainder was reversed by Act of Parliament in the 19th century. The earldom was then inherited by Alexander Carnegie, 6th Baronet.

But the most celebrated bearer of the name of Carnegie was Andrew (1835—1919), elder son of William Carnegie, a damask linen weaver in Dunfermline. The family emigrated to Allegany city, Pennsylvania, during the Hungry Forties. Here Andrew began work at the age of 13 as a bobbin-boy in a cotton factory, and moved from this job after a few months to fire a furnace in a cellar. By 1850 he was messenger boy in the Pittsburgh telegraph office. Here he was able to read books in a free library founded by Colonel James Anderson, a privilege which was to inspire him to one of his most gigantic acts of philanthropy. In 1853 he was appointed a clerk and telegraph operator, and he began his modest investments in the burgeoning railroads. When Scott became Vice-President of the Railroad Company in 1859 he made Carnegie a divisional superintendant. Then the Civil War broke out, the first war in which railways were to play a vital part. Carnegie organised a railroad manufacturing company, and by 1881 he had made himself the foremost ironmaster in America.

The effect of enormous wealth on him was most curious. In 1900 he published his *The Gospel of Wealth*, in which he stated 'the man who dies rich dies disgraced.' He sold his steel concerns and spent much of the remainder of his life distributing the personal fortune of £60,000,000 which they had brought him. To it Scotland owes her Carnegie libraries, among many other benefits. Andrew Carnegie spent much of his time in the country from which he had emigrated as a child, and rebuilt Skibo Castle in Sutherland as his home there.

Chisholm

This Highland clan takes its name from the homely English term Cheese-holm, which was planted in the parish of Roberton in Roxburghshire at some time after the British kingdom of Gododdin was overrun by the English of Northumbria in the 7th century. During the Norman take-over it was promoted to be the name of a feudal barony, and so the name of Alexander of Chisholm appears among the witnesses to a charter in 1249. The border Chisholms of Chisholm continued until the extinction of the family in 1899.

But in 1359 Sir Robert Chisholm of Chisholm succeeded his maternal grandfather as constable of the royal stronghold which guards the pass to the western Highlands at the Urquhart peninsula on Loch Ness. This provided the opportunity for his eldest son Alexander to marry the heiress of Erchless and Comar. His younger son continued the house of the border Chisholms, while Thomas, son of Alexander and Margaret of Erchless, became the first Chisholm Chief of the clan which occupied Strathglass and Glen Cannich during the next four centuries. He was known in Gaelic as *An Siosalach*, and in English, too, the Chief came to be addressed as The Chisholm.

The clan remained Catholic, and a branch which was planted in Perthshire provided three bishops who opposed the Protestant reformation during the 16th century. But the chiefs changed their religion, and consequently did not support the Jacobite risings in the 18th century. So their clansmen remained safely in Strathglass and

Chisholm of Strathglass

Glen Cannich until their own chiefs evicted them in the 19th.

There had been extensive emigration from the Chisholm country to North America, both before and after the War of Independence there, as there was in many parts of the Highlands. It was caused partly by a rise in population, partly by the action of *Ruairidh*, 22nd Chief, who subjected his tenants to massive increases of rent. But he died in 1785, and his son Alexander, 23rd Chief, granted leases of eighteen years. Although further rent increases followed, the new Chief resisted the temptation to evict his clansmen and when an odious Lowland grazier called Thomas Gillespie turned up with tempting offers, he was chased from the Chisholm lands. But Alexander died in 1793, leaving his widow, his only daughter Mary, and his leases to protect his people against the greed of the next Chief, his half-brother William.

The leases expired in 1810. Gillespie was invited back, and settled with his sheep in the lands of Strathglass from which the Chisholms were evicted by their own Chief. Bishop Angus Chisholm wrote to the widow of Alexander: 'Oh Madam, you would really feel if you only heard the pangs and saw the oozing tears by which I am surrounded in this once happy but now desolated valley of Strathglass.' The local bards added their testimony, amongst them, *Alasdair Òg* of Guisachan: 'The abode of warriors has withered away. The son of the Lowlander is in your place.' Alastair Chisholm of Chisholm (b. 1920) is the present Chief.

Clarke

Among the Ossianic ballads that were written down in the Book of the Dean of Lismore over four centuries ago are several that take the form of conversations between the bard and Saint Patrick. Ossian, the poet-son of Fionn (or Fingal, as his name has been altered in modern times), is a legendary figure of the 3rd century. Saint Patrick lived in the 5th; the earliest literary sources of Fingalian tradition belong to the 8th; the ballad swept Europe as a form of entertainment in the 13th; and Ossianic ballads have passed by oral tradition alone into the present century. In one of the ballad conversations, Ossian addresses Patrick:

> A chléirigh nam bachall mbreac—
> O Clerk of the speckled croziers,
> It would be a great enterprise of your generation
> To place on record forever
> All the valiant deeds of Fionn's warrior company.

This verse must have pleased Dean MacGregor, as he carried out Ossian's instructions early in the 16th century.

It was only a few years after he had done so that a clerk living in the far north of Scotland wrote a remarkable letter to Henry VIII in English. He did so in 1543 shortly after the death of James V, King of Scots, whose high-handed treatment of Highland and Border chiefs was revenged by such disloyalty to him when Henry of England invaded his country. The clerk's letter reflects the attitude of a Gael (whose voice is rarely heard in this period) to the repressive policies of the central government.

He describes himself as a redshank, the opprobrious Lowland term for a wearer of Highland dress, besides giving his personal name in the signature—John Eldar, Clerk, a Redshank. He also describes the Gaels of Scotland as Irish, according to the usage of the time. 'The Babylonical bishops and the great courtiers of Scotland repute the foresaid Irish lords as wild, rude, and barbarous people, brought up (as they say) without learning and nurture; yet they pass them a great deal in faith, honesty, in policy and wit, in good order and civility.'

These two contrasting illustrations show how the Latin name for a cleric passed through Gaelic into English and became over the centuries the term for a man of literacy or learning. Within the ancient diocese of Caithness to which John Eldar belonged there is still a township on the north coast called Clerkhill, whose older inhabitants are Gaelic-speaking to this day. At Durness in the far north-west, a family using the name of Clarke can be traced back to the 17th century.

But while the term became transformed into an inherited family name, it was still used also in its original context, as a form of description. Hector Maclean, who succeeded as the laird of the island of Coll in 1558, was known as An Cleirich Beag—The Little Clerk. There is no single learned dynasty of Clarkes, however, to compare with the Beatons or the MacMhuirichs, nor did any Clarke found a Highland clan.

(*Above*) Clarke; (*below*) Blue Clergy

51

Cochrane

The earliest recorded and most prominent family to bear this name assumed it from the five merk lands of Cochrane near Paisley in Renfrewshire: though it was said that some MacEacherns who had been removed to the Lowlands adopted the name, while its affinity to the Irish Corcoran is suggestive.

In 1456-7 Robert Cochrane of Cochrane, son of John, resigned the lands of Cochrane to Allan his son, who thereupon received a charter for them from James II. His descendant, William Cochrane of that Ilk, added a tower to the manor house before his death in 1594, after which it was called Cochrane Castle. It was a notable period for such architecture.

William's grandson and heir through a female line was Sir William, created 1st Earl of Dundonald in 1669, whose second son became a

Calvinist and crossed from Holland with William of Orange at the Revolution of 1688. It was his descendant who succeeded as 8th Earl on the failure of the senior line.

But the most remarkable by far was Thomas the 10th Earl (1775–1860), though during most of his career he bore the courtesy title of Lord Cochrane. He entered the Royal Navy, and before long was court-martialled for disrespect, and cautioned to 'avoid flippancy'. In 1801 he attended a fancy-dress ball dressed as a seaman, and fought a duel against one of the men who evicted him. That same year, with a brig and its crew of 54 men, he boarded and captured a Spanish frigate with thirty-two heavy guns and a crew of 319, a feat unparalleled in naval history.

In 1807 he had the singular honour of being returned to Parliament as a Member for Westminster, where he did not endear himself to the Admiralty when he introduced a motion on naval abuses. The next year he carried out his brilliant defence of Trinidad castle against the French and in 1809 his equally outstanding offensive against the fleet off the coast of France. But he brought a well-merited accusation of incompetence against the Commander-in-Chief as well as continuing his attacks on Admiralty abuses. Cochrane was prosecuted on a charge of financial swindling of which he was undoubtedly innocent, sentenced to a year's imprisonment and a fine of £1000, evicted from the House of Commons and struck off the Navy List. Though his electors immediately returned him again as their Member and declared him guiltless, he was compelled to serve his sentence.

In 1817 he accepted an invitation from Chile to organise and command the navy which played such an essential part in securing the independence both of Chile and of Peru. The Spanish Viceroy at Lima was amazed 'that a British nobleman should come to fight for a rebel community unacknowledged by all the powers of the globe'. Next he was invited to take command of the Brazilian navy and played a leading part in securing Brazil's independence from Portugal. Then came an invitation to command a fleet to secure the freedom of Greece from Turkey, but this did not materialise. In 1832 a more liberal government restored him to his naval rank, and in 1854 he was Rear Admiral of the United Kingdom. He used his authority to promote the use of steam and screw propellers, and to urge the Admiralty to study the problems of naval architecture. He was never given an opportunity to test his skill in command of a large fleet, but his courage and ingenuity with the limited strengths at his disposal have rarely been surpassed, while his assaults on incompetence led to far-reaching reforms in the future although he incurred such odium at the time.

Past ambiguity concerning the Cochrane tartan has been resolved by the present Chief of the name, the 14th Earl of Dundonald, who has ordained the sett here illustrated.

Colquhoun

The lands of Colquhoun in Dunbartonshire were granted to Humphrey of Kilpatrick in 1241 by Malcolm, Earl of Lennox, and Ingram, son of Humphrey, was the first in historical record to assume the surname of Colquhoun. His descendant, Sir Robert Colquhoun, acquired the property of Luss by Loch Lomond about a century later when he married the heiress who descended of the ancient Celtic house which included Maldwin, Dean of the Lennox, in 1150. Their grandson Iain Colquhoun of Luss married Margaret, daughter of Duncan, Earl of Lennox a few years before the King of Scots, James I, returned from his long captivity in England in 1424.

The King descended like a whirlwind upon the magnates who had failed to secure his release earlier, and among those he destroyed was the house of Lennox. Into the vacuum stepped Iain of Luss, appointed by James I to capture and hold Dumbarton Castle, once the capital of the British kingdom of Strathclyde, and now key fortress of the Lennox. In 1427 he was made Sheriff of Dumbarton. But in 1439, two years after James I himself was murdered by a band of the nobles whom he had treated with such severity, Iain of Luss met his death on the island of Inchmurrin in Loch Lomond at the hands of the Macleans of Duart. His grandson Sir Iain of Luss was compensated by James II, who erected Luss into a free barony in 1457, with a capital jurisdiction that his descendants continued to exercise until after the Forty-Five.

It was this Chief, the 11th of Luss, who built the castle of Rossdhu that still stands, a ruin, beside Loch Lomond. He became Great Chamberlain of Scotland and an ambassador to England, while his younger son Robert was Bishop of Argyll from 1473 until 1495. The Bishop's stone effigy has survived in the church of St Kessog at Luss, to whom it is very likely that he was related.

One of the most notorious episodes in the clan's history is the conflict with Clan Gregor which occurred during the lifetime of Alasdair Colquhoun, 17th of Luss. The dispossessed MacGregors lived by raiding the lands of others, and after one particularly savage sortie into Luss the Colquhoun women brought the blood-stained shirts of their menfolk (and, it is said, others dipped in the blood of sheep) to James VI. A few months later about 400 MacGregors came to Glenfruin, where they defeated the Colquhouns in 1603. The consequence was the proscription of Clan Gregor.

Sir Iain, 19th of Luss, was created a baronet of Nova Scotia amongst the first creations of 1625, when Charles I inherited the crown. But in 1718, for the first time since a Colquhoun had married the Fair Maid of Luss in the 14th century, the entire property passed to another house with the heiress Anne Colquhoun of Luss. This was the house of another Chief, that of Clan Grant. But special arrangements were made to preserve the two offices and properties separate from one another, and accordingly James Grant was recognised by Lyon in 1781 as the 25th Colquhoun of Luss, and a new baronetcy was created for him in 1786. Meanwhile, in 1774 the descendants of the heiress Anne began the building of the neo-classical house of Rossdhu in which they still live by Loch Lomondside.

Of all the custodians of a property owned for so many centuries by a single family, perhaps none will be remembered with deeper gratitude than Sir Iain Colquhoun, 31st of Luss, who died in 1948. The record of the Highland chiefs as guardians of clan properties is an extremely varied one. The Colquhouns of Luss were particularly exposed to temptation to exploit the lands whose charters they held, so close to the burgeoning city of Glasgow, and in such incomparable surroundings. Their comparatively unspoilt appearance today is largely Sir Iain Colquhoun's achievement. So far from making a fortune for himself at the expense of his country and of posterity, the 31st Chief of Luss played a dominant part, as Chairman of the National Trust, in holding the speculators at bay, and advocating principles of conservation.

Crawford

This name derives from the barony of Crawford in Lanarkshire. In the mid-12th century John of Crawford witnessed a charter, and a little later Sir Reginald of Crawford was appointed Sheriff of Ayr during the reign of William the Lion. With three of his sons he was witness to a grant in favour of Kelso Abbey, while a fourth son named Reginald was parson of Strathavon. Many other Crawford names appear in the charters of the 13th century and in 1296 another Sir Reginald Crawford appears as Sheriff of Ayr. During this century two Crawford girls made marriages which were to produce very remarkable offspring. In 1248 Sir John of Crawford died leaving two daughters, one of whom married David Lindsay, ancestor of the Earls of Crawford. The sheriff of Ayr in 1297 had a sister Margaret who married Sir Malcolm Wallace of Ellerslie, and gave birth to William Wallace, Scotland's greatest patriot.

Three principal branches are traced from these times. One springs from a brother of the sheriff of 1297, whose family received a grant of Auchinames from Robert Bruce in 1320. The head of the family was reckoned to belong to this branch, whose representative Hugh Crawfurd, 21st of Auchinames, sold the property and died recently in Canada. Another branch is that of Craufurdland, which descends from a younger son of the earlier Sheriff of Ayr, and was confirmed in this property by Robert III in 1391. The third is traced from Sir John of Crawford, and acquired the estates of Kilburnie in 1499.

Two cadets of this house made an exceptional stir. Thomas Crawford of Jordanhill (?1530–1603) was a sixth son of Lawrence of Kilburnie, and consequently required to seek his own fortune. He took part in the battle of Pinkie in 1547 where he was captured but ransomed, and then went to France to serve under Henry II, the future father-in-law of Mary, Queen of Scots. He returned with Queen Mary in 1561, and became a member of Darnley's household when he married the Queen. Crawford was well-placed to know who were the real instigators of the murder of Darnley, and in 1569 he had the courage to accuse Maitland of Lethington and Sir James Balfour: naturally without effect, since by this time the guilt had been fastened wholly upon Bothwell and the deposed Queen. When Darnley's father Lennox succeeded to the Regency in 1570 Crawford became an officer of his guard, and in the following year he performed the almost incredible feat of capturing Dumbarton from the adherents of Queen Mary with 150 men. Just before dawn they scaled its precipitous rock with ropes, ladders and grappling hooks. Archbishop Hamilton was captured there, and it is not the least horrible incident in the holocaust of Calvinism triumphant, that this aged prelate was hanged. Knox was recommending to Cecil that they should do the same with his Queen. 'If ye strike not at the root, the branches that appear to be broken will bud again.' Scotland's ghoulish prophet died before Thomas Crawford had played his part in reducing Edinburgh Castle in 1573, and thus extinguishing Marian resistence.

But the spirit of Knox passed to Lawrence Crawford (1611–45), sixth son of Hugh of Jordanhill. He had fought under the Scandinavian kings in the Thirty Years' War before he joined the rebellious English army which opposed Charles I. His intolerant Calvinism brought him into conflict with Cromwell, on whom he retaliated by bringing a charge of cowardice against him after the battle of Marston Moor. The quarrel was resolved by Crawford's death in action at Hereford in the following year.

In 1781 a baronetcy was conferred on the senior line of Kilburnie, and it has been held by two generals, two naval commanders, and a Fellow of King's College, Cambridge.

Cumming

This unpretentious name, probably derived from the herb called cummin, is in fact the most royal in Scotland of any that failed to attain the crown. Like so many others, it reached the country with David I, who made the grandson of one of William the Conqueror's knights Chancellor of Scotland after he had gone there from England as King. Richard Comyn improved upon this by marrying the grand-daughter of King Donald *Bàn,* and their son married the heiress of Buchan. So the Comyns were among the first Anglo-Normans to establish themselves in the old Celtic earldoms. As Lords of Badenoch they ruled from their impregnable castle on its island in Lochindorb. By 1286 when the last King of David I's line perished, they had become the most powerful family in Scotland.

During the time of troubles that followed the failure of the direct royal line the Comyns had a double claim to the succession. The first derived through their descent from Donald *Bàn*, but it was junior to those of the descendants of King Donald's elder brother, Malcolm Canmore (*Ceann Mór*: Big Head). Among these the senior line descended from Devorguilla, David I's great-grand-daughter. She married John Balliol who founded Balliol College at Oxford, while Devorguilla founded Sweetheart Abbey in her husband's memory. It was the son of this attractive pair who was raised to the throne as King John in 1292, while their daughter married John Comyn of Badenoch. Thus the Comyns as well as the Balliols stood between the Bruces, descendants of Devorguilla's younger sister, and the Scottish crown.

After King John had been deposed and the Balliols had left Scotland, Devorguilla's grandson John Comyn remained there, the most powerful man in the land, representing the legitimate royal line. Bruce invited him to Dumfries in 1306, far from his own territories, and there stabbed him to death at the church altar. In the following month Bruce was crowned King of Scots and in the following year the Hammer of the Scots died, leaving Edward II his unwarlike son to succeed him. But although this eased the pressure from England, it was many years before Bruce had destroyed the Comyns and their adherants in Scotland. John Comyn's only son fell in battle against his father's murderer at Bannockburn.

John Comyn's uncle Sir Robert had also been killed in the church at Dumfries, while trying to save his nephew's life. But there was no need to persecute Sir Robert's descendants. Although King Donald *Bàn* was their ancestor, they did not descend from Devorguilla. It is this branch which acquired the estate of Altyre in Moray which it has held ever since, and which has provided the chiefship of a clan that generally uses the Cumming spelling. The house of Altyre later acquired by marriage the property of Gordonstoun founded by Sir Robert Gordon (1580–1656), one of the most successful scoundrels of the Sutherland branch of this family. But although the present Chief's name is hyphenated with that of Gordon, he does in fact descend in a continuous male line from the knight who crossed the Channel with William the Conqueror, and from his grandson who married King Donald *Bàn*'s grand-daughter.

Cunningham

At some time before Hugh de Moreville, Constable of Scotland, died in 1162, he granted to Warnebald, presumably a Fleming, the property of Kilmaurs in the district of Cunningham in Ayrshire. When Haakon IV of Norway brought his fleet to this coast in 1263, to assert his sovereignty over the western isles, Harvey Cunningham of Kilmaurs was among those who helped to repulse him at Largs. The family property was increased by Robert Bruce as a reward for their support. Hugh Cunningham of Kilmaurs was granted the lands of Lamburgton in 1321 by King Robert. His grandson Sir William married the heiress of the Denniestons of that Ilk and thus added the property of Glencairn also. Sir William's grandson was raised to the peerage by James III, first as Lord Kilmaurs in 1462, then as Earl of Glencairn in 1488. The King's favour is perhaps indicative of the new Earl's character, for James III bestowed it upon men of culture and talent, to the fury of the older nobility. When they hounded James III to his death in 1488, the 1st Earl perished with him.

Alexander Cunningham, 5th Earl of Glencairn, played a very different part. He was a member of the band which called itself the Lords of the Congregation of Jesus Christ, and whose activities included embezzling church property, and furthering England's political aims in Scotland in return for English gold. Glencairn was a particular patron of Knox, who sent Cecil military information and begged for money in return. These were the instruments which enabled the Tudors to destroy both the Regent Mary and her daughter Mary, Queen of Scots, under the cloak of supporting a creed which they themselves persecuted in England as neither Mary nor her mother ever did in Scotland. In 1565 Glencairn joined Moray's rebellion against his sister, and he held a command among her enemies at Carberry, where she surrendered to them in 1567, only to be imprisoned in Loch Leven Castle. While Moray secured the Regency, looted his sister's jewellery, and sent her famous pearl necklace to Queen Elizabeth as her share, Glencairn went on his own initiative to the chapel of Holyrood and smashed all its furniture and works of art in an orgy of destruction. He has since been much praised by Protestant historians, not merely for his religious zeal, but more strangely, for his patriotism.

The 9th Earl of Glencairn returned to the traditions of the 1st when he played his gallant and forlorn part in raising a rebellion in the Highlands for Charles II in 1653. The King had fled back to the Continent after the defeat at Worcester, and Scotland was now under the military government of Cromwell's generals. Glencairn's rising could hardly succeed, but after the Restoration in 1660 he was made Lord Chancellor of Scotland.

In the time of Robert Burns, the Cunninghams, including their Chief the 14th Earl and two of his more humble clansmen, stepped upon quite a different stage. The two were the brothers Allan and Thomas Cunningham, born to an unsuccessful farmer in Dumfreisshire in 1785 and 1776. Allan was the more successful poet and writer of the two, and he enjoyed the friendship of James Hogg, Sir Walter Scott and Chantrey the sculptor, as well as that of Burns himself. But Thomas also made his contribution as a poet and songwriter to this golden age of Scottish literature, while Glencairn himself earned from Burns this tribute:

The bridegroom may forget the bride
Was made his wedded wife yestreen;
The monarch may forget the crown
That on his head an hour has been;
The mother may forget the child
That smiles sae sweetly on her knee;
But I'll remember thee, Glencairn,
And a' that thou hast done for me!

Currie

This Hebridean name is the corrupt English form of one of the most ancient and distinguished in Scotland's history. Its Gaelic form is *Mac Mhuirich*, and bearers of it descend from the Irish family of *Úi Dálaidh* (O'Daly) whose descent can be traced historically from an 8th-century King of Ireland. The O'Dalys were established in their literary role as a bardic family by the 12th century. When *Mael Íosa Ua Dálaidh* died in 1185, he was described in the contemporary Irish annals as *Ollamh* (chief man of learning) of Ireland and Scotland.

Of *Mael Íosa's* great-grandsons, two are especially memorable. *Donnchadh Mór* was the most notable Gaelic religious poet of the Middle Ages, while his brother *Muireadhach Albanach* (Murach of Scotland) is the reputed progenitor of the Scottish Mac Mhuirichs. At least twenty poems are ascribed to *Muireadhach Albanach*, and it is significant that one of them is addressed to an Earl of the ancient Gaelic province of the Lennox, who died in 1217. Another of them can be seen from its contents to have been composed in the Adriatic, and provides supporting evidence that *Muireadhach* took part in the Fifth Crusade. By 1259 a *Cathal Mac Mhuirich* signs as witness to a document by virtue of his residence in the Lennox. His name is spelt *Kathil Macmurchy*, and he is almost certainly the son of *Muireadhach Albanach*.

Such were the already ancient origins of Scotland's longest learned dynasty. Naturally it attached itself to the Lords of the Isles when these maintained a virtually independent Gaelic principality in mediaeval Scotland. At the decisive battle of Harlaw in 1411, when the Lord of the Isles sought to enforce his claim to the lands of the Earldom of Ross against the parvenu dynasty of Stewart, it was *Lachlann Mór Mac Mhuirich* who composed the incitement to battle. Two related texts of this poem survive.

Niall Mór is the first who appears under Clanranald patronage, and the earliest dateable poem from his pen belongs to the year 1613.

The Clanranald bards produced the largest corpus of Mac Mhuirich writings. *Niall Mac Mhuirich* (*c*.1637–1726) chronicled the wars of Montrose in the last body of Gaelic prose to be written in Scotland in the ancient Irish script style. He was also the last fully competent poet of his family, and a hard core of ten of his poems survives, besides others that are attributed to him. He lived in Uist, a Catholic, and it was here that *Lachlann Mac Mhuirich* was found in 1800, who claimed to be 18th in descent from *Muireadhach Albanach*. But the long persecution of his society and its religion and culture had at last reduced this dynasty to illiteracy: its great collection of manuscripts was dispersed, many of them cut up for tailors' strips.

It was in the 17th century that the forms McVurich and McCurrie began to appear in historical records. By the end of the 18th century the form Currie had become common in Islay; by the 19th, the same form was in general use in Uist. Currie was the name that emigrants carried with them across the Atlantic: the name that Lauchlan D. Currie used, who was Chief Justice of Nova Scotia and one of the Governors of St Francis Xavier University before his death in 1969.

Davidson

It is a curious fact that even in the heart of Gaelic-speaking societies an English form of patronymic was sometimes adopted. But although the Davidsons were members of the Clan Chattan confederation, they do not descend from a man called David of the Mackintosh clan nor, apparently, of any other clan within this alliance. They seem to have been a totally independent tribe which was led by a Moses of the name of David Dubh into the relative safety of the Mackintosh fold.

Before that time the great massif of the northern Grampians and the plains of Buchan and Moray had been dominated by the Comyn family, the most powerful in Scotland until Robert Bruce destroyed it. In the hiatus that followed Bruce's devastation of Buchan and the plantation of his supporters throughout this region, it was natural that communities which had flourished under the Comyns should seek new protectors. It is particularly understandable that they should seek it in the old Celtic tribal context that was familiar to them, rather than under new alien feudal overlords. Such, at any rate, were the circumstances in which David Dubh led the clan which has ever since been called the Davidsons into the association of Clan Chattan.

In the long run it brought them neither security nor prosperity. They were involved in many an unprofitable clan conflict, in one of which they were thought to have been very nearly annihilated in 1396. Few of their name are any longer to be found in the Highlands.

Dewar

The term Dewar is a title of office like Toiseach. The difference is that whereas a son of the Toiseach was called *Mac an Toiseich* (Mackintosh), the Dewar simply adopted the office as his surname. Inasmuch as this office involved the custody of a saint's relics, the particular relic was generally specified after the surname.

The relics were those of Saint Fillan, a prince of the royal house of Dalriada who died in 703, leaving the MacNabs as his heirs. There were five of these relics: the bell, the missal, an arm-bone, the pastoral staff, and a lost relic of uncertain identity called a *Fearg*, which is Gaelic for Wrath. The Gaelic for a bell is *Bearnan*, and nearly a thousand years after the death of Saint Fillan the property of its custodian at Suie in Glendochart was referred to in 1640 as Dewar-Vernon's Croft. The bell has no clapper, and probably never had one. These bells were generally struck with an independent instrument to summon the faithful to worship. Saint Fillan's was borne in the pageant which celebrated the coronation of the young King James IV in 1488. It is now in the Scottish National Museum of Antiquities.

The other relic to have survived amongst those which the Dewars guarded for so many centuries is the pastoral staff. Originally this was a simple shepherd's crook of wood, but during the Dark Ages its head was encased in bronze, and a beautifully ornamented mediaeval crozier-head of silver was added to that. The Gaelic for a crozier is *Coigreach*, and in 1336 Donald *McSobrell Dewar Cogerach* was confirmed in possession of the lands he held by virtue of his office. The Dewar of the staff received his confirmation of title from a Menzies, rather than from the saint's original successors, the MacNabs. These had failed to jump on the Bruce band-wagon, and consequently their ancient lands of Glendochart had been sequestered to one of Bruce's Norman supporters, from Mesnières near Rouen. Although the MacNabs were restored to their Glendochart properties, the Dewars have been offered the option of regarding themselves as septs either of Menzies or of MacNab.

Other options are open to them. In 1575 the Dewar of the staff sold his lands to Campbell of Glenorchy. A century later he was driven to sell the staff itself to MacDonald of Glengarry, so that a MacDonald became a Dewar. But the original Dewars of the staff took the trouble to recover it, and by bringing it home to Breadalbane presumably gave themselves an equal option to regard themselves as a sept of the Campbells. By 1782 the custodian of the staff had sunk to the status of a labourer at Killin, where Presbyterians who had been taught otherwise travelled long distances to obtain the virtues of water that had been poured through the crozier case. In 1818 Alexander Dewar emigrated with his staff to Canada. Here Highlanders visited him to collect water in which it had been dipped, to cure their sick cattle. The last Alexander Dewar of the staff sent the staff back to Scotland in

1876, to be placed in the National Museum of Antiquities. And Saint Fillan himself could hardly have made a more graceful gesture of appreciation if it had been himself who rewarded his faithful Dewars by granting them the continuing power to create water of life, for which the Gaelic is *Uisge Beatha*, and its anglicised form Whisky.

Black Douglas

This Douglas tartan has been composed of the two colours from which the clan takes its name: *dubh* is Gaelic for black, *glas* for grey. How this originated is unknown, despite a variety of legends. Nor have any antecedents been established with certainty for the first William of Douglas who witnessed charters between 1175 and 1199, and again in about 1200 and 1211. Between 1198 and 1239 flourished Archibald Douglas, apparent progenitor of those great families that were to play such a resounding part in Scotland's history. He was succeeded in the lands of Douglasdale by William, of what was to become the senior line of the Black Douglases. William was the father of Sir William the Hardy, the companion of Wallace who was captured and died in the Tower of London in 1298.

His son, the Good Sir James Douglas, occupies the third place among the heroes of the Scottish wars of independence. Indeed, in Barbour's 14th-century epic poem *The Bruce*, the Good Sir James occupies a place equal to that of King Robert himself. He attended Bruce at his death in 1328 and promised to take his heart to the Holy Land. But in Spain he was killed in battle, and then his son fell fighting against the English at Halidon Hill in 1333. But the Good Sir James left a bastard son also. Meanwhile, his brother Sir Archibald became Regent during the minority of Bruce's son and also perished at Halidon Hill, leaving the son William who was created Earl of Douglas in 1358. The 2nd Earl married a daughter of the first Stewart King, Robert II, but he was killed at the battle of Otterburn in 1388; and so the second legitimate line of the Black Douglases was extinguished. It was now that the remarkable bastard son of the Good Sir James, Archibald the Grim, entered into his father's inheritance as the 3rd Earl of Douglas. He had already received huge grants from Bruce's son, David II, in Galloway. There he governed with strength and justice, and there the ruins of his castle of Threave still stand as a memorial to the Black Douglas Lords of Galloway. Archibald the Grim fought against the English at Poitiers in 1356, where he was captured and escaped. He died in about 1400, leaving as his most enduring monument the Church property which he did so much to build, restore and endow.

His son the 4th Earl fought at the battle of Shrewsbury with Harry Hotspur against Henry IV of England in 1403. The Percy was killed and the Douglas taken prisoner. After he had regained his freedom he continued the fight against England as a general of Joan of Arc's Dauphin, Charles VII of France. There he was rewarded with the duchy

Grey Douglas

of Touraine, but died in battle. His young grandsons were lured to Edinburgh after their father's death and executed in the castle by enemies of the overmighty house of Douglas; and so the earldom passed to the second son of Archibald the Grim.

James the 7th Earl proved to be violent and impetuous, and nemesis struck the Black Douglases in the time of his sons. William the 8th Earl succeeded in 1443 and was made by James II Lieutenant General of the kingdom. When he travelled to Rome in 1450 to attend the Papal Jubilee, he passed through Europe with regal magnificence. On his return he resumed his alliance with the earls of Crawford and Ross. James II sent him a safe-conduct and invited him to dinner in Stirling Castle. After dinner James ordered him to break his alliances. When Douglas refused, the King stabbed him, the attendants finished him off, and his body was flung over the battlements. A few weeks later his brother James, now 9th Earl of Douglas, rode through Stirling, dragging the dishonoured safe-conduct at his horse's tail. Three years after the Stirling murder the curtain fell on the house of the Black Douglas. First James II secured the submission of the 9th Earl, then he raised a charge of treason against his family and brought an army against them. The Earl fled to England, and of his brothers one joined him there, one was killed, and the third was executed. Archibald the Grim's island stronghold of Threave was forced to surrender, the entire Douglas estates were forfeited, the earldom extinguished.

Douglas

It is presumed that the Archibald Douglas who disappears from historical record in 1239 was the father of a younger son called Sir Andrew, founder of the senior cadet branch of the family. In 1315 his grandson Sir James Douglas was granted the property of Morton, originally a small-holding in East Calder, Linlithgow-shire. Soon greater honours and properties were added to this branch of a house to which the dynasty of Bruce owed so much. David II raised Sir William, son of Sir James, to the ancient earldom of Atholl in 1341, but then arranged for him to exchange it for Liddesdale. He was celebrated as the flower of chivalry, and known henceforth as the Knight of Liddesdale. His descendants became first lords of Dalkeith, then in 1458 earls of Morton in Dumfries-shire. So when the Black Douglases were forfeited in 1455, a phoenix was already rising from their ashes.

Nor was it the only one. The 1st Earl of Douglas had left a bastard son called George who had married a daughter of King Robert III, and been raised to the earldom of Angus as befitted the husband of a princess. By the time the Black Douglases were forfeited, the 4th Earl of Angus represented the line of what were known as the Red Douglases and his heir, Archibald 'Bell the Cat' had been born. The Red Douglases began to occupy the centre of the stage of Scottish history almost as soon as the Black Douglases had departed from it. Indeed, by siding with the crown against their clansmen, they succeeded in acquiring much of the forfeited Douglas property.

The 5th Earl acquired his nickname, according to tradition, in a manner that does him little credit. A clique of nobles was conspiring to undermine the King's favourite Cochrane, reputed architect of the palace of Stirling. One of them told the story of the mice who put a bell round the neck of the cat to warn them of its approach. 'I will bell the cat,' said Angus. The nobles then hanged the talented favourite from Lauder bridge under the very eyes of James III. In 1488 the King himself was murdered, and Archibald Bell the Cat became Guardian of the Realm in the name of the young James IV, and subsequently Lord Chancellor. His two elder sons died with James IV at Flodden, while his youngest lived to be one of the ornaments of the Renaissance. Indeed Gavin Douglas, Bishop of Dunkeld, is the first person who ever translated a Latin classic into the English language. First he translated a work of Ovid, now lost, then he completed his Aeneid of Virgil. This, and his original poetry, place him in the highest ranks of Scotland's early poets. At the same time he played an active part in the political activities of his house. These prospered for a time when his nephew, the 6th Earl of Angus, married the widowed Queen of Scots, Margaret Tudor. But when Angus fell from power and fled to England, Gavin Douglas was forced to share his exile. He died of the plague in London in about 1522, a denounced traitor.

The branch of the earls of Morton also suffered from the hatred of James V for all of his stepfather's family of Douglas. But in the reign of his daughter, the 4th Earl of Morton (c. 1516–1581) stepped into the centre of the stage once occupied by Black and Red Douglases. His part is one of the most sinister of all, including complicity in the murders of both Darnley and Rizzio. After Queen Mary's deposition he became one of the Regents during the minority of her son James VI, who executed him when he came of age. It was then established that the Countess of Morton had been insane for the previous twenty-two years: only daughters survived these parents.

Among the innumerable Douglases who have depended upon their abilities, rather than on their connection with these great parent houses, for their claim to attention, David Douglas is one of the most bizarre. He was born at Scone in Perthshire in 1798, the son of a working mason, and became a gardener. First he increased his knowledge of botany by touring all over Scotland, then he carried his researches across the Atlantic. At Rio de Janeiro he encountered the form of orchid named after him, the *G. Douglasii*, and from Cape Horn to Vancouver he collected specimens that secured his election as a Fellow of the Geological, the Zoological and the Linnaean Societies. Then he visited the Sandwich islands, and dug traps for wild bulls. In 1834, when he was thirty-five years old, he fell into one which already contained a trapped bull, and was torn to pieces.

Douglas of Drumlanrig

The Red and the Black Douglases were not the only branches of this prolific and powerful clan to descend from a bastard. The earldom itself had reverted to the natural son of the Good Sir James when the 2nd Earl was slain at Otterburn in 1388. But before that event the Earl of Douglas had bestowed the barony of Drumlanrig on his illegitimate son William, founder of a house that was to become as mighty and far-flung as any of the others. Sir William the 9th of Drumlanrig entertained James VI there in 1617, on the solitary visit which that monarch paid to Scotland after he had inherited the throne of Elizabeth Tudor. When Charles I succeeded to his father's two crowns, he created Sir William Earl of Queensberry in 1628.

So once again a cadet branch of the Douglases had moved into the room vacated by its seniors. On the downfall of the earls of Douglas, the house of Angus had advanced: after the Earl of Angus fell, Douglas of Morton had risen to supreme power in the state. The very King who ordered Morton's execution bestowed his favours on Drumlanrig. From this moment its rise was spectacular and rapid. The 2nd Earl of Queensberry was a zealous royalist during the wars which cost Charles I his head, and his eldest son William reaped the reward after the Restoration of Charles II. In 1680 he became Justice-General of Scotland. Two years later he was appointed Lord High Treasurer and raised to the rank of Marquess. In 1684 he became 1st Duke of Queensberry, just before Charles II was succeeded by his openly Catholic brother James VII.

It was now that the Duke made the crucial decision which sealed his family's fortunes. Despite all he owed to the Stewarts, he was one of those who offered the crown to William of Orange, and thus placed himself on the winning side in the Revolution of 1688. A few years later he died, only fifty-eight years old, leaving his son, the 2nd Duke, to play an even more resounding part in the history of his country. For it was James, 2nd Duke of Queensberry (1662–1711) who was principally responsible for securing the incorporating union between England and Scotland in 1707. Such a measure had become increasingly unpopular in Scotland, and it required considerable skill on Queensberry's part, as well as bullying and bribery, to force it through the Scottish Parliament.

His vast properties were passed to a younger son. But since then the English titles have become extinct while Drumlanrig and the dukedom have passed to the Dukes of Buccleuch. The senior line has continued, however, with the rank of Marquess of Queensberry, and it was the 9th Marquess who gave his name to the Queensberry Rules of boxing. He was the father of Alfred Douglas, who brought such misfortune to Oscar Wilde, while he greatly over-estimated his own stature as a poet. But his taste for the arts has continued in the family. The present Marquess of Queensberry is a Professor of Ceramics, his brother Lord Gawain Douglas a musician.

Drummond

Drummond of Perth

Tradition asserts that the founder of this clan was the admiral who transported Margaret the Atheling's sister from her exile in Hungary, long before she became the second wife of Malcolm Canmore, King of Scots. But the earliest historical evidence suggests a noble Celtic origin, for the earliest certain ancestor is *Maelcolm Beg*, Little Malcolm, who appears in charters from about 1225 as Seneschal of the Lennox. He took the surname by which the clan is now called from Drymen, a place associated also with the Highland Mores and the Buchanans. To this day the name of the Chief is *An Drumanach Mór*, The Great Man of Drymen. Malcolm of Drymen's son Malcolm was twice captured during the wars of independence against Edward I of England, and his grandson, the third Malcolm Drummond, fought at Bannockburn. Thus the Drummonds were among the clans which increased in prosperity through having backed the winner. In about 1345 John, the Drummond Chief, married the heiress of Stobhall, the beautiful mediaeval mansion in which his descendant, David Drummond, 17th Earl of Perth, lives today.

John Drummond of Stobhall's sister Margaret married David II, son of the Bruce, but they left no heirs. However, his daughter Annabella Drummond married the second of the Stewart Kings, Robert III, and was the mother of the poet-King James I. Her brother Sir John Drummond became Justiciar of Scotland and his great-grandson was created Lord Drummond in 1488. It seemed likely that

Margaret, daughter of the 1st Lord Drummond, might become a third Queen of Scots of this family, so violent was the affection of the young King James IV for her. But Margaret and her three sisters all died in mysterious circumstances—it was generally believed that they had been poisoned—and James IV made his dynastic marriage with Margaret Tudor which led to the Union of England and Scotland. Two years after the marriage had taken place in 1503, the 4th Lord Drummond was created Earl of Perth.

The most distinguished member of his clan at this time was William, son of Sir John Drummond of Hawthornden, a Gentleman Usher to James VI descended from the Drummonds of Carnock who were cadets of Stobhall. William was born in 1585, and inherited on his father's death in 1610 the estate of Hawthornden which was later described as 'a sweet and solitary seat, and very fit and proper for the Muses'. Here William lived his literary life, shunning the opportunities which his family connections offered him. 'If we believe some schoolmen,' he wrote, 'that the souls of the departed have some dark knowledge of the actions done upon earth, which concern their good or evil; what solace then will this bring to James I, that after two hundred years, he hath one of his mother's name and race that hath renewed his fame and actions in the world?'

In 1618 Ben Jonson made the long winter journey to Hawthornden, and William Drummond scribbled his rough draft of the English poet's malicious comments on his contemporaries, his strictures on Shakespeare and Donne, on Michael Drayton and Sir John Harington and Sir Walter Ralegh. He did not even spare his host. Thirty years later, when the rebellion had broken out against Charles I, William Drummond sat in Hawthornden calmly prophesying exactly where it would lead. 'During these miseries, of which the troublers of the state shall make their profit, there will arise (perhaps) one, who will name himself Protector of the liberty of the kingdom: he shall surcharge the people with greater miseries than ever before they did suffer.'

He did not live to see it, dying in 1649, the same year as Charles I. After the Restoration his eldest son William was knighted by Charles II. But William Drummond of Hawthornden had preferred to erect his own memorial in privacy, the harmonious poetry in the style of Spenser, the outstanding sonnets, and more surprisingly, the sixteen mechanical inventions which he patented.

An Drumanach Mór remained loyal to the Catholic religion and to the Stewart dynasty. The 4th Earl of Perth was James VII's Lord Chancellor; the 5th commanded the Jacobite cavalry at Sheriffmuir in the 1715 uprising; the 6th died at sea in his flight from Culloden. But Stobhall is still theirs, its ancient furnishings undesecrated by Calvinists.

John Drummond, 17th Earl of Perth (b. 1907), is the present Chief.

Dunbar

The family which first adopted the name of Dunbar after surnames came into use in Scotland was one of the great Celtic houses that continued to flourish throughout the centuries of Normanisation. It descended from Crinan of Dunkeld, probably the grandson of Duncan, the lay-abbot who was killed in 965. By the reign of Malcolm Canmore its representative was Gospatrick, Earl of Northumberland, to whom the King granted the lands and earldom of Dunbar, whose sea-girt stronghold was to witness so many dramas in Scotland's history.

It was Patrick the 10th Earl who received Edward II of England into Dunbar Castle after his flight from Bannockburn, and enabled him to return to his own kingdom. If he had detained Edward, the English might have been compelled to recognise King Robert and make peace, saving both countries from years of bloodshed. But Earl Patrick himself came to terms with the Bruce soon after, and was one of the signatories of the Declaration of Arbroath in 1320. When Edward Balliol returned as the rival (and rightful) King of Scots during the reign of the Bruce's son David II, Earl Patrick supported him briefly in 1333–4. But finding that he was little more than an English puppet-king, he returned to David II's allegiance. The English brought an army to invest his castle of Dunbar during his absence in 1337, but his Countess, Black Agnes, held the fortress until a relieving force succeeded in reaching her by sea. A ballad preserves the exasperation of the English commander:

She kept a stir in tower and trench,
That brawling boisterous Scottish wench.
Came I early, came I late,
I found Agnes at the gate.

The 11th Earl was one of the victims of the greed of James I. After nearly four hundred years the property of the Celtic earls of Dunbar was annexed to the crown, and the last Earl, Sir George Dunbar of Kilconquhar, died in 1455. But by this time his house had established its branches of Mochrum in Moray and Westfield in Wigtownshire, and moved into the earldom and bishopric of Moray. The grandson of Earl Patrick and Black Agnes was Columba Dunbar (?1370—1435), Bishop of Moray, whose effigy is still to be seen in the ruins of Elgin Cathedral. By the mid-15th century Dunbars of the Westfield line were established as far north as Caithness.

Several Dunbars made memorable contributions to the Renaissance when it reached Scotland. Gavin, Bishop of Aberdeen (?1455—1532) was the 4th son of Sir Alexander Dunbar of Westfield. By 1503 he was in the Privy Council of that ornament of the Renaissance, James IV, and in 1518 he received his bishopric in succession to his great predecessor Elphinstone, founder of the university of Aberdeen. Gavin Dunbar completed his work there, and beautified the cathedral of St Machar, where his marble effigy was smashed at the Reformation. Bishop Gavin had a nephew of the same name, 3rd son of Sir John Dunbar of Mochrum. Through his uncle's influence he followed him in the Deanery of Moray, and became tutor to the young King James V after his father's death on the field of Flodden. In 1524 he was made Archbishop of Glasgow, then Lord Chancellor, and died in 1547 to enjoy a posthumous fame in the scurrilities of John Knox.

William Dunbar, 'the darling of the Scottish Muses', as Walter Scott called him, belonged to an obscure branch of the name that gave him no social advantages. Although James IV gave him a small pension for his poetry, he remained poor all his life, and his sweetest songs are those that tell of saddest thought. While he attained no Church rank other than that of a Friar, his better-connected namesake Alexander Dunbar, Prior of Pluscarden at the time of the Reformation, was able to transfer its ample funds and lands to his own family. Well might William Dunbar comment on the world's instability:

Belief does leap, trust does not tarry,
Office does flit, and courts do vary,
Purpose does change as wind and rain;
Which to consider is an pain.

The people so wicked are of feiris (manners)
The fruitless earth all witness bears,
The air infected and profane;
Which to consider is an pain.

Duncan

This is the Gaelic personal name *Donnchadh*, which appears in Scotland's oldest records. Dunchad was the eleventh Abbot of Iona and died in 717. Duchad, Abbot of Dunkeld, was killed in about 965. The two Scottish kings of this name were equally unfortunate. Duncan I's grandfather had killed off several of his senior relatives to secure his succession. But there remained his senior cousin Thorfinn the Mighty, Earl of Orkney, his uncle Macbeth, and the most senior of all, Macbeth's wife Queen Gruoch. With competence Duncan might have survived, but he provoked his relatives until he was murdered in 1040 and Macbeth succeeded to his realm. Duncan II ought to have fared better because he was the eldest son of Malcolm Canmore. But he too was murdered by his relatives in 1094, and although he had a son it was his junior half-brothers, the English Queen Margaret's children, who usurped the throne.

By 1367 the name Duncan had moved to Berwick, Scotland's greatest port, perilously close to the English border. In that year John Duncan held property in Berwick, while the mayor, John Duncanson, was very probably his son. Earlier in the same century Duncan the Fat in Atholl (*Donnchadh Reamhar*) had given his name to Clann Donnchaidh, by which title the Robertsons call themselves to this day.

Adam, 1st Viscount Duncan (1731–1804), the Admiral, was the second son of Alexander Duncan of Lundie in Perthshire.

Elliot

It is thought that at least some bearers of this name derived it from the village of Eliot in the county of Forfar: and one of the most outstanding of them, the poet T. S. Eliot, used this spelling. On the other hand the Border clan of the Middle March possessed a Chief in the late 15th century whose name was spelt Robert Elwold. He was Captain of Hermitage Castle, and his son fell at Flodden and was father of another Robert Elliot, Captain of Hermitage in 1531. His brother Archibald was ancestor of the branch represented by the late Walter Scott Elliot of Arkleton.

But the branch which has been decided, after some uncertainty, to represent the senior line of the Chiefs of this name is that of Stobs. Its prosperity, if not its very survival, was due to the Revolution of 1688 which engulfed so many others in ruin. For Gilbert Elliot of Stobs (1651—1718) was convicted of high treason in 1685, and was only enabled to return from his exile in Holland after William of Orange had seized his uncle's throne. 'Gibbie wi' the gowden gartens', as he was called, was made clerk to the Privy Council and rose to the office of a judge. His senior grandson Gilbert was created first baronet of Stobs and is ancestor of the present Chief.

It was George Elliot (c. 1718—1790), a younger son of the 3rd baronet, who formed and trained the first regiment of light horse, called by his name until its outstanding services earned it the title of the King's Royal Regiment of Light Dragoons. Its founder drank no alcohol and ate no meat: and he was noted for his humanity. After serving in the West Indies and Ireland and rising to the rank of general, he performed his most outstanding feat in holding Gibraltar with a handful of men against the utmost power of Spain. For this he was created Lord Heathfield and Gibraltar.

Meanwhile a younger son of Gibbie Elliot, Sir Gilbert Elliot of Minto, followed his father's profession of the law and likewise became a judge. He was also musical, and it is said that in about 1725 he first introduced the German flute into Scotland. His son took to politics, became Sir Gilbert Elliot, 1st baronet of Minto, and also something of a poet. But his once-popular song, 'My sheep I neglected', has not attained the immortality of his sister Jane's song of Flodden, 'The Flowers of the Forest'.

Such was the cultured family background in which the baronet's son Gilbert, 1st Earl of Minto (1751—1814) grew up. Burns was his contemporary, Niel Gow the interpreter of popular airs in his youth. Minto followed his father into politics, and in 1794 was made Viceroy of Napoleon's island of Corsica, where he first showed his gifts as a proconsul. In 1807 he was appointed Governor-General of India, which already contained those other borderers, John Malcolm and John Leyden, the poet of the Turnbull country so close to Minto. Leyden was one of the principal architects of the expedition to Java in which he himself died, while Minto returned to receive the thanks of both Houses of Parliament for this, above all his other services, together with an earldom. But before he could return to Scotland and the wife to whom he had written such wise and delightful letters, the Earl died and was buried in Westminster Abbey.

The 4th Earl followed his forebear as Viceroy of India 1905–10 after serving as Governor-General of Canada. However, his line is not the most senior of the house of Stobs. The Chief of the name, using a different spelling, is Sir Arthur Eliott, 11th baronet (b. 1915).

Westminster Hall is perhaps the finest mediaeval hall in Europe, its hammer-beam roof with carved angels constructed in the late 14th century when the poet Chaucer was Minister of Works. In the early hours of 11 May 1941 the chamber of the House of Commons was set on fire by a high explosive bomb and incendiaries. Chief Superintendant C. P. MacDuell summoned additional pumps to meet the emergency at about the time when Colonel Walter Elliot, M.P., who was engaged in fire-fighting in a neighbouring street, looked up and observed that the roof of Westminster Hall was ablaze. He hurried to the spot, and arranged with the Chief Superintendant that all the pumps should be used to save this precious building, while the relatively modern chamber of the House of Commons was destroyed. So two Scots saved the hall in which both William Wallace and King Charles I were sentenced to death. Walter Elliot filled many offices, including that of Secretary of State for Scotland, but his service on that night of 1941 is perhaps the most memorable.

Erskine

The first to bear this name in historical record was Henry of Erskine during the reign of Alexander II, and he took it from his barony in Renfrewshire. The family were supporters of Robert Bruce and prospered exceedingly as a result. Sir Robert of Erskine was Great Chamberlain of Scotland before his death in 1385, while his two sons each founded powerful dynasties. Malcolm, the younger, was ancestor of the house of Kinnoull. Sir Thomas, the elder, married Janet Keith, great-grand-daughter and heiress of Gratney of Mar. Their son Robert assumed the title of this earldom, which had evolved from the office of the Pictish Mormaers of Mar without ever having been created as such by a King of Scots. But he was stripped of his title in 1457, and created Lord Erskine instead ten years later. His younger brother John became the founder of the cadet house of Dun.

After the 4th Lord Erskine had died at Flodden in 1513 in the company of James IV, his son the 5th Lord became the custodian of James V during his minority. So well did he discharge this trust that he was next given the custody of James V's daughter, the infant Mary, Queen of Scots, and he conveyed her to France before his death in 1552. Mary showed her appreciation by restoring to his son John, 6th Lord Erskine, the ancient earldom of Mar; and lest this title should ever again be cancelled, she also invested him with a new earldom of Mar. The strange consequence of this is that today there is a 30th Earl of Mar representing the direct line from the Pictish Mormaers, and a 13th Earl of Mar who is also 15th Earl of Kellie and who descends from John's younger brother Alexander.

John himself, 18th and 1st Earls of Mar, was a man of incorruptible integrity. His wife Annabella was a particular friend of Queen Mary, which may help to explain Knox's description of her as 'a very Jezebel.' It is noteworthy that Erskine favoured the marriage of Queen Mary to the Earl of Leicester which Queen Elizabeth proposed and Queen Mary dismissed with scorn—although it would almost certainly have gained her the English crown which she craved. When she had instead made her disastrous marriage to her cousin Darnley and given birth to their son James, she placed him in the custody of the Earl and Countess of Mar. Bothwell tried to gain possession of the child after his marriage to the Queen, and there was a serious danger that, should he succeed, the baby might disappear in favour of an heir of Bothwell's. But Mar frustrated his attempts, and it was he who carried the infant James VI at his coronation in 1567. Mary's treacherous bastard brother Moray became Regent until his murder, when he was succeeded by the child-King's grandfather the Earl of Lennox. After he had been murdered too, the Earl of Mar was raised to the Regency, only to die in 1572, a year later. But his widow Annabella remained in charge of the little King, and although Sir James Melville described her as 'wise and sharp, and held the King in great awe' he could not have resented it, because he later placed his eldest son in her charge. Thus the house of Erskine possesses the unique distinction of having been entrusted with the care of four infant heirs to the Scottish throne in succession.

The Regent's son John (1558—1634) was appointed by James VI Lord Treasurer of Scotland in 1616. It was he who built the beautiful castle of Braemar in 1628, while his sons added to the cadet houses of the Erskines. Henry became Lord Cardross, Sir Charles was ancestor of the Earls of Rosslyn, while Sir James married the Countess of Buchan in her own right, so that his descendants inherited that earldom. Sir Alexander was less fortunate. He was blown up at Dunglass in 1640, to be immortalised as the hero of the song 'Baloo my Boy'.

The 23rd and 6th Earl of Mar was raised to a Jacobite dukedom in circumstances that do him little credit. In 1715 he raised the standard of rebellion in the Braes of Mar, but he fled from the field of battle to Saint Germains, and there betrayed his associates. The attainder of his earldoms was reversed in 1824, when George IV himself had become an ardent Jacobite under the influence of Sir Walter Scott. By this time the credit of the name of Erskine had been restored by a member of the Buchan branch whose outstanding gifts as an advocate raised him to the office of Lord Chancellor in 1806.

John Erskine, 13th Earl of Mar and 15th Earl of Kellie (b. 1921), is the present Chief of this name.

Farquharson

A grant of arms made by Lord Lyon in 1697 stated that John Farquharson of Invercauld was 'lawfully descended of Shaw son of Macduff Thane of Fife whose successors had the name of Shaw until Farquhar Shaw son to Shaw of Rothiemurchus chief of the whole name came to be called Farquharson about ten generations ago.' Thus the Farquharsons branched from Clan Shaw, which was itself a member of the Clan Chattan confederation under the leadership of the Mackintosh clan. It was Farquhar's son Donald who married the heiress of Invercauld, and their son Finlay who gave to the Farquharson chiefs their style, *Mac Fionnlaidh*.

Finlay *Mór* was killed carrying the royal standard at Pinkie in 1547, the defeat which led to the removal of the baby Mary, Queen of Scots to France for safety. But his widow Beatrix Garden has an even greater claim to remembrance. She was said to have been an outstanding performer on the little harp or *clàrsach*, so that Queen Mary presented one of these instruments to her. It came into the possession of the Robertsons of Lude, who also inherited the Lamont harp. This instrument may be almost a century older still, but Queen Mary's harp is the more beautifully constructed of the two. Both are now preserved in the National Museum of Antiquities in Edinburgh, and are the sole surviving examples of the musical instrument which Celtic Scotland shared with Ireland before the music of the bagpipe had achieved its full popularity and sophistication.

Moving into their Deeside inheritance of Invercauld, the Farquharsons became vassals of the earldom of Mar. But in the early 17th century they were able to purchase feu charters to their lands, and after the attainder of the Earl of Mar who led the Jacobite rising of 1715, they held these directly of the crown. Today the castle of Braemar which was built in 1628 by James Erskine, Earl of Mar, is owned by Captain Alwyne Farquharson of Invercauld. This result, and the fact that the chiefship of the clan is vested in the house of Invercauld at all, is partly due to the eccentric and auspicious part which it played in the Jacobite rebellions.

The eldest son of Finlay *Mór* who died at Pinkie, and of his wife who played the clarsach, was named Donald. From him descended many branches, of which that of Inverey had already taken first place by the time William Farquharson, 2nd of Inverey, fought with Montrose. 'The main body of the Royalists' battle was given to Inverey,' wrote the contemporary chronicler, 'a man whom they both loved and understood, for he had their language.' This was of some importance, since it is doubtful whether Montrose himself possessed any fluency in Gaelic, the language of most of his troops. Inverey's son John, the Black Colonel, fought with Bonnie Dundee for James VII in 1689, and his grandson Colonel Patrick led the men of Mar in the Jacobite rising of 1715. At this time the chiefship was rightly held to be vested in the house of Inverey. For the family of Invercauld descended from a younger son of Finlay *Mór*.

But during the Jacobite period John of Invercauld was able to show that his house had become involved unwillingly in the 1715 rebellion, as vassals of the Earl of Mar. He preferred commercial to political activities, and avoided taking part in the Forty-Five. His daughter was married to the Mackintosh, and although she was only twenty years old, she played a leading part in raising her husband's clan for Prince Charles. The Farquharsons of the senior line also rose for the Prince; so that after Culloden it was fortunate for the clan to possess a rich and powerful member who had supported the winning side. Even when the inheritance of Invercauld passed through the female line in 1805, the Lord Lyon recognised Catherine Farquharson of Invercauld as Chief of the clan, in granting her supporters to her arms, despite the senior representatives of the direct male line.

Fergusson

There is no evidence that those who bear this name descend from a single progenitor of the name of Fergus, or that they have ever been organised as a Fergusson clan. Indeed, families of this name, apparently unconnected, have been long settled as far afield as Aberdeenshire and Dumfries-shire, Fife, Perthshire and Ayrshire. Dr Adam Ferguson (1723–1816), the distinguished philosopher and historian, belonged to the house of Dunfallandy whose Chief was

Fergusson

called Baron Ferguson. His father was the minister at Logierait in Perthshire, and Adam himself became chaplain to the 42nd Regiment and was present at the battle of Fontenoy. Subsequently he was Professor of Mathematics, then of Moral Philosophy, at Edinburgh University. During the American War of Independence he was sent across the Atlantic with the commission which attempted to make terms with the rebellious colonists in 1778—9. He lived to become the close friend of Sir Walter Scott.

Robert Fergusson was, by contrast, the son of a bank clerk who had moved to Edinburgh from Aberdeen. He died in 1774, at the age of twenty-three, on a bed of straw in an asylum cell, his ears filled with the shrieks of the insane, and was buried in an unmarked grave. But when Robert Burns came to Edinburgh he sought out Fergusson's burial-place, uncovered the head and embraced it. He then obtained permission to raise a monument above it. For in his short life Fergusson had composed a body of poetry which ranks with that of Burns himself.

The present Chief of the name is Sir Charles of Kilkerran, whose uncle Sir Bernard Fergusson was the outstanding guerilla leader of the Chindits in the Far East during the 1939—45 war. A former Governor-General of New Zealand, Sir Bernard was made a Life Peer in 1972, taking the title Baron Ballantrae of Auchairan.

Fletcher

Fletcher of Dunans

Like other trade-names, Fletcher is found throughout the British Isles, for it signifies an arrow-maker. The bow was an obsolescent weapon of war by the time the men of Mackay's regiment were depicted in Germany in 1631 with the explanantory note: 'besides muskets, they have their bows and arrows and long knives.' The army of Montrose shot arrows at Tibbermore in 1644 for the last time in a British battle, although they were discharged once more in a clan fight between Mackintosh and MacDonald of Keppoch in 1688.

Naturally many clans possessed their families of hereditary arrow makers, so that in its Gaelic form of *Mac an Fhleistear* there is no reason why it should have constituted a separate clan, and in fact it did not evolve in this way as the clan of the carpenters, the Macintyres, did. On the other hand it appears that the Fletchers might well have done so, and in the very region in which the Macintyres flourished, for there was a tradition that it was the Fletchers who first raised smoke or boiled water on the braes of Glenorchy. And long after the erosion of Gaelic society in the aftermath of Culloden, a Fletcher of Glenlyon demonstrated that he was as much a Gael as any clansman. He was Archibald son of Angus Fletcher, born in Glenlyon in 1746, and after attending school at Kenmore in Breadalbane he went to Edinburgh to pursue his studies. There in 1778 he was deputed to negotiate with some MacRaes who had joined the army and were now objecting to the order to embark from Leith for foreign service in America. The reason why he was appointed to this task was that he was a native Gaelic speaker in a capital that had never troubled to study the language of half the population of Scotland. Archibald Fletcher himself favoured the cause of American independence, became 'the father of Burgh reform', and was sent to London in 1787 as a delegate of the Scottish Burghs, where he gained the friendship of Charles James Fox. As a lawyer he was described by Lord Brougham as 'one of the most upright men that ever adorned the profession'. It is a career that contrasts dramatically with the record of the Fletchers of Glenlyon who had made arrows for the MacGregors and even saved Rob Roy, once, from a dragoon.

As a lawyer he had been anticipated by Andrew Fletcher, son of Robert of Innerpeffer, a burgess of Dundee. He rose to the bench as Lord Innerpeffer during the stormy years of the Civil War but was stripped of his offices before his death in 1650. A few years later another Andrew Fletcher was born in East Lothian, son of Sir Robert of Saltoun whom Bishop Burnet praised for his learning and high character. Andrew of Saltoun opposed the regime of Lauderdale during the reign of Charles II, and had troops quartered on him as a punishment. He retired abroad and in 1686 took part in Monmouth's rebellion. After its failure he was forfeited, but his property was restored after the Revolution. He then associated with another Scot, William Paterson, the founder of the Bank of England, in launching the Darien scheme in 1690. Its failure inflamed his nationalism, and at his entry into the Parliament of 1703 he moved that 'after the demise of Her Majesty' (Queen Anne) 'we will separate our crown from that of England.' Thereafter he was one of the most eloquent opponents of the Union of 1707. When it had been enacted he turned to agricultural improvement, and to the introduction of new barley mills from Holland. The finest writer of his age, one of Scotland's outstanding patriots, he was generally admired for what David Hume called his 'signal probity and fine genius'. His example was followed by a third Andrew Fletcher, son of Henry of Saltoun, who was born in 1692 and had become a judge as Lord Milton by the time of the Forty-Five. He treated the Jacobites with the greatest possible leniency. He also worked strenuously to promote trade and agriculture, while his wife introduced the manufacture of fine linen from Holland to Saltoun.

Forbes

This clan originates in the lands of Donside that had once lain in the northern Pictish kingdom, and its very name is held to derive from the Gaelic *Forba*, meaning a field, with the Pictish place-name suffix *-ais*. The earliest historical reference is a charter of the reign of Alexander III who died in 1286, and this does not record the planting of a new family, but the confirmation of Duncan of Forbes' title to his lands. His descendants were raised to the peerage in 1445 when Sir Alexander Forbes married a grand-daughter of Robert III. But this was the very year in which the Gordons became earls of nearby Huntly, and thenceforth Clan Forbes were constantly menaced by their powerful and predatory neighbours.

They enjoyed a certain advantage through embracing the reformed faith while the house of Huntly remained Catholic, but this was complicated by the marriage of the 8th Lord Forbes to a daughter of the Earl of Huntly. Both of her sons renounced their worldly possessions and ended their days as Capuchin friars, leaving their Protestant half-brother to succeed as the 9th Lord Forbes. By the 17th century Arthur, the 10th Lord (1581–1641), was described as a Chief much decayed, 'an naked life-renter of an small part and portion of his old estates and living of Forbes.' But his cousin Patrick (1564–1635), of the house of Corse and O'Neil which descended from the 2nd Lord Forbes, brought a novel distinction to the name. He entered the reformed ministry at a time when a number of lairds possessed the same sense of vocation, and became Bishop of Aberdeen and then Chancellor of King's College. In both university and diocese he proved to be an administrator of outstanding ability.

But it was during the Forty-Five that the name of Forbes shone with greatest lustre. There was Robert Forbes (1708–1775), Rector of the Episcopal church at Leith, who attempted to join the Jacobites but was intercepted and imprisoned in Stirling Castle. He was the son of a schoolmaster in Aberdeenshire of uncertain pedigree. Having failed to take an active part in the cause, he determined instead to be its chronicler, and assembled the invaluable collection of eye-witness accounts which was published long after his death as *The Lyon in Mourning*. He met Flora MacDonald in Edinburgh after her release from captivity, and she was one of the many people who provided first-hand material. In 1762 he was appointed Episcopal Church Bishop of Caithness.

Alexander Forbes, 4th Lord Pitsligo (1678–1762), escaped attainder for his part in the 1715 rebellion, only to become a hunted rebel for raising a troop of horse for the army of Prince Charles in 1745. By this time he was an asthmatic old man, and the story of his privations and hair's-breadth escapes is among the most romantic of the Forty-Five. The last occurred as late as 1756, while he enjoyed asylum at the house of Auchiries. He was hidden behind the wainscotting at the back of an elderly Miss Gordon's bed, and while the soldiers felt her chin to make sure she was not a man, she managed to cough violently enough to drown the noise of Pitsligo's asthmatic breathing behind her. 'A poor prize, had they obtained it,' he remarked after the troops were gone, 'an old dying man.'

Most distinguished of all was Duncan Forbes of Culloden (1685–1747), President of the Court of Session, a consistent opponent of Jacobitism. In the 1715 he and his brother raised a force for the government, but he protested to Sir Robert Walpole against the severe treatment of the rebels. He advocated the policy of raising Highland regiments, later adopted by Pitt, and when he was the sole remaining representative of the Hanoverian government in the north during the Forty-Five, he acted with sense and courage. After Culloden he attempted to restrain the bestialities of Butcher Cumberland.

From a younger son of the 2nd Lord Forbes descend the distinguished lines of the baronetcy of Pitsligo, created in 1626, and of Craigievar, created in 1630. It was Sir William Forbes, the 1st Baronet of Craigievar, who built the castle of that name, one of the outstanding masterpieces in the custody of the National Trust for Scotland. The Pitsligo branch produced John Forbes, Lord Medwyn, the Judge and his son Alexander (1817–75) the Bishop, who moved the episcopal seat from Brechin to Dundee. James Forbes (1809–68) the physicist and Professor of Natural Philosophy at Edinburgh University was a son of the 7th baronet of Pitsligo.

The Chief of the clan Nigel, 23rd Lord Forbes (b. 1918), is the premier Baron of Scotland.

Fraser

This name was brought to Scotland by a knight who bore the name of Frezel from the lordship of La Frézelière in Anjou. In about 1160 Simon Fraser gave the church of Keith in East Lothian to the abbey of Kelso, and Simon has been a favourite name of the Frasers ever since. His lands of Keith passed with his grand-daughter to the family who became the Earls Marischal of Scotland after having adopted Keith as their name. For a time the Frasers compensated themselves with Oliver Castle and Tweeddale, won and lost with other heiresses. But after the wars of independence they moved north and burgeoned into a Highland clan.

In those wars the Frasers played a heroic part. Sir Simon Fraser defeated the English at Rosslyn in 1302 as an adherent of Wallace, and was captured fighting for Robert Bruce. Like Wallace, he was executed with notable cruelty, as the processes of hanging and quartering made possible. His kinsman, Sir Alexander Fraser, fought at Bannockburn, married King Robert Bruce's sister Mary, and became Chamberlain of Scotland. In 1375 their grandson Alexander obtained the castle of Cairnbulg and the lands of Philorth in Buchan with the hand of Joanna, daughter of the Earl of Ross. So the line of Fraser chiefs was established which has inhabited Cairnbulg to this day. Sir Alexander the 8th of Philorth founded Fraserburgh, which is a thriving fishing port, despite the rivalry of the larger port of Aberdeen to its south. Fraserburgh might also have become a university town, for

James VI granted the Fraser Chief charters in 1592 and 1601 to establish one there: but this enterprise did not survive Aberdeen's rivalry. In the meantime Alexander the 9th of Philorth married the heiress of Lord Saltoun, and the chiefs of clan Fraser have borne this title ever since.

The chiefship was for a time disputed by another branch of the Frasers who sprang from Oliver Castle and the supporters of the Bruce. These settled in Mar where their seat of Castle Fraser was completed by Andrew Fraser shortly before he was created Lord Fraser in 1633 by Charles I. But the 4th Lord Fraser joined the Jacobites in 1715 and died a fugitive soon after their defeat.

The most famous cadet branch of the clan was the one which inherited the Bisset properties in Ross-shire. Here John Bisset had founded Beauly Priory in 1200 and built Lovat Castle. When he died without a son in 1258, his eldest daughter carried the Lovat inheritance to her husband David Graham. But once again it passed through an heiress, and so reached the younger brother of King Robert Bruce's Chamberlain, Sir Simon Fraser. The chiefs of this branch have been called *Mac Sìmi* (Son of Simon) ever since. Among the junior stems of this branch was one that originated with the second son of the 5th Lord Lovat in the 16th century. He settled at Strichen in Buchan, the province of the senior house. Here the religious order had lived which was said to have been named the Monastery of Tears by Saint Columba. Here the Book of Deer had been kept, with its glosses in the earliest surviving Scottish Gaelic prose. Here Lord Strichen the judge was reared, whose son entertained Johnson and Boswell so hospitably in 1773, and whose descendants were to inherit the title of *Mac Sìmi*.

Fraser of Lovat

Hugh the first *Mac Sìmi* did homage to the Bishop of Moray for some of his properties on 11 September 1367 as *'Dominus de Loveth et portionarius terrarum de Aird'*. In 1431 Sir Hugh Fraser of Lovat was Sheriff of Inverness and at a time when many magnates were suffering from the punitive policies of James I he was raised to the peerage. His successor obtained a charter in 1539 which was to have far-reaching consequences, for it altered the succession from the heir of line to the heir male.

The issue which this raised could hardly have become a matter of dispute in more dramatic circumstances. Hugh, 9th Lord Lovat, had only daughters as his heirs just when the Revolution of 1688 placed William of Orange on the throne. Their mother belonged to the powerful house of Atholl—all the more so when the Marquess of Atholl became William's Secretary of State for Scotland. The male heir was the 9th Lord's great-uncle Thomas of Beaufort, and his cause was naturally supported by Atholl's great rival, Campbell of Argyll. When the 9th Lord died prematurely in 1696 his eldest daughter

Amelia was offered by the Atholl family to the senior branch of Saltoun in marriage. Thomas of Beaufort correctly adopted the style of 10th Lord Lovat, while his son Simon kidnapped the young widow (she was four years older than himself) of the 9th Lord and went through a form of marriage with her. But if he hoped to ingratiate himself with the house of Atholl by this means, he was disappointed. A conviction for treason was secured against Simon by gross abuse of legal procedures, while his father was so terrorised by the steps which the Privy Council took to capture him that he fled to Skye, where he died in 1698. His son Simon, the most famous of all the Lovats, became the 11th Lord.

Argyll secured a pardon for the treason charge against him, but the Atholls pressed a charge of rape, and so in 1703 the new Lord Lovat fled to the Jacobite court in France. Amelia's marriage to the Saltoun heir had been foiled, but she was styled Baroness Lovat and married to a MacKenzie who hopefully assumed the name of Fraser of Fraserdale. Nor did his optimism appear misplaced when Lovat quarrelled with the Jacobites and was flung into a French prison while he was still a fugitive from British justice. Ten years later he contrived to return, just as the death of Queen Anne led to the Hanoverian succession. He reached the northern Highlands as a loyal Hanoverian when the MacKenzies were defeated in the Jacobite rising of 1715. The 300 Frasers whom Fraserdale had taken to the Jacobite camp at Perth deserted to their natural chief, and Simon of Lovat entered at last into his inheritance with encomiums.

But *Mac Sìmi* was a Catholic, and was disposed to favour a King of the same religion, especially one who created him Duke of Fraser and appointed him Lieutenant of all the Highlands. When Prince Charles arrived in 1745 without the promised French army, Lovat hesitated to keep his own promise of support, but he sent his son to maintain his cause with the Jacobites. In 1747 he was made prisoner, a crippled fugitive of eighty, and taken to London to display his remarkable powers of mind at his trial before being beheaded in the presence of an immense crowd.

The Lovat title was attainted, but although the 11th Lord's son had commanded his clansmen at Culloden he was pardoned. In 1757 he raised the Fraser Highlanders in the service of the Hanoverian King, and as General Simon Fraser he commanded them at the capture of Quebec. His younger half-brother, Colonel Archibald Fraser, raised the 'home-guard' of the Fraser Fencibles, and eventually succeeded to the remaining honours and estates of *Mac Sìmi*. But by 1803 the line of the 11th Lord Lovat was extinct.

During this period in which his title was abolished and his sons were raising regiments of their clansmen, Dr Johnson and James Boswell passed through their country in 1773, and left a vivid picture of the home of one of the poorer amongst them. 'By the side of Loch Ness I perceived a little hut, with an old-looking woman at the door of it,' Boswell recorded. The two travellers entered. 'It was a wretched little hovel of earth only, I think, and for a window had only a small

Hunting Fraser

hole, which was stopped with a piece of turf, that was taken out occasionally to let in light. In the middle of the room or space which we entered was a fire of peat, the smoke going out a hole in the roof. She had a pot upon it, with goat's flesh, boiling. There was at one end under the same roof, but divided by a partition made of wattles, a pen or fold in which we saw a good many kids.' Although the woman looked old, and her husband was said to be eighty, the oldest of their five children was only thirteen unless Boswell misunderstood. For the woman 'could hardly speak any English except a few detached words'.

The family were tenants at will of Fraser of Balnain. 'This contented family had four stacks of barley, twenty-four sheaves in each. They had a few fowls. We were informed that they lived all the spring without meal, upon milk and curds and whey alone. What they get for their goats, kids and fowls maintains them during the rest of the year.' Such was the home of an ordinary Fraser clansman who had escaped Butcher Cumberland's holocaust and now witnessed the tide of emigration and the raising of the clan regiments. The woman's comment to her two distinguished visitors is memorable. 'She said she was as happy as any woman in Scotland.'

On the failure of the 11th Lord's line the title of *Mac Sìmi* passed to the cadet branch of Strichen. In 1837, the year of Queen Victoria's accession, Thomas of Strichen was created Lord Lovat in the peerage of the United Kingdom, and his Scottish dignities were subsequently restored also. The 22nd *Mac Sìmi* still lives in Beaufort Castle. The ruins of Beauly Priory nearby, in which the earliest memorials of his forebears lie, are well tended. His record as a Commando leader in the Second World War continued the distinguished military traditions of his house; while the record of his younger brother, the Right Hon. Hugh Fraser, as a cabinet minister with an outstanding reputation for integrity, has provided a refreshing contrast to that of the wily *Mac Sìmi* who was the last nobleman to lose his head on Tower Hill.

The heir to the chiefship of Clan Fraser itself was one of the most admired of his generation. Freddie Fraser, Master of Saltoun, possessed a natural goodness and modesty combined with high intelligence which found their expression in his skill as a musician, and his charm as a companion. He was killed in action in the Second World War and his sister Flora is the 20th Lady Saltoun.

Galbraith

After the British (Welsh-speaking) kingdoms of southern Scotland had been extinguished in the Dark Ages, some record of the Men of the North was preserved in Wales. It may be assumed that British society was not entirely destroyed in Scotland, particularly in Strathclyde, which lay furthest from the Northumbrian English. Its capital had been Dumbarton, the precipitous rock called in Gaelic the Fortress of the Britons. In nearby Loch Lomond lies the island called Inchgalbraith, Gaelic for the Island of the British Foreigner. Strathclyde was united with the kingdom of Scotland in 1124, and it is at the end of this century that the first Galbraith Chief appears, in circumstances that suggest he was the social equal of the Gaelic royal house of the Lennox. His name was Gilchrist Bretnach and he married a daughter of *Alwyn Òg*, son of Muireadhach, 1st Earl of Lennox in the new order. Their son Gillespic was father of a 3rd Chief of Galbraith who bore the suggestive name of Arthur. The family stronghold stood upon Inchgalbraith. Arthur's son, Sir William, moved into the centre of the national stage when he became one of the co-regents of Scotland.

Sir William died shortly before the outbreak of the Scottish wars of independence, but his son Sir Arthur supported Robert Bruce and outlived the victory of Bannockburn. Thereafter the fortunes of the Galbraiths varied with those of the house of Lennox. James the 9th Chief was the first of Culcreuch in Strathendrick, a cadet branch until then. It was in his time that James I returned from his 18-year captivity in England and decimated his own Stewart relatives. Chief among these were the ducal family of Albany and their Lennox kinsmen. James of Gilcreuch is said to have helped them to sack Dumbarton in 1425, and to have fled west to Kintyre and Gigha with 600 Galbraiths and their families to escape the King's wrath. After James III had been murdered in 1488, Thomas the 12th Chief took up arms with Lennox against the regicides. But these possessed the person of the young King, and after the defeat of Talla Moss Thomas

Galbraith

was hanged in 1489. His brother escaped from the field and received the estates in the general remission which followed. Andrew the 14th Chief once again joined Lennox in 1526, when he attempted to rescue the young King James V from the Douglases. Lennox was captured and killed, but the King remained grateful. The last office in the long association between the houses of Galbraith and Lennox was performed by James the 16th Chief, who administered the Lennox on behalf of Esmé, its absentee first Duke.

Robert the 17th Chief proved to be an unscrupulous rogue who brought nemesis upon his house. In 1592 he was given a commission to pursue the Clan Gregor, and he misused his powers to persecute the Chief of MacAulay, who had married his widowed mother against his wishes. His subsequent misdeeds led finally to his being denounced as a rebel. In 1622 he fled from an order for his arrest, and died in Ireland sometime before 1642. His heir inherited nothing and his grandson James the 19th Chief is the last traceable member of his line.

A generation after the sack of Dumbarton in 1425, *Giolla Críost*, a member of the family of hereditary Galbraith harpers in the island of Gigha, was composing the poems that survive in the Book of the Dean of Lismore. This ancient tradition is represented today by the Gaelic singer Carol Galbraith, wife of the poet *Ruaraidh MacThómais*.

Gordon of Huntly

Huntly, Old Colours

This is another of Scotland's territorial surnames, and it was carried to the north-east from Gordon near the southern border when Sir Adam of Gordon was rewarded for his rather belated support of Robert Bruce. He was granted the lordship of Strathbogie, that fertile basin among the eastern foothills of the Grampians. This had been held with the ancient Celtic earldom of Atholl, which eventually passed to the Stewarts. From Strathbogie the Gordons were able to expand into that northern world in which the Comyns had been paramount until Bruce destroyed them.

The senior male line died out in 1402, and the heiress Elizabeth Gordon married another magnate from the south of Scotland, Alexander Seton. In 1445 their son was created Earl of Huntly—the burgh which stands in the centre of Strathbogie—and the former Comyn lordship of Badenoch was added to their possessions. At this time the Stewart kings were investing the houses of Campbell and Gordon with increasing power, to which they added vice-regal authority in those great areas of the north and west which barely acknowledged the Scottish crown. So it was that while the power of the crown remained weak in the north, the Gordons used its delegated authority to build their private empire. Their most spectacular success was the seizure of the earldom of Sutherland in 1514, immediately after Flodden had cut off the King and many of Scotland's ablest leaders. It is significant that they did not adopt the surname of

92

Sutherland in the conventional manner, though they claimed (falsely) to have inherited the earldom by marriage with the heir of line. The Sutherland earls remained Gordons.

They were not always successful. In 1560 John Gordon, the third son of the Earl of Huntly, made an ingenious plan to acquire the castle and lands of Findlater, later erected into an earldom. He informed the Ogilvie owner that his own son and heir was plotting to deprive him of his reason by locking him up and then preventing him from sleeping. Cecil was sent the details by the English ambassador in Scotland. 'This being revealed and sure tokens given unto his father that this was true, he thought just cause to be given unto him why his son should not succeed, and having no other issue, by the persuasion of his wife (who was a Gordon) gave the whole land unto John Gordon, who after the death of the said Findlater married her and so had right unto the whole living. To see also how God hath plagued the iniquity of the same woman, which in one month after her marriage John Gordon casteth his fancy unto another and locketh her up in a close chamber, where she yet remaineth.' As step-mother of the dispossessed heir she had contributed to the Gordon plot by accusing him of having made sexual advances. Now she and her step-son were rescued when the Gordons over-reached themselves in another of their enterprises. Mary, Queen of Scots returned to Scotland to begin her personal reign, and bestowed on her half-brother the earldom of Moray, which the Gordons desired for themselves. They took up arms against the sovereign and were defeated by her at Corrichie in 1562. The Earl of Huntly died of apoplexy on the field, being 'gross, corpulent and short of breath'. His son John was taken to Aberdeen to be beheaded, and the Ogilvies recovered their property.

Queen Mary's son James VI built up the Gordon power once more, making Huntly a Marquess. When he was granted a royal commission to extend the Gordon enterprises into the Hebrides, the Lords of the Privy Council were moved to protest in 1605: 'they think it unreasonable that the King's power should be put in the hands of a subject to conquer lands to himself.' The project failed. But it was in this century that the Gordons obtained the overlordship of the enormous Mackay province of Strathnaver, and used it to assault the Sinclair earldom of Caithness. The evil genius behind these operations was Sir Robert Gordon, Tutor of Sutherland during its earl's minority. Sir Robert left a detailed chronicle of the events of his time, a bare-faced tissue of lies and libels that is still quoted as a historical document as he would have wished. Charles I's civil war interfered with his projects, and he ended his days a baronet in his property of Gordonstoun, now occupied by a famous school. The parent house of Huntly was raised to a dukedom after the Restoration, but this was extinguished in 1836.

Douglas Gordon, 12th Marquess of Huntly (b. 1908), is the Chief of the clan.

Gordon

Elizabeth Gordon, who married Sir Alexander Seton and gave birth to the line of Huntly, possessed a cousin named Sir John Gordon of Strathbogie. He died in about 1395, leaving a son remembered as Jock Gordon of Scurdargue. Jock possessed three sons, of whom James, the youngest, was the grandfather of another James who acquired the estate of Haddo. There were thus many Gordons in the north-east of Scotland who did not belong to the Seton house which had adopted their name. And although the family of Haddo was to acquire the highest distinction amongst these, it was not the senior branch of them.

This pre-eminence asserted itself early. One of James of Haddo's sons was Alexander, Bishop of Aberdeen, while Patrick, his elder brother, was so long-lived that he was able to obtain charters to his properties from James III, IV and V. James the 3rd of Haddo remained faithful to Mary, Queen of Scots, and the longevity of his house led to his being succeeded by his grandson when he died in 1582. James the 4th of Haddo was likewise succeeded by his grandson when he died in 1623. It was John the 5th of Haddo who was created a baronet by Charles I as a reward for his conduct at the battle of Turriff in 1642. In the following year he was captured and imprisoned at Edinburgh in a recess of St Giles Cathedral, still called Haddo's Hole. In 1644 he became the first royalist to suffer execution by the forms of a judicial sentence. The family estates were sequestered, but they were restored after the Restoration of Charles II in 1660, and towards the end of his reign the 3rd Baronet of Haddo became Lord High Chancellor of Scotland and 1st Earl of Aberdeen.

It was during this period that another cadet house of the Gordons shone with sudden lustre. Robert Gordon of Straloch (1580−1661) made his earliest appearance in national affairs when he became involved in the negotiations between Huntly and Montrose. Huntly was then a royalist (though King Charles correctly described him as 'feeble and false'), while Montrose was still a soldier of the Covenent. Charles I appointed Straloch and his son James Gordon, the parson of Rothiemay, to complete the maps of Scotland which Timothy Pont had prepared for Bleau's atlas. The parson also kept the invaluable chronicle called *Scots Affairs*, while the training which his father gave him as a geographer made him the first to preserve views of particular places and buildings in his country. In addition to the maps, he left a pictorial survey of Edinburgh, illustrated with his own skilful drawings, while his plan of Aberdeen is graced with his pen and ink sketches.

In the 18th century Haddo House, one of the earliest and finest of Adam masterpieces, was built; and its policies and woods were beautified in the 19th by that lover of trees, George, 4th Earl of Aberdeen (1784−1860). He is one of the most attractive men of his name, without genius or ambition, but possessing the simple virtues of compassion and integrity. When he became Prime Minister in 1852 he found himself drawn into the war in the Crimea which he was then accused of having bungled. In fact his pacifism was no match for the jingoism of the day and its exponent, Palmerston. In 1855 Aberdeen resigned and retired to run Haddo as a model estate. He made a lake where there had been a morass. He built new stone houses for almost all the 900 farms, he planted thousands of trees. He remembered the battlefield over which he had once ridden, and the screams of the wounded. 'It must be owned that a victory is a fine thing, but one should be at a distance.'

The 7th Earl of Aberdeen (1847–1934) served as Lord Lieutenant of Ireland and Governor General of Canada and was created a Marquess. David, 4th Marquess of Aberdeen, organised the conveyance of Haddo to the National Trust for Scotland, and after the succession of his brother Archibald, the 5th Marquess, these arrangements were completed in 1980.

Gow

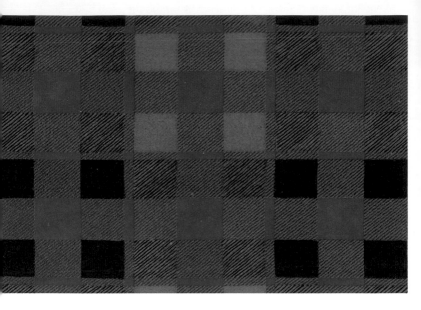

This name is merely one of the corruptions of the Gaelic *Gobhan*, meaning a Smith. But just as there is a Rob Roy tartan, different from that of MacGregor, so the celebrity of Niel Gow (1727–1807) has invested his name with a separate tartan. The greatest Scottish portrait painter of his day also played a part in this, for Sir Henry Raeburn painted Niel Gow four times, always in the same tartan knee-breeches and hose. Whether Gow's father, a plaid weaver, designed the sett is unknown. It is the most primitive surviving after that of Rob Roy.

Niel was born at Inver near Dunkeld in Perthshire, where he also died. He began to play the violin when he was only nine years old; and was introduced to Dunkeld House, where the Duke of Atholl became his patron. He was soon a favourite with the nobility.

Nathaniel, the youngest of Niel's five sons, was born at Inver in 1766 and taught by Niel until he was sent to Edinburgh for further instruction. He became leader of a band that was in frequent demand in Edinburgh and London. It often performed at private parties of the Prince of Wales who became Regent in 1811. Nathaniel was held to be as superlative an exponent of Scottish music as his father, and was also a prolific composer. With his father he published their compositions in three volumes called *Niel Gow and Son*, and he later added several more. Of Nathaniel's numerous family it was only his son Niel who promised to continue this family tradition. But he died in 1823, eight years before his father, leaving the still popular air 'Cam' ye by Atholl?'

Graham

Graham of Montrose

The English manor of Grey Home is to be found in William the Conqueror's Domesday Book. Its name was carried to Scotland when England's premier baron succeeded to the Scottish crown as David I, and William de Graham accompanied him. He witnessed the foundation charter of the Abbey of Holyrood in 1128. In the next century the Grahams gained their first foothold in the Highlands through a marriage into the princely Celtic family of Strathearn, and before it closed they had laid the foundations of their long tradition of military leadership.

Sir Patrick Graham of the Strathearn marriage died in 1296, carrying the royal banner in battle against the English during the war of independence. His nephew Sir John was the right arm of William Wallace until he fell in 1298 at the battle of Falkirk. But the most outstanding of all the Graham commanders in the field was the descendant of Sir Patrick who succeeded in 1626 when he was a mere youth as 5th Earl of Montrose. At first he was a prominent supporter of the Covenanters who rose in rebellion against the high church policies of Charles I. But when Argyll treated the defeated King with increasing severity, Montrose suspected that he was attempting to dethrone King Charles and to set up King Campbell, so he offered his sword to his sovereign. By the time Montrose made his way alone from Oxford to the Highlands, the royal cause there was almost lost. But he encountered a force of Catholic MacDonalds, under their leader

Alasdair, called after his father, Colkitto. It was long since such men had enjoyed the sanction of a royal commission to legalise their resistence movement against Campbell and Calvinist persecution, and under Montrose they made good use of it. In a year of incredible victories Montrose with his tiny army won the reputation of the most brilliant general in Europe. But outside the Highlands he could not win, and when he attempted the impossible he was defeated. The opposing general gave his men quarter for their lives, but Calvinist ministers persuaded the general to break his military oath, and they were slaughtered in cold blood with the women and children who accompanied their menfolk to war in those days. When Montrose was finally captured in 1650 he was conducted to a felon's death in Edinburgh with every possible ignomity. On the eve of his execution he composed one of his most famous poems:

> Let them bestow on every airt a limb,
> Then open all my veins, that I may swim
> To Thee, my Maker, in that crimson lake;
> Then place my parboiled head upon a stake,
> Scatter my ashes, strew them in the air.—
> Lord! Since Thou knowest where all these atoms are,
> I'm hopeful Thou'lt recover once my dust,
> And confident Thou'll raise me with the just.

The limbs of Montrose were displayed in the principal cities of the kingdom until Charles II was restored ten years later. They were then collected for a magnificent state burial, while Argyll was executed. Nemesis caught up with the Calvinist Covenanters who had behaved with such consistent intolerance and barbarity during the days of their power, and its instrument was another Graham.

His admirers called him Bonnie Dundee; his enemies, Bloody Claverhouse. John Graham of Claverhouse, Viscount Dundee, was one of the commanders of the dragoons which suppressed the assemblies of the faithful remnant of the Covenanters; until these were revenged in the Revolution of 1688 which brought the Calvinist King William of Orange to the throne. Bonnie Dundee died in 1689, fighting for the last Stewart King in the pass of Killiecrankie.

Montrose and Dundee were both Lowlanders, commanding Highland troops, and this exceptional relationship of the Grahams with the Gaels was given expression in a fitting manner after the defeat of the Jacobites in 1746, and the proscription of Highland dress in the following year. It was James Graham, later 3rd Duke of Montrose, who in 1782 piloted the Bill through Parliament which restored the kilt and the tartan to Scotland.

The 6th Duke of Montrose (1878–1954) married Mary, daughter of the 12th Duke of Hamilton, with whom he lived in Brodick Castle, ancient seat of the Dukes of Hamilton in the isle of Arran. In 1958 the castle and its possessions were accepted in lieu of death duties by the Commissioners of Inland Revenue, and in 1980 the National Trust for Scotland took custody of them at the request of the Treasury.

The 7th Duke of Montrose is the present Chief of Clan Graham.

Grant

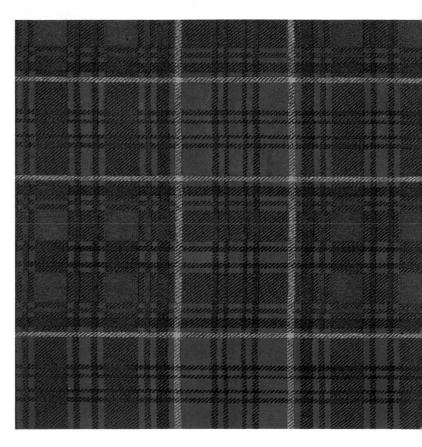

Grant is a name of the same meaning as More; the one being French, the other Gaelic, for Great or Big. In 1246 William le Grand held property in Nottinghamshire in England, and also Stratherrick in the Highlands, through his marriage to a Bisset heiress. Twelve years later Sir Laurence le Grand was Sheriff of Inverness. By the time Sir Iain Grant became Sheriff of Inverness in 1434 a clan of his name had spread from Stratherrick into Glenmoriston and Glenurquhart, north of Loch Ness. Sir Iain himself married an heiress of the Glencarnies, a cadet branch of the ancient Celtic dynasty that had held the earldom of Strathearn since before the earliest written record. Through this alliance the Chiefs of Clan Grant obtained Kinveachy and the lands of Strathspey that they have possessed ever since. Sir Iain's eldest son Sir Duncan was the first to be styled 'of Freuchie', a designation that was followed until, in the 16th century, the Chief became known as Grant of Grant. Sir Duncan's younger brother Patrick became the founder of the cadet house of Tullochgorm.

Two centuries separate the original Grant of Nottinghamshire from Sir Duncan of Freuchie, and during this period the number of people bearing the name of Grant had multiplied prodigiously. As in the case of Sinclair, the question naturally arises whether all these people descended from a single Norman ancestor, or whether they simply adopted the name of the foreign feudal overlord who became assimilated into their world as a tribal Chief. On this question Gaelic tradition may not have an accurate answer, but it has an emphatic one. It asserts that the Grants are of the aboriginal stock of *Siol Ailpein*, to which Kenneth Mac Alpin, first King of the Picts and Scots, belonged. This involves kindred with the MacGregors: and it was universally believed that Clan Grant descended from the 12th-century Gregor More MacGregor.

The strength of this conviction may be assessed from an incident which took place at a time when the MacGregors were a proscribed and hunted clan, the Grants prosperous. For a fortnight members of the two clans met at Blair Atholl to discuss reunion, and the adoption of the old clan name MacGregor, if the government could be persuaded to lift the proscription that forbade its use. Alternatively, it was agreed to use MacAlpine or Grant. Not unnaturally, the negotiations foundered over the question of the chiefship.

Clan Grant rose to the summit of its power at the end of the 17th century, with the eclipse of the Gordons in the north. For his support of the Revolution of 1688, King William granted the chief the Regality of Grant in 1694, when Freuchie was renamed Castle Grant. It stands, untenanted, but not yet a ruin, beside the burgh of Grantown-on-Spey which was created in 1766. But despite the clan's support for the house of Hanover in 1715 and 1745, the regality was abolished with all such independent jurisdictions after Culloden.

In 1811 Sir Lewis Grant of Grant inherited the Ogilvie earldoms of Findlater and Seafield through his grandmother, and in 1858 the earls were enabled to sit in the House of Lords by the creation of the United Kingdom peerage of Strathspey. But today these titles are divided, since Scottish peerages can pass through the female line. Sir Patrick Grant of Grant is 5th Lord Strathspey and 32nd Clan Chief, while his cousin is the 13th Earl of Seafield.

Gunn

The far north of Scotland is extremely rich in prehistoric remains. On the threshold of the historical period stand the mysterious brochs of the proto-Picts and the superb stone sculpture of the Picts themselves. Their intricately carved monuments survive along both shores of the Moray Firth, while Caithness possesses the largest concentration of brochs in Scotland.

When the Picts were overrun by the Gaelic Scots of Dalriada in the south, and by Vikings from the north, the survivors would naturally have taken refuge in inaccessible hinterlands behind the areas in which such substantial evidence of their presence remains. It is precisely here, in the heights of the Caithness-Sutherland border, that Clan Gunn is to be found. For centuries their name has been offered a variety of Norse pedigrees. Perhaps this is not surprising: no Pictish records survive, so that their very language is a matter of controversy. The earliest literature of the area is a Norse saga of the Orkney earls. From this quarry the distinguished historian Sir Iain Moncreiffe of that Ilk has extracted the theory that the Gunns descend from Gunni of the saga. The late Lord Lyon King of Arms, Sir Thomas Innes of Learney, has stated by contrast that the name derives from the Norse *Gunnr*, meaning war. In the same way, Norse and Gaelic derivations are found for many local place-names that may survive, in fact, from a lost prehistoric language.

Throughout the Middle Ages the territories of the Gunns became more and more heavily indented by their neighbours in the west, north and south. Their very survival as a distinct tribe was increasingly menaced, particularly during the great conflict between the Sinclair earls of Caithness and the Gordon earls of Sutherland, which continued throughout the 16th and 17th centuries. By the mid-15th century the chief had acquired the Gaelic patronymic *Mac Seumais Cataich* (Son of James of Caithness). From this period the chief also held the office of hereditary coroner or Crowner of Caithness. His insignia of office gave him his Gaelic title, *Am Braisdeach Mòr* (Wearer of the Big Brooch).

The Gunns suffered severely in the Highland clearances of the early 19th century, particularly those who lived in the strath of Kildonan and other territories within the Gordon earldom. In 1821 the 10th *Mac Seumais* presided over the formation of a Clan Gunn society. But he was the last officially recognised Chief of this clan, and one of the most aboriginal tribes in Scotland had been swept from its fastnesses at last. Many of the Gunns moved down to the coast, and took to fishing from little villages in the nooks and crannies of its cliffs. It was in one of these villages, Dunbeath, twenty-one miles south of Wick, that a member of the Gunn clan was born who has immortalised the name and way of life of his clan at the very moment of its final disintegration.

Neil Gunn (1891–1973) was the son of a skipper who generally engaged his crews from the west, and was a Gaelic-speaker himself. Of the novels he wrote, the German scholar Kurt Wittig states: 'Modern Scottish fiction reaches its highest peak in the novels of Neil M. Gunn.' The American Professor Francis R. Hart has gone even further: 'For me, Neil Gunn's twenty novels are the finest body of work as yet produced by a Scottish novelist.' The long struggle for survival since the Picts were overrun by later colonists has left a monument as imperishable as those carved symbol stones which still stand so inscrutably around the Moray Firth. It has been augmented in 1981 by the publication of F. R. Hart and J. B. Pick's definitive biography, *Neil M. Gunn: a Highland Life*.

Hamilton

At the time when the wars of independence began, Sir Walter, son of Gilbert of Hameldone, possessed properties in Renfrewshire. But King Robert Bruce rewarded him for his support with forfeited Comyn property that was in due course renamed Hamilton. Sir Walter's son Sir David was captured by the English at the battle of Neville's Cross in 1346, in company with his namesake David II, son of Bruce. Like the King, Hamilton was not released until a heavy ransom had been paid.

But an even closer association with the royal house began in about 1474, when James, 1st Lord Hamilton, married Princess Mary, daughter of James II, King of Scots. For over a century thereafter a Hamilton stood next in succession to the crown, while during much of this period the King was a minor. The son of the 1st Lord Hamilton and Princess Mary was created Earl of Arran, the Gaelic-speaking island in the Forth of Clyde on which, from 1503, the family made their Highland home at Brodick Castle.

It was the second Earl of Arran who acted as Regent for the baby Mary, Queen of Scots, as next heir to the crown. In this office he plundered the royal revenues, switched his allegiance between France and England according to the bribes he received, and was largely responsible for the provocations which led to Henry VIII's atrocities in Scotland. Among Arran's prizes was the French dukedom of Châtelherault. His claim to the throne was challenged by the Stewart Earl of

Lennox, who played the same game, and was Henry VIII's quisling claimant at the time of the Rough Wooing.

Arran possessed two remarkable brothers, bastard sons of the first Earl. One of these, John Hamilton (?1511–1571), became Archbishop of St Andrews. In this office he attempted to reform the Church from within, and issued a catechism in English. He baptised Queen Mary's son, the future King James VI, in 1566, and remained loyal to the Queen after her downfall. But when her brother the Regent Moray was assassinated by a Hamilton, the party of Lennox hanged the archbishop in his pontifical robes from a common gibbet.

The fate of the 1st Earl of Arran's other remarkable bastard was little different. Sir James Hamilton of Finnart was wild and impetuous, but he possessed a personality that enabled him to retain the friendship of the fickle King James V, begun in youth, through almost his entire reign. It was partly because they shared a passion for the renaissance architecture which both men had admired in France, and which Finnart had the skill to plant in Scotland. It was he who carried out the incomparable renaissance work on the palaces of Linlithgow and Falkland, for which James V presented him with letters of legitimation amongst other rewards. But Finnart was also a leader of the deadly brawl in Edinburgh in 1520, known as 'cleansing the causeway'. In 1526 he murdered the Earl of Lennox after the latter had surrendered his sword to him—a crime that the Earl's son revenged on Finnart's brother the archbishop. In 1528 he played a prominent part in bringing his cousin Patrick Hamilton to the stake for his Lutheran heresies. Patrick's father was a bastard of the 1st Lord Hamilton, so that he did not possess the blood of the Princess Mary. On the other hand, Patrick's mother was a grand-daughter of James II, while he himself was legitimate. Perhaps Finnart was moved by jealousy. He met his deserts in 1540 when Patrick's brother revealed to James V a plot to murder the King in which Finnart was alleged to be involved. He was instantly arrested and executed, and all his estates confiscated.

The royal connection continued to augment the family's fortune without other noticeable merit. The third Earl became the first Marquess of Hamilton: the third Marquess became the first Duke: and it was this Duke who contributed so much, by his stupidity, arrogance and deceit, to the downfall of Charles I.

The part of the Duke of Hamilton in securing the Union of Scotland with England in 1707 is particularly disreputable, for he professed to oppose it, and repeatedly undermined the opposition by treachery, to his own immense profit. Once again, it was a bastard line, descending from the first Lord Hamilton, that restored the credit of his name. John Hamilton, 2nd Lord Belhaven and Stenton (1656–1708), made speeches against Union which are Scotland's supreme examples of parliamentary oratory. He was imprisoned in Edinburgh with other opponents of Union, and taken a prisoner to London in 1708 on a charge of favouring a French invasion. He died there a few days after being granted bail.

Hay

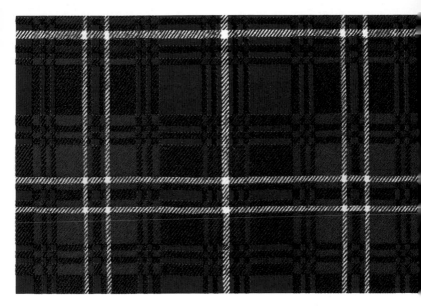

The Norman place-name La Haye derives from *haie*, meaning a hedge. In English it was not translated, but remained Hay. However it is one of the Norman names that was translated into Gaelic, rather than merely corrupted, so that the Chief of Clan Hay is known to this day as *Mac Gàraidh Mór*. *Gàradh* means a wall or dyke, as well as a garden, and thus preserves the more significant meaning of La Haie, a defensive stockade. The river Garry has the same name as the Great Son of the Stockade.

The rise of the Hays in Scotland was early and rapid. The first to appear there was William de la Haye, who was at the court of Malcolm IV in about 1160. He became first lord of Erroll, Butler of Scotland: and more significantly still, he married an heiress of the old Scoto-Pictish stock, Eva of Pitmilly. His son David improved upon this by marrying a daughter of one of the ancient Scottish earldoms, Ethna of Strathearn. So the third Hay of Erroll was only a quarter Norman in blood, and took the name of his Gaelic grandfather, Earl Gilbert Mac Ferteth. He became Sheriff of Perth, held the office of co-Regent of Scotland on two occasions, and married into the great family of Comyn, Earl of Buchan, and descendants of King Donald *Bàn*. His brother-in-law was Constable of Scotland, an office that King Robert Bruce bestowed on Sir Gilbert Hay, 5th lord of Erroll, and his descendants as a reward for his support. Thus the Hays rose in a century and a half to be one of the most powerful families in Scotland, possessing the blood as well as the lands of those they had supplanted.

Amongst these was the former Comyn stronghold of Slains on the coast of Buchan, from which the officer-of-arms of the Lord High Constables of Scotland derives his title, Slains Pursuivant. It was occupied by the Hays until James VI demolished it in 1595, when the Hay chiefs enlarged their tower of Bowness further north and called it Slains Castle. But now this gigantic pile of masonry is a ruin also. Diana Hay, *Nic Gàraidh Mhór*, 23rd Countess of Erroll, Lord High Constable of Scotland, lived in a modern house that has been built within the ruins of the original of Slains until her death in 1978.

The family has overcome many hazards in the interval. It was raised to the earldom of Erroll in 1452, and in 1559 the 7th Earl was appointed Lord Lieutenant of central Scotland when Mary, Queen of Scots married the heir to the French throne and her mother Mary of Lorraine was Regent of Scotland. After Queen Mary had been murdered by the English at Fotheringhay, the 9th Earl joined with Angus and Huntly in attempting a Catholic coup d'état, and it was this that led to the demolition of old Slains Castle by James VI in 1595. But as the King was equally anxious to free himself from the control of his Calvinist subjects, his rebellious Catholics escaped lightly.

The usurpation of the Calvinist King William in the Revolution of 1688 proved more serious. The 13th Earl, last of the male line, vigorously opposed the Union of 1707, and brought the Old Chevalier (*de jure* James VIII) to the coast of Scotland for the first unsuccessful Jacobite uprising. He was succeeded by his sister as 14th Countess, who used Slains Castle as a centre for Jacobite conspiracy and raised her clan for Prince Charles in the Forty-Five. When she died in 1758 she was succeeded by her great-nephew Lord Boyd. His family had lost three earldoms through their loyalty to the Stewarts, but he took the surname of Hay and became the 15th Earl of Erroll.

Branches of the family have become earls of Kinnoull and marquesses of Tweeddale. James Hay, created Earl of Carlisle, was also proprietor of what were called the Carlisle islands. But these were annexed to the crown in the 17th century and are now called Barbados. John Hay enjoyed the Jacobite title of Duke of Inverness and was Secretary of State to the King at Saint Germains. The Hays of Delgatie in Aberdeenshire provided one who lost his life for Charles I as chief of staff to Montrose; and their castle of Delgatie with its fine painted ceiling of 1597 is now administered by the Clan Hay Society as its international headquarters.

The present Chief is Merlin, 24th Earl of Erroll (b. 1948).

Henderson

The forms of Henry, Hendry and their sons have many variants and diverse geographical origins. The Gaelic form is *Mac Eanruig*, and the Hendersons of Glencoe possessed a legendary ancestor in *Eanruig Mór Mac Righ Neachtan* — Great Henry, son of King Nechtan. It appears that the chiefship passed to an heiress, and that she became united in a handfast marriage with Angus *Óg* of Islay. Their son was known as *Iain Fraoch* (Heather John), and he evidently settled in the lands of the grandfather to whom he was heir, Dugald MacHendry, at Inverlochy in Lochaber. Here his son was born and became known as *Iain Abrach* (John of Lochaber). It was he who gave the patronymic MacIain to the MacDonald chiefs of Glencoe. But recognition was given to precedence of the Hendersons in various ways that satisfied Highland pride. They formed the chief's bodyguard, and they were the first to carry a dead chief's coffin in the funeral procession. They were hereditary pipers to Maclain, and one of them, *Iain Breac MacEanruig*, composed the well-known air *Gabhaidh sinn an rathad mór*. The assimilation of Hendersons and MacDonalds after the chiefship had passed with an heiress to another name is in stark contrast to what occurred when the Campbells obtained a similar footing in the lands of the MacGregors.

In the far north another tribe of Hendersons emerged of equally ancient, but entirely different origins. Here the chiefs of Clan Gunn had become hereditary coroners of Caithness and one of these, George Gunn, possessed a younger son Hendry, from whom the Henderson sept came into being in the 15th century. The corrupt Gaelic form of the name, Mackendrick, does not appear to have been favoured in this area, as Gow was in place of Smith, and as it would be logical to expect in all such areas in which forms of English and Gaelic have existed side by side for upwards of a thousand years.

At the opposite end of the country, in Dumfries-shire, lived the Hendersons of whom James became Lord Advocate in 1494 and founder of the line of Fordell in Fife. It is thought that the man who played the greatest part in Scottish history of any of this name belonged to the branch of Fordell. Alexander Henderson was born in about 1583 and attended St Andrews University, where he became a professor of philosophy. He was appointed to Leuchars, whose church still possesses its Romanesque chancel built before 1200. Despite the influence of its beautiful architecture, Henderson was one of those who opposed Charles I's attempt to restore the beauty of vestments and ritual in Scottish religious observance. With Archibald Johnstone he drew up the historic National Covenant of protest that was exhibited for signature in Greyfrairs churchyard in Edinburgh in 1638. 'We have now cast down the walls of Jericho', declared Henderson. In 1643 he was among the Scottish commissioners to the Westminster assembly, who tried to force Presbyterianism on the unwilling English as the price of Scotland's military support against Charles I. He died in 1646, just as his party reached the summit of its success.

The name has also shed extraordinary lustre upon Scottish literature. Henry the Minstrel (Blind Harry, as he is called) is perhaps the best known of all those wandering bards who recited the deeds of their countrymen in Gaelic and English in the firelight of centuries. He lived in the 15th century and recreated William Wallace as a folk hero of singular strength and ferocity, quite unlike the statesman and skilled strategist of history. The same century produced Robert Henryson, the schoolmaster of Dunfermline whose poetry ranks in quality with that of his contemporaries William Dunbar and Gavin Douglas. All three lived in that period between the death of Chaucer in 1400 and the publication of Tottel's Miscellany in 1557, during which England produced no comparable poetry, and founded the literature of a northern dialect of English which came to be called the Scots tongue. But neither Blind Harry nor Henryson can be connected with any other family of their name.

Home

Whether this name is spelt Home or Hume, it derives from Home in Berwickshire, and first occurs in historical record as a personal designation during the 13th century. The earliest certain progenitor of the later earls was Sir John, father of Sir Thomas Home of that Ilk, who flourished in 1385 and acquired the barony of Dunglass in East Lothian by marriage with the heiress of the Pepdie family. Their descendant Sir Alexander founded the collegiate church of Dunglass in 1450 and became an ambassador to England. He played an unsavoury part in hounding James III to his death in 1488 and died as the 1st Lord Home sometime after 1490. Alexander the 3rd Lord Home was executed for treason in 1516 after he had intrigued with the English against the Regent Albany in the aftermath of Flodden, when the King was a minor. The 5th Lord was a supporter of the Reformation, but he joined the adherents of the deposed Queen of Scots in 1569. The 6th Lord became a member of her son's Privy Council and accompanied him to London in 1603 when he became James I of England and VI of Scotland. He was created 1st Earl of Home and thereafter there is little noteworthy to record of his descendants until Sir Alexander, 14th Earl of Home, disclaimed his peerage titles in 1963 on taking office as Prime Minister. In the following year his party was defeated in a general election, but it returned to power in 1970 when Sir Alexander Douglas Home became Secretary of State for Foreign Affairs. In 1974 he was created a life peer as Baron Home of the Hirsel, so he has had four designations, including the title he bore before succeeding as earl.

Many other Homes, all belonging to Berwickshire, though not all of them possessing any traceable connection with the senior stem of their name, have made their contribution to Scottish culture. Alexander Home (?1560—1609) was born at Polwarth and became a respectable poet of the post-Reformation era. At the same time he warned Scottish youth against 'profane sonnets and vain ballads'. It is not certain whether he or his brother Lord Polwarth was the protagonist in *The Flyting betwixt Montgomerie and Polwart*. The 19th century produced two other minor poets of the same name.

David Hume (?1560—?1630), a younger son of Sir David of Wedderburn, became the historian of his house and composed Latin poetry which earned the commendation of the greatest Latinist in Europe, George Buchanan. He also possessed the spirit to attack the English historian Camden for his derogatory remarks about Scotland. However, his fame was overshadowed in the following century by his namesake David Hume (1711—1776), son of Joseph of Chirnside, again in Berwickshire. As a philosopher and historian he has been judged the acutest thinker in Britain during the 18th century—that age of vast intellectual achievement. His outstanding compatriot and contemporary Adam Smith said he came as near to the 'character of a perfectly wise and virtuous man as perhaps the nature of human frailty would permit.'

In his own day John Home (1722—1808) earned a comparable celebrity, which has not stood the test of time. He was the son of the town clerk of Leith, and one of the comparatively few Lowlanders who fought for Prince Charles in the Forty-Five. He was taken prisoner at the battle of Falkirk and imprisoned in Doune Castle. But he escaped to enter the ministry and to write in his manse the play which earned such an astonishing success. His *Douglas* is a turgid drama. But the tradition founded by Lindsay's *Three Estaits* with such promise had been blighted by two centuries of Calvinism, and an inferiority complex goaded Scots to hail this pretentious piece as a masterpiece. 'Where's your Willie Shakespeare now?' they asked the English. Home became tutor to the future King George III and even had the temerity to attempt a drama about the great English King Alfred. The theatre has been better served in this century by William Douglas Home, brother of the 14th Earl.

Innes

This clan, recognised as such by the Scottish Privy Council in 1579, took its name from the barony of Innes which lies between the Spey and the Lossie in Morayshire. It was granted to Berowald Flandrensis by Malcolm IV in 1160, and Berowald's grandson Sir Walter of Innes received a charter of confirmation in 1225. Since then their descendants have won exceedingly varied distinction, and have proved fertile in creating new branches.

John, Bishop of Moray from 1407 until 1414, was a son of Sir Robert, 8th of Innes. It was he who rebuilt much of Elgin Cathedral after it had been destroyed by the Wolf of Badenoch, King Robert II's evil son. William, 15th of Innes, attempted in 1554 to murder Alexander Dunbar, Prior of neighbouring Pluscarden, on the very altar steps of the same cathedral, while the 16th baron sat in the

Parliament of 1560 which abolished the Catholic Church in Scotland.

It was left to later Inneses to continue the tradition of the mediaeval bishop. Outstanding among these were the two brothers Lewis and Thomas, descendants of the 11th Baron. Father Lewis (1651–1738) was appointed Principal of the Scots College at Paris, where many of the mediaeval Scottish records had been brought for safety during the iconoclasm of the Reformation. He devoted himself to the task of their preservation and arrangement, with his brother's help; and their collaboration also produced *The Life of James II*, the exiled Catholic James VII of Scots. At his court of Saint Germains Father Lewis acted as a confidential secretary besides holding the posts of Lord Almoner to the Chevalier and Secretary of State for Scotland in 1690. His brother, Father Thomas Innes (1662–1744), had been born in Aboyne parish, and after helping Lewis to arrange the church records of Glasgow at the Scots College he returned to his country to work as a priest of the Scottish Mission. In 1701 he returned to Paris, where he died. The immense services of these brothers to the history of Scotland is commemorated today by *The Innes Review*. Meanwhile it was left to a clansman of a very different complexion to continue the tradition. Cosmo Innes (1798–1874) descended from the hereditary Keepers of Spynie Castle. He held Whig views, pursued a successful career as an advocate, and became Sheriff of Moray in 1840. But his passion was to rescue Scotland's historical documents. He devoted immense labours to arranging, editing and publishing his country's records, and became a professor of Edinburgh University.

In the sphere of public life, Sir James, 12th of Innes, was chief esquire to James III and entertained that very mobile monarch James IV at Innes Castle in 1490. During the troubled times that followed the deposition of Mary, Queen of Scots, the 16th Baron was so unlucky as to be beheaded by one of the Regents (most of whom suffered a similar fate). The 19th Baron shared the interest of James VI in witchcraft, and was alleged to have entertained the Queen of Elphin. But he also had the practical sense to establish the port of Garmouth in the Moray Firth, and it was here that Sir Robert, 20th of Innes, welcomed Charles II in 1650 when he arrived to claim his kingdoms from Cromwell. As a reward Innes was made a baronet; and it was the 6th baronet who succeeded as Duke of Roxburghe in 1805. His descendant is the 29th Baron of Innes.

Of the many cadet branches, there are those who descend from William, second son of the 11th Baron. William's son was made hereditary Constable of Redcastle, whose ruins still stand beside the Beauly Firth. There Constable Robert Innes gave his support to Mary, Queen of Scots, was betrayed by his own son, and murdered in the castle. Nemesis struck in 1595 when his son was beheaded in turn for his part in the murder of the Bonnie Earl of Moray. Such were the antecedents of the 1st baronet of this branch, who built the magnificent castle of Balveny on Speyside, and whose family still flourish in Banffshire although they lost all for Charles I, and were out for the Young Pretender in 1745.

Johnston

The earliest certain use of this surname occurs shortly after 1174, when John gave his personal name to the property he had been granted in Annandale in Dumfries-shire. His son Gilbert adopted the name of the parish and barony of Johnstone, and his grandson Sir John of Johnstone was living in 1296. On the other hand it is extremely likely that others took their name from Johnston or St Johnston, as Perth was still called in those days. There can be little doubt that Jonystoun in East Lothian, now Johnstonburn, also gave rise to families of the same name, though of different stock. And while the Johnstones proliferated as one of the most turbulent clans of the western borders, they cannot be connected with the Johnstons of Strathspey in the Highlands. These originate with Stephen the Clerk, who married Margaret, heiress of Sir Andrew Garioch, in the

14th century, and so obtained the lands of Johnston from which their descendants took their name. On the other hand, the vagaries of spelling offer little guidance to the origins of those who bear it today.

George Johnston of the Highland line was created a baronet of Nova Scotia in 1626, and the 4th baronet took part in the Forty-Five, while his son was killed at the battle of Sheriffmuir. Sir Thomas Alexander Johnston, the 11th baronet, lives in the United States. Of the border clan, Sir James Johnstone was created Lord Johnstone in 1633 and Earl of Hartfell in 1643. His son was created Earl of Annandale also; his grandson Marquess of Annandale in 1701. But all these titles became dormant on the failure of male heirs. The senior line of the border name was continued in the cadet branch of Westerhall, raised to a baronetcy in 1795, and to the barony of Derwent in 1881.

But no Johnstone, whether from the Borders or from the Highlands, made a greater impact upon the history of Scotland than Archibald, son of James Johnstone of Beirholm in Annandale. He was born in Edinburgh in about 1610, and in 1637 his astute mind was enlisted amongst those of five advocates to plan the resistance to Charles I's church liturgy. It was he who drew up the historic National Covenant with Alexander Henderson and became its most powerful propagandist. When Charles I made the mistake of seeking the support of his Calvinist opponents in Scotland in 1641, as a weapon against the rebellious English, he made Johnstone a judge with the courtesy title of Lord Warriston, knighted him, and gave him an annual pension of £200. He gained nothing by it, for Johnstone was a delegate to the Westminster conference of 1643 which attempted to seal an alliance between the Presbyterians of England and Scotland against the King.

When Charles I was executed, Johnstone was among those who supported Charles II as a 'Covenanted' King and earned his hatred by lecturing him on his morals. He was equally hateful to Cromwell for his wish to enforce Calvinism in the two kingdoms, but he helped Cromwell considerably through his part in purging the Scottish army of 'malignants' (those who did not share his own religious views) and so enabling Cromwell more easily to defeat it. Yet in 1657 he accepted judicial office under Cromwell, and played a leading part in the debates of his House of Lords.

Charles II, generally so forgiving, did not forget Johnstone of Warriston. At the Restoration in 1660 he was excepted from the general pardon, and sentenced to forfeiture and death. He escaped abroad but was taken in Rouen and sent home to be hanged in Edinburgh, in 1663. His nephew Bishop Burnet wrote of his 'unrelenting severity of temper'; and it proved effective in awakening an equal severity in a King usually remarkable for his tolerance.

In the present century the most distinguished bearer of this name has been Thomas Johnston C. H. (1881–1965). Appointed by Sir Winston Churchill to be secretary of state for Scotland 1941–5, he proved one of the ablest in the history of that office. He instituted hydro-electric development and promoted hospital schemes in Scotland.

Keith

Keith and Austin

During the centuries in which human civilisation depended so largely upon horses, it is natural that the highest offices of state should have involved their training and welfare. Thus the *Comes Stabuli*, Companion of the Stables, evolved into the High Constable, and the keeper of the royal mares into the Earl Marischal of Scotland.

The earliest recorded appointment of a member of the Keith family to the office of Marischal occurs in the reign of Malcolm IV. The part played by his descendant in the same office was one of the most decisive in settling the issue of Bannockburn. For Edward II of England had advanced on Stirling with the great horse that William had introduced, and that had played a major part in his victory at Hastings, a horse large enough to bear the weight of a fully armoured knight. It is the ancestor of the English Shire horse and of the Scottish

Clydesdale: but at the time of Bannockburn there were no such horses in Scotland. For one thing, the country was then too poor to feed them. Marischal met the chivalry of England mounted on their great horses with a small detachment of indigenous Scottish ponies, ancestors of the garron, which still bears the primeval eel-stripe along its back. On such a small steed Robert Bruce encountered and killed Bohun on his great horse. With such resources Marischal was only able to perform the vital part of scattering the Welsh archers when they might have caused havoc amongst the unbreakable Scottish hedge-hogs of unmounted spearmen.

It was this Marischal's great-grandson who founded the castle of Dunnotar on its sea-girt precipice south of Stonehaven on the east coast. In 1458 the office of the Keiths was erected into a functional earldom, and the family continued to grow in wealth and importance. Their castle expanded until it could accommodate an army. In 1495 the 3rd Earl entertained James IV, the King who founded Aberdeen university, at Dunnottar. The 4th Earl received his grand-daughter Queen Mary at the castle after she had defeated the Gordons at Cor-richie in 1562. Her son James VI held a Privy Council there and ap-pointed the 5th Earl his proxy at his marriage to Anne of Denmark. This Marischal founded Marischal college of Aberdeen university in 1593.

When Charles II landed in Scotland after his father's execution in 1649, the 7th Earl welcomed him to Dunnottar. Here were brought the state papers, the crown and sceptre of the Scots, the royal furniture and hangings. After Charles II had been defeated by Cromwell and had fled back to the Continent, Dunnottar became the last stronghold in Scotland still flying the royal standard. By the time it surrendered, the royal correspondence had been smuggled out in a woman's skirts, and the Scottish regalia had been let down the cliffs to an old woman gathering seaweed on the rocks. She carried it beneath the dulse in her creel to a nearby church, where it was hidden until the Restoration.

The 9th Earl Marischal strongly opposed the incorporating Union with England in 1707, but died in 1712, two years before the Hanov-erian succession. So it was George Keith, 10th and last Earl Marischal (?1693–1778) who fought with the Jacobites in 1715. After their defeat he escaped to Europe, was attainted for treason, and all his property was forfeited. Dunnottar was disposed of to the York Buildings Com-pany, which dismantled it. Marischal returned to fight for the Jacobites in 1719, when he was severely wounded in Glenshiel but again man-aged to escape. So did his brother James Keith (1696–1758), who was made a Field Marshal by Frederick the Great of Prussia before being killed in action, while Frederick appointed the Earl Marischal ambassa-dor to Spain. George II granted him a royal pardon and George III received him at court. But King Frederick built a house in Potsdam for his friend, and there Scotland's last Earl Marischal died.

In 1919 Dunnottar was purchased by Viscountess Cowdray who re-paired the ruins, which are now open to the public. The mausoleum erec-ted in 1582 by the 5th Earl has been restored by Aberdeen university.

Kennedy

> Twixt Wigtown and the town of Ayr,
> Portpatrick and the Cruives of Cree,
> No man need think for to bide there
> Unless he court with Kennedy.

This clan which dominated Carrick for so many centuries probably derived from a branch of the Celtic lords of Galloway. John Kennedy of Dunure had already acquired Cassillis by the time he married Mary, heiress of the Carrick earls. Their son, Sir Gilbert Kennedy, took a favourite personal name of those earls, and was the father of James Kennedy who married Robert III's daughter. Their son was not unnaturally created Lord Kennedy, as the grandson of a King, while his younger brother James was appointed Bishop of St Andrews.

Bishop Kennedy, born in about 1406, was one of the most outstanding prelates in Scottish mediaeval history. His uncle, James I, placed him in the See of Dunkeld in 1437, where he did much to reform that rather turbulent Highland diocese before he was transferred to St Andrews in 1440. Here his predecessor Bishop Wardlaw had secured the foundation of Scotland's first university, to which Bishop Kennedy added the college of St Salvator's. He extended his work of reformation in his new diocese. After the murder of James I he continued to act as adviser and administrator throughout the reign of his son. When James II was accidentally killed by a cannon in 1460, Kennedy assisted his widow Mary of Gueldres in the government of the country and undertook the education of the infant James III. Only after the Queen Mother had died in 1463, and the Bishop in 1465, did anarchy return. His brother Lord Kennedy then took part in the palace revolution which gave power to the Boyds until James III came of age.

Although this made Lord Kennedy one of the regents of James III's minority, it did not recommend him to the new sovereign. But David, 3rd Lord Kennedy, found favour with James IV, who created him Earl of Cassillis four years before he fell with his King at Flodden in 1513.

At the Reformation the last Abbot of Crossraguel, Quentin Kennedy, was the uncle of the 4th Earl of Cassillis. He appointed the Earl lay administrator of the abbey properties—the first step to their embezzlement. But on the Abbot's death Allan Stewart was made Commendator, which threatened to deprive the Earl of his prize. He therefore carried off Stewart to Dunure Castle and roasted him over a slow fire in order to compel him to sign a deed in the Earl's favour. According to his own testimony, Stewart withstood the treatment. 'When then seeing I was in danger of my life, my flesh consumed and burnt to the bones and that I would not condescend to their purpose, I was relieved of that pain, wherethrough I will never be able nor well in my lifetime.' Stewart was rescued from Dunure by his relatives the Kennedys of Bargany, who were at feud with their chief, but the Earl kept the lands of Crossraguel and merely gave the crippled Commendator a pension.

But the 6th Earl earned himself the surest place in his country's folklore when he scotched his wife's love affair with Johnnie Faa. According to many accounts he was Sir John Faa of Dunbar, of whom there is no historical record, although he came with a party of gypsies to carry off the Countess from Cassillis. But Johnnie Faa was the name of the gypsy king to whom James V had granted the right to rule his followers in 1540, nearly a century earlier. And the ballad may well be correct in making the Countess declare: 'I'll follow the gypsy laddie.' She was disappointed. Her husband caught the eloping party, hanged Johnnie Faa and his companions before her eyes, and incarcerated her for the remainder of her life.

From Cassillis, where the Countess had been compelled to watch from a window as her lover was hanged from the Dule Tree, and from Dunure, in whose Black Vault the Commendator had been roasted, the Kennedy chiefs moved into a new castle at Culzean on the shore of the Firth of Clyde. It is one of the strangest of Adam achievements, half Gothic and half classical. Opposite its windows rises the dramatic island from which the 12th Earl in 1806 chose his new title of Marquess of Ailsa. It was at this time that the family provided for one of the numerous children of Mrs Jordan and the future King William IV of England and III of Scotland.

Archibald Kennedy, 7th Marquess of Ailsa (b. 1925), is the present Chief.

Kerr

The first of this name to be recorded in Scotland lived in the reign of William the Lion at the end of the 12th century, and since then the forms of Kerr, Ker and Carr have become numerous in the Border country. Tradition gives the Kerrs a Norman descent and derives their two main branches from Ralph and John, two brothers who were living near Jedburgh in the 14th century. The senior branch of the Kerrs of Ferniehurst claims descent from Ralph. Their rivals were possessed of Cessford from 1467. The collision between these two houses of the same name is one of the dramas of 16th-century Border history, and it is heralded by the appointment of Sir Andrew Kerr of Ferniehurst as Warden of the Middle March in 1502, before the battle of Flodden, and of Sir Andrew Kerr of Cessford to the same office two years after that battle.

The death of James IV and the rapid remarriage of his widow, Margaret Tudor, to the Douglas Earl of Angus brought national politics into the heart of the Border country. Queen Margaret had been an English agent throughout her life in Scotland, and now Angus became the same, while the young James V grew up to detest all Douglases and to despise his mother. Cessford chose the pro-English faction of Margaret Tudor and the Douglases; Ferniehurst the party of the young King. First it was Cessford's turn to flee to the court of Henry VIII when Angus was exiled. Next, when James V himself died in 1542, Angus returned to Scotland with the support of English arms, which deprived Sir John Kerr of Ferniehurst of his castle. The Scots were rescued from the terrible devastations that followed by the auld alliance with France, and the French officer Beaugué has left a graphic account of the recapture of Ferniehurst in 1549. The atrocities committed by the English, and in particular the violation of women, had made Sir John Kerr's men extremely anxious to take their enemies alive. 'I myself,' Beaugué related in his memoirs, 'sold them a prisoner for a small horse. They laid him down upon the ground, galloped over him with their lances at rest, and wounded him as they passed. When slain, they cut his body in pieces and bore the mangled gobbets in triumph on the points of their spears. I cannot greatly praise the Scots for this practice. But the truth is, that the English tyrannized over the Borders in a most barbarous manner; and I think it was but fair to repay them, according to the proverb, in their own coin.'

The rivalry between the two branches continued. Sir Walter of Cessford was among those who fought against Queen Mary at Langside in 1568. After she had fled into her English captivity Sir Thomas Kerr of Ferniehurst remained loyal to her cause for as long as there was any hope of restoring her. Then the rivals turned to disputing their rights to the offices of Warden of the Middle March and Provost of Jedburgh. Finally they were united by marriage. The Cessford branch had acquired Newbattle Abbey at the Reformation, whose properties were erected into the earldom of Lothian. In 1631 Anne Kerr of Cessford married William Kerr of Ferniehurst, and from them descend the earls and marquesses of Lothian. The 11th Marquess presented Newbattle Abbey to be a residential college of adult education, and it has already won a prominent place in the cultural life of Scotland. The second title of nobility bestowed upon the Kerrs was the earldom of Roxburghe, and this was enlarged to a dukedom as a reward for supporting the Union of 1707. This title had already passed through the female line to a Drummond who adopted the name of Kerr, and in 1805 it devolved upon Sir James Innes of Innes, who joined his own ancient surname to that of the dukedom.

Peter Kerr, 12th Marquess of Lothian (b. 1922), is the present Chief.

Lamont

This clan descends from the original Scots who crossed the sea from Ireland to found the kingdom of Dalriada. One of its districts was named after King Comgall, killed in 537, a generation before the coming of Saint Columba, a prince of the same royal house of O'Neill as the Lamonts themselves sprang from. In the ancient Gaelic *Senchus Fer nAlban* (Account of the Men of Scotland) three principal kindreds are named in 7th-century Dalriada, and the kindred of Comgall is one of them. Its territory is called Cowal to this day, though its islands then included Bute and perhaps Arran also. In about 1200 Ferchar was a chief in Cowal, and a generation later his sons Duncan and Malcolm granted lands to the monks of Paisley. Malcolm's son Ladman is the progenitor from whom Clan Lamont derives its name. That this was the original kindred of Comgall emerging under a new name in a new era is attested by the Gaelic designation of its chief, *Mac Laomain mór Chomhail uile*—Great Ladman's Son of all Cowal.

The most precious heirloom with which his name is now associated is the Lamont harp—*Clàrsach Lumanach*—the oldest surviving example of Scotland's most ancient musical instrument. It has been dated to at least as early as 1464, and was said to have been taken to the Robertsons of Lude in Perthshire by a daughter of the Lamonts who married into that family. It is just over thirty-eight inches in height and sixteen inches wide at its broadest point. It was almost certainly tuned to the diatonic scale, and the number of its tuning pins gives it a compass of just over four octaves. Five hundred years ago it was playing an entire repertoire of music that was already ancient when it was new.

By this time the Lamont chiefs lived in Toward Castle, now no more than an extensive ruin. Cadet branches were established at Knockdow and Otter and Silvercrags. The junior branch of Cowston descends from Patrick Lamont who was coroner of Cowal in 1450.

But situated as they were in the heart of Argyll, they were among the natural targets for Campbell aggression, and this reached its appalling climax in 1646. The chief at this time was Sir James Lamont, who established a school at Toward in 1634, sat in the Scottish Parliament, and supported Charles I's attempt to restore a liturgy in the Scottish church and to recover the church properties which the nobility had embezzled. Campbell of Argyll, leader of the Calvinist opposition to these measures, was easily able to overawe a chief whose clan lived in the heart of the Campbell lands. Lamont even fought for him at Inverlochy in 1645, when Argyll was routed by Montrose and Lamont taken a prisoner. His clansmen now took the same opportunity that Montrose had given to the long-persecuted MacDonalds, to revenge themselves on the Campbells. Montrose later testified that his troops had killed none but men capable of bearing arms, and although atrocities were undoubtedly committed, it was nothing to the act of revenge that followed. After the defeat of Montrose a Campbell force invaded the Lamont country, besieged the castles of Toward and Ascog, and after Sir James Lamont had surrendered upon written terms, began their work of genocide. The women and young girls were murdered, thirty-six of the principal men of the clan buried alive. About two hundred perished at the spot now marked by the Dunoon memorial stone. It would be wrong, however, to blame the perpetrators because they happened to be Campbells. It was Calvinists, and the ministers in particular, who committed such atrocities throughout Scotland, not only in this period of their triumph, but whenever they possessed the power to promote their doctrines in this characteristic manner.

After the destruction of Toward Castle in 1646 the Lamont chiefs lived at Ardlamont until it was sold in 1893 by the 21st of his line. Noel Lamont of that Ilk (b. 1928), the present Chief, lives in Australia.

Leslie

The absence of a Fleming clan in Scottish history is perhaps to be explained by the fact that Flemings preserved this name in the burghs, where people organised themselves in trades and commercial guilds rather than in clans, whereas in the country they adopted the names of their properties. Among the most successful and distinguished are those who took the name of their lands of Leslie in Aberdeenshire. It was as early as the 12th century that Bartholf the Fleming settled here. As the son who obtained a charter for Leslie from William the Lion was named Malcolm, it is evident that his father had made a prudent Celtic marriage. With equal prudence his descendants survived the downfall of the Comyns when Robert Bruce won the crown, and Sir Andrew Leslie was among the signatories of the Declaration of Arbroath in 1320. Before the century was over his family had become members of the royal house by marriage and blood, and magnates of the first rank as earls of Ross. But Alexander Leslie, Earl of Ross, died in 1402 leaving an only daughter who became a nun. His sister's husband Donald of the Isles came to Harlaw in 1411 to fight for his rights in the earldom. It passed with the blood of the Leslies to his heirs until the forfeiture both of the earldom and of the Lordship of the Isles itself. But long before this the 6th Leslie chief, Sir Andrew, had been created Earl of Rothes by James II, and this less contentious title has survived the storms of history. The 20th Earl of Rothes is chief of the clan today.

One of these storms centred upon the murder of David Beaton, Cardinal Archbishop of St Andrews, in 1546. Scotland was then being ravaged by Henry VIII of England during the childhood of Mary, Queen of Scots. To Scotland the English despatched George Wishart as a treasonable agent and would-be assassin. He was, however, taken at his own profession as a reforming preacher and burned in St Andrews as a heretic. Soon afterwards Beaton was murdered in his palace there in what was represented as revenge for the death of a Protestant martyr, though in fact it was the crime of a private Leslie vendetta. Norman, Master of Rothes, one of the culprits, died in battle in France in 1554, and the 4th Earl died at Dieppe in 1558. But the 5th Earl took an active part in Queen Mary's personal reign without mishap, and the 6th Earl survived the hazards of Charles I's Civil War. It was he who called out prophetically to Montrose when the National Covenant was being signed in the Greyfriars churchyard in Edinburgh: 'James, you will never be at rest till you are lifted up above the rest in three fathoms of a rope.' At the coronation of Charles II in 1651 he carried the sword of state which had been added to the Honours of Scotland by Pope Julius II in 1507.

By this time two members of his clan had reached the summit of their military careers. Alexander, son of George Leslie of Balgonie, had entered the service of Gustav Adolf of Sweden in the Thirty Years' War. In 1628 he successfully defended Stralsund against Wallenstein, where Mackay's regiment was also engaged. At the outbreak of the Civil War he returned a field-marshal, and was appointed general of the army of the Covenant. Charles I created him Earl of Leven at the time when he created Argyll a Marquess, in an attempt to win the Covenanters to his side. With him in the Covenanting army fought the much younger David Leslie, son of Patrick of Pitcairly, who took over the command from Leven in time to be defeated by Cromwell both at Dunbar and at Worcester. In gratitude Charles II created him Lord Newark after his restoration.

But it was the cadet branch of Balquhain which produced in John Leslie, Bishop of Ross, the greatest ornament of this name. He was born in 1526 and became the most loyal of all the supporters of Mary, Queen of Scots, throughout a lifetime of increasing disappointment and persecution. The *History of Scotland* which he wrote for her in the Scottish vernacular is his imperishable monument.

Lindsay

Lindsay had once been one of the little kingdoms of England. It lay in Lincolnshire and flourished from the 6th until the 9th century, when it was occupied by the Danes. The Norman Conquest followed, and in 1086, the year before the Conqueror's death, Baldric of Lindsay was tenant of his manors under the Earl of Chester. The name was by this time in current use in England. In about 1120 Sir Walter of Lindsay, proprietor of Fordington, was a member of the council of England's greatest magnate, David Earl of Huntingdon. While Earl David succeeded his brother as King of Scots in 1124, Sir Walter was succeeded either by his brother or his son William of Lindsay. William accompanied David to his kingdom, where presently he was in a position to grant lands in Ayrshire to Dryburgh Abbey. His son Walter was a justiciar of Scotland and sat in the Parliament of 1145; his grandson Sir William, the first to appear as proprietor of Crawford, was described by Wyntoun as 'the greatest that of our land were seen.' He also married a rich English heiress, and so the family continued to branch prosperously both sides of the border. Sir David Lindsay of Crawford and the Byres adventured further. He became one of the Regents of Scotland in 1255 and High Chamberlain in the following year. Then he joined the crusade of St Louis, King of France, and died in Egypt in 1268.

It was in such families that the war of independence presented a particularly painful choice. The Lindsays responded with exceptional patriotism. The crusader's son, Sir Alexander, had been knighted by Edward I of England, but despite his English properties and allegiance he was the companion of Wallace and the supporter of Bruce. His English lands were forfeited, his three sons taken prisoner. But they survived, and Sir David, the eldest, was among the signatories of the Declaration of Arbroath in 1320. One of his grandsons was ambassador to England in 1357, the year in which the English released the Bruce's son David II from his eleven years of captivity to reign again as King. Another died on pilgrimage to the Holy Land in 1382.

It was the pilgrim's son Sir David Lindsay who was created Earl of Crawford in 1398. Eight years earlier he had represented the chivalry of Scotland in a passage of arms on London Bridge on St George's Day, when he fought before Richard II of England and his queen. This splendid figure from the world of Froissart also became Admiral of Scotland, and once served with the French fleet in an action at Corunna. The heads of the great house of Lindsay continued in their loyalty to the Stewart sovereigns. The 6th Earl died very near to James IV on the field of Flodden in 1513. The 10th Earl was a faithful adherent of Mary, Queen of Scots. The 16th Earl commanded a regiment of horse for Charles I until he was captured. When he died in 1652 the title passed to a cadet branch first of Spynie, then of Balcarres, which had already been raised to the earldom of Balcarres in 1651 for its loyalty to the royal house. This line continued the same tradition at the Revolution of 1688, and in the Jacobite rising of 1715. But it secured an indemnification, and in the 18th century the lines of Crawford and Balcarres were united.

The services to Scotland of the late Sir David Lindsay, 28th Earl of Crawford and 11th of Balcarres, would have received the approval of James III. He was a Trustee of the Tate Gallery, the National Gallery, and the British Museum. From 1943 until 1957 he was Chairman of the Royal Fine Arts Commission. He was also Chairman of the National Trust and a Trustee of the Pilgrim Trust.

Among those of his name who have done so much to enrich Scotland's heritage before him, two are especially noteworthy. Sir David (1490–1555), son of David Lindsay of the Mount in Fife and of Garmylton near Haddington, was an attendant of James V's earliest childhood. In 1529 the King appointed him Lyon King of Arms, an office in which he blazoned the nation's follies in his play, *An Satyre of the Three Estaits*. He composed it in the popular vernacular, which he was so far-sighted as to advocate as the language of religion and law as well as of poetry. Although he was a courtier and a royal favourite he rebuked court vices and displayed popular sympathies: and both James V and his remarkable Queen Mary of Lorraine gave him public approval. But paradoxically, the Reformation, which he promoted, killed the infant school of drama which he founded in Scotland. His contemporary, Robert Lindsay of Pitscottie (?1500–?1565), that delightful, humorous, but unreliable historian, belonged to one of the cadet branches of the great family of Crawford.

Livingstone

Here is one of the clearest illustrations of how a Lowland name such as Gordon or a Norman name such as Sinclair might be planted in Gaelic Scotland by feudal charter. The Livingstons of Livingston in Lothian were earls of Linlithgow and hereditary Keepers of the royal palace there. It was not until 1641 that Charles I granted to one of this family a lease of the lands and rights of the bishopric of Argyll and the Isles, which made a Livingston overlord in Lismore.

To this island Saint Lughaidh had come from Bangor to found an abbey over a thousand years before. He was remembered as Moluag, and among his relics was the pastoral staff which became known as the *Bachuil Buidhe* or Yellow Staff, because it was encased in copper. Its hereditary guardians might have called themselves Dewars to this day, as those of the relics of Saint Fillan did: and a *Tigh nan Deora* (House of the Dewars) on Lismore remains as evidence that the title of Dewar was used there. But the keepers of the staff, the only certain relic of Saint Moluag to have survived, were generally known as Macleays—until James Livingston moved into Achanduin Castle on Lismore sometime after 1641. It was not until this late date that they added a letter to the name of a new overlord with whom they had no previous connection, and called themselves Livingstone. At least they seem to have done this of their own volition. Over a century earlier the Dean of Lismore, Sir James MacGregor, had made his priceless collection of bardic poetry and Ossianic ballads on the eve of the persecution which outlawed his very name. The Dean's Book survives, as though by a miracle, like Saint Moluag's staff; and it is possible that the bell shrine from Kilmichael Glassary is also one of the saint's relics.

The most famous of the Macleay Dewars whose name had become altered is Dr David Livingstone the African traveller and missionary after whom Livingstone in Malawi is named. The most distinguished today of those who did not change their name is the former Secretary of State for Scotland, John Maclay, now Viscount Muirshiel. Among his many services, that which best recalls the tradition of Saint Moluag may be seen at Quarrier's Homes near the Bridge of Weir, where the children of poorer parents have a Dewar in their midst.

Logan

Although the names Logan and MacLennan often appear in clan books as though they were virtually interchangeable, there is no historical evidence whatever to connect them. The most famous of the southern Scottish Logans were Sir Robert and Sir Walter, who accompanied the Good Sir James Douglas to the Holy Land with the heart of King Robert Bruce, and died with Douglas in Spain in 1329. Sir Robert Logan of Restalrig married a daughter of Bruce's grandson Robert II and was appointed Admiral of Scotland, but the dynasty of Restalrig was later outlawed and extinguished. However, Logans have lived in Lothian from that day to this, such as the minor 18th-century poet John Logan, son of a small farmer. Of greater consequence were the Logans of Logan in Ayrshire: George Logan, the 18th-century Moderator of the General Assembly and controversialist, has been supposed to belong to this house.

It is a far cry from such folk to the legendary Gilligorm, leader of Lobans, Lobhans or Logans in Easter Ross, killed in a feud with the Frasers in no particular century. His widow gave birth to a deformed son, who was called *Crotair Mac Gilligorm*, and who entered the Celtic church in which priests were permitted to marry. He was educated by the monks of Beauly Priory, founded the churches of Kilmuir in Skye and Kilchrinin in Glenelg, and fathered a son whom he named *Gille Fhinnein* — the Devotee of Saint Finnan. At this point light breaks upon the confusions of tradition, suggesting an origin for *Clann Mac Gill'innein* long before Frasers or Logans were to be seen in the Highlands. While the Lobans of Drumderfit in Easter Ross survived until the Jacobite rising of 1715 (when a wooden effigy of Gilligorm was destroyed with their house), the MacLennans of Wester Ross lived cheek by jowl with the MacRaes and became standard bearers to the Mackenzies of Seaforth. Roderick and his brother Donald MacLennan were killed defending the banner at the battle of Auldearn in 1645, during the Montrose wars.

More recently Sir Hector Ross MacLennan (1905–1978) was a distinguished gynaecologist and obstetrician. His son, Robert

Logan

MacLennan, a former Government minister representing Sutherland and Caithness, is one of the founders of the Social Democratic Party.

The alternative name of Logan deserves a very special place in any history of the Highland tartan. In 1826 a certain James Logan embarked on a tour of Scotland, collecting all the information he could find about the setts of tartans, amongst other antiquities. After years of wandering and analysis his two volumes of *The Scottish Gaël* were published in 1831: the first scientific attempt to place on record details of the most colourful folk costume in the world. It is unfortunate that Logan did not live before the suppression of Highland dress, or even before the tartan mania which followed George IV's visit to Edinburgh in 1822. But he published his systematic definitions of fifty-five tartans before the illustrated books appeared, before the Sobieski Stolberg Stewarts issued their more dubious *Vestiarium Scoticum*. Between 1843 and 1849 he collaborated with Maclan in the illustrated *The Clans of the Scottish Highlands*. Its brawny, sentimentalised clansmen have since enjoyed an incomparable vogue. By the time Logan died in 1872 the tartan enthusiasm was running riot, and the anchorage which he had given to a sober study of the subject could be seen to have been invaluable. The name of Logan is one of those to whom the Highland heritage owes a supreme debt.

MacAlister

Alasdair Mór was a younger son of Donald of Islay, the founder of Clan Donald and grandson of King Somerled. According to the Irish annals, Alasdair was killed in 1299 in conflict with his cousin Alasdair MacDougall, of the senior line of Somerled. By this time the Scottish war of independence had broken out, in which the MacDougalls were to suffer for their opposition to Bruce, while Clan Donald rose to power as a result of their ruin. The descendants of *Alasdair Mór* settled in Kintyre, where Charles MacAlister was invested with the stewartry in 1481 by James III. His son was called John of the Lowb: *lùb* is Gaelic for a creek or bend in the shore, and it had given its name to his patrimony. John himself provided the name of the subsequent chiefs, who were henceforth styled *Mac Eoin Duibh*. Thus the Chief was designated in 1515, in the garbled Gaelic of the day, Angus Vic Ian Dhu M'Alastair of the Loup.

During the 15th and 16th centuries the MacAlisters of Kintyre spread into the neighbouring islands of Bute and Arran. One cadet branch became the hereditary Constables of the royal castle of Tarbert between the Loup and Loch Fyne, the key to Kintyre. Another established the family of the MacAlisters of Glenbarr in Argyll.

But a branch which settled in Clackmannanshire and held their property of Menstrie from the Earls of Argyll adopted the name Alexander, although they claimed descent from *Alasdair Mór*. *Alasdair* is the Gaelic for Alexander, just as *Iain* is the Gaelic for John.

The English name of the Menstrie line became appropriate when it gave birth to William Alexander in 1567. For he followed James VI to London when he inherited the English throne in 1603, and there published his sonnets in the language and style of the English poets. In 1614 he published his *Doomsday, or the Great Day of Judgment*, and in admiration for his poetry, James VI knighted him. He was the principal promoter of the order of Baronets of Nova Scotia, instituted by Charles I in 1625, who created Alexander first a Viscount, then Earl of Stirling. Before his death in 1640 he published his collected works. But although they possess considerable merit, were composed in the language of Shakespeare, and preserved in print, they have not stood the test of time so well as the poems of his younger kinsman Iain *Lom* MacDonald. Iain *Lom* composed in a language understood by relatively few and now spoken by fewer still. He could not hope to see his work published. Yet the fire of his Gaelic poems on the wars of Charles I, and the subsequent misfortunes of the Stewart kings is not extinguished yet.

The senior line of *Mac Eoin Duibh* of Loup remained loyal to the Stewarts, but were not rewarded as the London courtier had been. Alasdair, 8th of Loup, fought for the dethroned King James VII at Killiecrankie, and afterwards at the battle of the Boyne in Ireland which defeated the Jacobite cause there in 1690. But a century later the fortunes of *Mac Eoin Duibh* were very considerably increased when the 12th Chief of Loup married the heiress of the Somervilles of Kennox in Ayrshire. The chiefs of Clan MacAlister have lived at Kennox ever since.

MacAlpine

It was the fortune of King Alpin of Dalriada to beget the son who became the first sovereign of the Picts and Scots and the founder of the royal dynasty of what was to evolve as the modern kingdom of Scotland. Kenneth Mac Alpin's achievement has remained a matter of some surprise ever since, and the explanations for it have been various. The British (Welsh-speaking) kingdoms of Strathclyde, Gododdin and Rheged in southern Scotland were of ancient and firm foundation: yet they vanished utterly. The Picts had been considered the most formidible military power by the Romans, and they had repelled the Northumbrian English who conquered the Britons. Yet it was Kenneth the Scot who took over Pictland in 843, and not the Picts who conquered Dalriada. By the time he died in 858 he had established the Scottish hegemony so effectively that the very Pictish language soon disappeared in favour of Gaelic.

This can be explained partly by the cultural infiltration which followed the mission of Saint Columba to the King of the Picts in the late 6th century. On the other hand, another Pictish king was adopting the rival Roman religious customs from Northumbria over a century later, in place of those of the Columban church, which must have

MacAlpine

diminished its influence considerably. In 741, according to the Gaelic annals, King Oengus of the Picts 'utterly destroyed' the Scots. Yet a century later Kenneth Mac Alpin's takeover occurred. Perhaps he was assisted by the ancient law of matrilinear succession which gave him a claim to the Pictish crown through female descent. But probably the dominant factor was the onslaught of the Vikings from Scandinavia early in the 9th century. The Picts were already weakened by their assaults by the time the Scots began to move eastwards, towards the safety of the hills, as the Norsemen made life in the western islands and firths increasingly precarious. Such were the contributory factors which caused Britain's northern peninsula to be called Scotland, and the ancient Scottish form of social organisation by kindreds to spread and evolve into the clan system.

Although MacAlpine is used as a surname to this day, there is little trace of an effective clan of that name in historical record. Generally the term employed is *Siol Ailpein*, the descendants of Alpin, and among those who have claimed this distinction are the Mackinnons and MacQuarries, the MacGregors, Grants, MacNabs and Mac-Aulays. The paradox is that these clans did not combine to make *Siol Ailpein* an effective confederation like that of Clan Chattan. The most ignominious fate of all that befell Alpin's descendants was suffered by the MacGregors: whose motto is *Is rioghal mo dhream*, my blood is royal.

MacArthur

After the Roman legions had left, the British kingdoms of southern Scotland fought to maintain themselves against the Picts and the Scots to their north, and against the expansionist English of Northumbria to their south. In their Welsh language the earliest surviving Scottish poem was composed, telling of the defeat of the Gododdin heroes by the English; and this poem contains far the earliest reference to the British resistence leader, Arthur. When the old British kingdoms of Gododdin, Strathclyde and Rheged had vanished, the traditions of the Men of the North were preserved in Wales—the only part of the once predominantly British isles in which their language remains to this day. The story of Arthur travelled south until he was given a new setting as far south as Tintagel in Welsh-speaking Cornwall.

Meanwhile Arthur's Seat commemorated him in the lands of the Gododdin, while to the north of Strathclyde the MacArthurs were tracing their descent in the 13th century from the legendary hero. It was a MacArthur who at this time married the heiress of Duncan *mac Duibhne* of Loch Awe. This was before the nickname *Cam beul* gave rise to the surname of Campbell, who are also called the *Clanh Ua Duibhne*. MacArthur may therefore be regarded as an earlier name of the same race. It was also one of considerable consequence until James I returned from his long captivity in England, and fell like a thunderbolt on the magnates of his realm. In 1427 Iain MacArthur shared the fate of the king's nearest relatives who had suffered execution and forfeiture. Thereafter it was the surname of Campbell which flourished in this region beyond the ancient capital of Strathclyde on Dumbarton Rock.

But in modern times the name of MacArthur has been carried to the ends of the earth. John MacArthur (1767–1834) belonged to a family that had already emigrated, since he was born in Devonshire. In 1790 he arrived with his regiment in New South Wales, where he was Commandant at Parramatta from 1793 until 1804. In 1794 he laid the foundations of the wool industry in Australia by crossing Bengal with Irish sheep, and then introducing merino sheep from Africa. Later he travelled throughout Europe with his sons, studying wine production, and in 1817 he planted the first Australian vineyard. When Bligh of the *Bounty* was appointed Governor, he attempted to arrest MacArthur in 1807, but he had met his match. MacArthur arrested Bligh in turn. He was a quarrelsome man, as two Scots who followed Bligh in the post of Governor, Sir Thomas Makdougall Brisbane of Brisbane and Lachlan MacQuarie, were to discover to their cost. But he founded a continent's two great industries of wine and wool, and justly ranks as a Father of Australia.

His name has been carried to even greater renown in the United States of America, where it was brought in about 1840 by an emigrant from the former lands of Strathclyde, in which Glasgow now lies. His son Arthur MacArthur entered the army, a career that was followed by his son General Douglas MacArthur (1880–1964).

MacAulay

Here is a clan name which, like Morrison, derives from two different progenitors. One of these is believed to have been *Amhlaidh*, a younger son of Alwin, Earl of Lennox. His name appears as a witness to charters granted by his brother Earl Maldowen to a Graham and a Galbraith, at the time when the father of the MacMhuirichs first brought his bardic art to the Lennox soon after 1200. *Amhlaidh Mac Amhlaidh* (or Aulay MacAulay) appears in the Ragman Roll at the end of this century, and in 1587 Sir Aulay MacAulay of Ardencaple is included in the roll of landlords of Gaeldom, as a principal vassal of the earldom of Lennox. The historian Skene dismissed the claim that the two men could be connected across the gap of three centuries. He pointed to a bond of friendship between MacAulay of Ardencaple and MacGregor of Glenstrae in May 1591 in which MacAulay owns himself to be a cadet of MacGregor at a time when there could be little profit in such an admission. Indeed, by 1594 the MacAulays join the MacGregors in the roll of broken clans. But no less an authority than Sir Iain Moncreiffe states that the Lennox MacAulays probably were descended from Earl Alwin's younger son. At any rate, Lennox protection saved them from the fate to which their connection with the MacGregors exposed them, and they retained the castle and lands of Ardencaple until these were sold for debt to Campbell of Argyll in 1767.

MacAulay

In the outer Hebrides the MacAulays of Lewis are believed to have taken their name from the Norse Olaf. Here Norse invasion, settlement and intermarriage had produced a half Celtic, half Germanic stock which finally reverted to the Gaelic language and culture. Moncreiffe suggests that the Hebridean MacAulays came from the mainland of Ross, where Ullapool commemorates Olaf's Place. The suggestion that their progenitor was Olaf the Black, King of Man, is speculative. King Olaf reigned before the battle of Largs in 1263 led to the surrender of the western isles to the Scottish crown. The earliest historical reference to a MacAulay in Lewis relates to Donald *Cam* (Crooked) in 1610. His son Angus was one of those who died at Auldearn in 1645 during the Montrose wars. Thereafter his descendants joined the virtually hereditary profession of the Calvinist ministry, until the Rev. John MacAulay of Inveraray produced as his grandson the prolific Whig historian Thomas, Lord Macaulay. One of the most remarkable of his qualities was his indifference (which bordered upon aversion) for his Highland background.

His totally un-Scottish poetry contrasts with that of his clansman of today, Donald MacAulay. When his collection, *Seobhrach as a'Chlaich* was published in 1967, the distinguished Lewis poet Iain Crichton Smith concluded his review by writing: 'In my opinion MacAulay's poetry is as good as anything that is being produced by anyone of his generation in Britain.'

MacBean

Three quite different Gaelic names have become corrupted into an even greater number of English forms, and it is by no means always easy to establish which Gaelic original gave rise to each of the English names. One of these is *Mac a'ghille bhàin*, Son of the Fair Lad: another is *Mac Maol Bheatha*, Son of the Servant of Life: the third, *Mac Beathain*, Son of Beathan. It might appear obvious that the MacBeans are the last of these, yet the MacBeans of Alvie were known as *Clann Mac Maol Bheatha*. The spelling in historical records sometimes identifies sons of Beathan without ambiguity, as when *Duncan mc behan* in *Dunmakglass* was baillie to the Earl of Moray in 1539, and *Malcolm Makbahing* was a servant of the Bishop of the Isles in 1585.

The mis-pronunciation which results in MacBain has been common among the non-Gaelic speaking peoples of Scotland. The noun *Cabar* and the province of Badenoch both have their initial vowels barbarised in this way. Shakespeare's Donald *Bàn* is the most celebrated instance of all. Early examples in Scottish records are *Ferquhar M'Bane* who took part in the assault on Petty in 1513: there was a *Sorle M'Conill M'Allane M'Baine* in Balloch in 1564. The aspiration of the initial letter produces the other range of names represented by *Roy M'Veane*, a cattle farmer in Glenorchy in 1594, and *John M'Vane* from Inverness among the Jacobite prisoners of the Forty-Five.

MacCallum

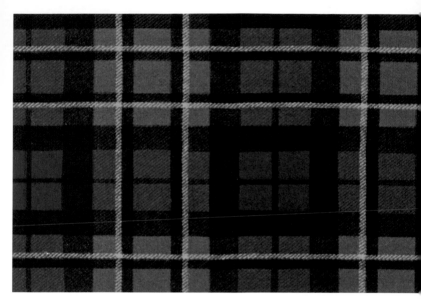

Saint Columba's name was *Colm* in its original Gaelic form, and he was distinguished from others of the same name by the suffix meaning a cell: *Columchille*. This suffix has made it easier to identify Columba's own foundations among those of a namesake. MacCallum means Son of Colm; and although it does not indicate descent from Columba, the MacCallums do originate in the ancient kingdom of Dalriada settled by the first Scots from Ireland.

Nearly a thousand years separate Columba and the earliest historical reference to the MacCallums. By this time the Campbells had moved into the district of Lorne in Argyll named after one of the princes of Dalriada, and for so long settled by MacCallums. In 1414 Ranald MacCallum was made hereditary Constable of Craignish Castle by the Chief of the Campbells.

A charter of 1562 is particularly interesting. It was granted by Duncan Campbell of Duntrune, and gave title in the property of Poltalloch to 'Donald M'Gillespie vich O'Challum.' In correct Gaelic this reads: *Domhnall mac Gilleasbuig Mhic Ui Chaluim*—Donald son of Gillespie son of the grandchildren of Callum. The reference may be late, but the pedigree is that of the oldest stock, using the archaic form for a grandson of Callum. The MacCallums of Poltalloch have continued down to the present, and now live in the ancient castle of Duntrune from which their 16th-century charter originated.

MacCrimmon

This name will be associated forever with Scotland's most distinctive contribution to European music, the art of pibroch. Its instrument, the bagpipe, was indigenous among all the peoples of Britain; and is merely one development of the many reed instruments of Europe and the Middle East that derive from river civilisations. The very chanter on which the melody is played is called in Gaelic *Feadan*, which means also a channel or water course.

The MacCrimmons are thought to have come to Skye from Harris in the outer Hebrides, and were already numerous there when they became involved in the feud between the MacLeods and the Mathesons in 1580. It was Donald *Mór* MacCrimmon who found time amid his warlike interests to develop the new musical form now generally called Pibroch. In fact the term derives from *pìobaireachd*, which simply means piping; but the compositions which Donald *Mór* pioneered were a sophisticated form of theme and variation governed by strict rules. His new heights of invention were heard in 1601 when he performed his '*Fàilte nan Leòdach*' ('MacLeod's Welcome') at Dunvegan. The fact that no surviving pibroch belongs to a date much before this provides the conclusive evidence that Donald *Mór* was indeed the originator of this new art. By 1612 he had left Skye for the mainland, perhaps as a result of his more violent activities; for he was named in that year as piper to the Chief of Mackay in Strathnaver. A tradition was planted there which led to the preservation of the art of the MacCrimmons by Mackay pipers after it had died out in Skye.

Meanwhile it was continued there by his son Patrick *Mór* MacCrimmon, who celebrated the death of the revered MacLeod Chief Rory *Mór* in his famous song of sorrow, '*Tog Orm Mo Phìob*'. Patrick *Mór* was succeeded by Patrick *Òg*, whose most famous pibroch, perhaps, is his lament for John MacLeod of Raasay. Patrick *Òg*'s most gifted son was Malcolm, born in 1690. It was he who composed the lament for his brother Donald *Bàn*, when he was killed in the Forty-Five.

By this time the MacCrimmons enjoyed the estate of Borreraig in Skye, as hereditary pipers to the MacLeods of Dunvegan, and it had become a college for the teaching of piping and composition. The music was not written down, but was transmitted orally by an intricate system of mouth-sounds called *cainntearachd* (chanting). Malcolm's son *Iain Dubh* (1730—1822) was to be the last principal of the Borreraig college. When MacLeod withdrew a part of his endowment, MacCrimmon left in disgust, although he later returned to his island to die in Glendale. It was now that the MacCrimmons began to disperse throughout the world, as silence fell on Borreraig.

Iain Dubh's younger brother Donald *Ruadh* (1743—c.1823) emigrated to America in 1772. He was gazetted Lieutenant in the Caledonia Volunteers in 1778, and the pibroch was heard in many distant places before he returned to Skye to perform "*Rory Mór's*

Welcome' at Dunvegan in 1799. He was celebrating the return of General Norman MacLeod from India with his graceful reference to the ancient association between their two families. When Sir Walter Scott visited Dunvegan in 1815, he saw Donald *Ruadh*. 'He is an old man, a Lieutenant in the Army, and a most capital piper, possessing about 200 tunes, most of which will probably die with him, as he declines to have any of his sons instructed in the art. These Mac-Crimmons formerly kept a college in Skye for teaching the pipe music.' But Samuel Johnson had found it closed when he visited Skye in 1773.

After the deaths of Malcolm's two sons, the dispersal of the clan was rapid and far-flung. *Iain Dubh*'s elder son Patrick *Mór* became a piper in the Black Watch, and boxing champion of the British Army. He finally settled and died in West Africa. His younger brother Duncan also served in the Black Watch, and left one son John (Iain) who emigrated to New Zealand and another who settled in America. As for the sons of Donald *Ruadh* whom Scott had seen in Skye, Patrick MacCrimmon (1780–1837) became a Captain in the Caledonia Volunteers, and subsequently a Lieutenant in the Cameron Highlanders. After serving with distinction in the Peninsular War he was appointed barrack-master in Sierra Leone, where he died within the year. His brother Donald (1788–1863) emigrated to Canada, where his descendants multiplied in Ontario.

But oral transmission proved too frail for all these upheavals, and the responsibility for preserving the art of the MacCrimmons passed into other hands. The masterpiece of pibroch is the 'Lament for the Harp Tree' (that is, for the harp key), a tribute to that earlier instrument, the little harp, which the bagpipe superseded. The music of the Mac-Crimmons might well have shared the fate of the ancient *clàrsach* music. But it survived the closing of Borreraig and the other colleges, and flourishes once more.

MacDonald

In 1098 Magnus Barefoot, King of Norway, led an expedition to recreate the old Norse power that had once been paramount from Shetland to Dublin. In the peace which he made with Edgar, King of Scots, he acquired possession of all the islands of the west round which he could sail a ship with its rudder in position. Magnus ordered his men to drag a ship across the isthmus of Kintyre while he sat at the helm, and so added this mainland province to his realm. But fifty years later the Scots of Argyll under Somerled evicted the Norsemen, and in 1156 they defeated Godfrey, King of Man and the western Isles in a sea battle. In 1164 King Somerled conducted an expedition of the Gaels of Ireland and the west against Malcolm IV, the Anglo-Norman King of Scots, but he was defeated and killed.

He was succeeded by his eldest son Dougall as a virtually independent sovereign in the west. But Dougall's mother, daughter of Olaf, King of Man, also gave birth to a younger son Ranald, and

MacDonald

this was the father of Donald, progenitor of the great Clan Donald. Ranald himself inherited a kingdom, for although his father was almost certainly a Gael despite his Norse nickname, these territories still belonged to the Norwegian crown, and the Norse practice of dividing a patrimony amongst the sons was followed.

Thereafter, the senior line of MacDougall possessed Mull, while the Chief of Clan Donald enjoyed Islay. But the MacDougalls remained loyal to the legitimate line of Balliol during the wars of independence, while the MacDonalds supported the Bruce, the only man likely to succeed in restoring Scotland as an independent kingdom. The MacDougalls were forfeited and Mull passed to the MacDonalds. Iain of Islay, Lord of the Isles in 1354, made a marriage which brought further possessions to his house, both in the islands and on the mainland. His son by this heiress was Ranald; and when he begot a younger son Donald by a subsequent marriage to a daughter of Robert II, King of Scots, he nominated Donald to succeed him as Lord of the Isles, while Ranald was compensated with the inheritance of Clanranald. So it was that the senior line of the MacDonalds of Clanranald gave allegiance to the Lords of the Isles with their royal blood. And when Donald, Lord of the Isles (1387–1423) fought for the earldom of Ross on the field of Harlaw in 1411, his opponent was his own first cousin Alexander Stewart, both men grandsons of Robert II, and both noted in their day as men of culture and ability.

MacDonald of the Isles

Thirteen years after the battle of Harlaw James I, the first effective Stewart sovereign, returned from his captivity in England to begin his personal reign. He executed his most powerful relatives and in 1427 summoned the Highland magnates to a Parliament at Inverness. Donald of the Isles was now dead, but his son Alasdair and his widow the Countess of Ross attended, only to be flung into prison. Some, including their cousin Alasdair MacDonald of Garmoran, were even executed and their estates forfeited. For this act of perfidy, so characteristic of the rule of the Stewarts, Alasdair of the Isles raised a rebellion as soon as he was released. But he was defeated, and accordingly came to Holyrood to fling himself upon the King's mercy. It was granted, but the Lord of the Isles was imprisoned in the great fortress of Tantallon. After two years the men of the Lordship rose again, and taught James I the lesson that their ruler could keep the peace there better from Islay than from Tantallon. He was accordingly released and restored to his properties. In 1435 he succeeded peacefully to the earldom of Ross.

With the earldom of Ross, the Lordship now comprehended all the islands of the Hebrides as well as much of the Gaelic mainland. A sole surviving Gaelic charter attests that the ancient vernacular was a language of its administration, while the *Mac Mhuirichs* were the principal custodians of its history and literature, and the Beatons possessed medical treatises embodying Greek and Arabic science

MacDonell of Keppoch

not then current in Europe as a whole. But this promising era was short-lived. Alasdair's son, John of the Isles, declared the independence of the Lordship, and entered into the Treaty of Ardtornish with the King of England in 1462. This recognised the fundamental division between the Gaelic and English-speaking halves of Scotland, and provided that if England were to defeat the Stewart King, the English-speaking Lowlands would be ruled by the house of Douglas, Gaelic Scotland by the Lord of the Isles, under the English King as paramount sovereign.

The treaty became known. In 1476 John of the Isles was stripped of his mainland possessions. His successors attempted to win them back by force, and in 1493 the Lordship itself was forfeited to the Scottish crown.

Stripped at the same time of the apex of authority, and of security in the possession of their property, the tribal society of the Highlands and islands fell to violence and anarchy. 'It is no joy without Clan Donald,' sang the Gaelic poet. 'It is no strength to be without them.' His pessimism was to prove well grounded. 'For sorrow and for sadness I have forsaken wisdom and learning.' A century later, as Campbells and Gordons and acquisitive Lowlanders still scrambled for MacDonald property, Sir Alexander Hay referred to the survivors of the holocaust as 'these unhallowed people with that unchristian language.'

MacDonald of Sleat

Alexander of the Isles, who also succeeded to the earldom of Ross for which his father had fought at Harlaw in vain, left at his death three sons. John succeeded as Lord of the Isles. His brother Celestine received Lochalsh. Hugh the youngest received his portion of Sleat in Skye, where he died in 1498, just after the forfeiture of the lordship. His descendants lived in *Dun Sgathaich*, whose ruins are still to be seen on their steep rock. But in 1539 Donald Gorm, 6th Chief of Sleat, moved into Duntulm, a castle in an even more impregnable position on the north of Score bay in Kilmuir.

When the lordship was abolished the different branches of the clan grouped themselves under the authority of their separate chiefs. Meanwhile, with fatal persistence, successive attempts were made to restore the ancient island authority of MacDonald. A confederation of clans rose in favour of the deposed John of the Isles' grandson Donald *Dubh*. James IV launched an expedition by land and sea, where his distinguished admiral Sir Andrew Wood soon demonstrated the paramount importance of a navy as the source of authority in this island world. The claimant Donald *Dubh* was captured and kept in prison for forty years. The rebels rose again in favour of his nearest relative, and again were defeated. After this, the MacDonalds of Islay became loyal subjects of the crown, and it was Donald *Gorm* of the house of Sleat who made the next attempt to recover lost property.

Evidently he was a man of energy, for it was he who completed the expulsion of the MacLeods from Trotternish in favour of his own clansmen, and who moved to Duntulm. He now aspired to the lost lordship and received widespread support. He headed, however, for the earldom of Ross, where his opponents were naturally the MacKenzies. Donald *Gorm* perished before the castle of Eilean Donan, shot by a MacRae arrow. The following year, James V launched another expedition into the disaffected west. He sailed from the Firth of Forth to the outer Hebrides, and then visited Skye, where he admired the strength of Duntulm as he passed it on his way to Portree. Two years later he was dead, his heir a week-old daughter, his country defenceless at the feet of Henry VIII of England. Donald *Dubh* was rescued, declared Lord of the Isles, and died in Ireland, whither he had gone for assistance. With him died the senior line of the lordship. That of Lochalsh came second, but it had passed through a female. The house of Sleat now preserved the senior male stem of Clan Donald.

Donald Gorm's great-grandson, Sir Donald MacDonald, was knighted in 1617 and became the senior baronet of Nova Scotia in 1625. He died in 1643, just before 400 of his clansmen joined the army of Montrose. In 1689 the 3rd baronet sent 500 men to fight at Killiecrankie for James VII. By this time he was recognised as the head of the whole name, and instead of being designated as of Sleat was described as Sir Donald MacDonald of that Ilk. His barony of MacDonald (implicit in this term) was forfeited after the next act of loyalty to the Stewarts in 1715, but it was soon restored, and in 1776 the 9th baronet was created Lord MacDonald in the peerage of Ireland. Unhappily, his titles include a place called Slate in Antrim: and rather oddly, one of his descendants is a baronet and Chief of the MacDonalds of Sleat, another Lord MacDonald and head of the whole Clan Donald.

MacDonald of Clanranald

While the muniments of the Lordship of the Isles disappeared, almost without a trace, and the fertile island of Islay, its seat of government, fell to the Campbells, the MacDonalds of Clanranald remained in possession of their inheritance. The original Ranald, son of Iain of Islay, left five sons of whom Allan succeeded as Chief of Clanranald, while a younger son Donald founded the cadet branch of Glengarry. Both remained loyal to the Lord of the Isles: and when he was a prisoner in Tantallon Castle it was Clanranald's son, Donald Balloch, who invaded Lochaber on his behalf, and secured his chief's freedom at the cost of his own life.

Another of this branch was less estimable. Dugald, 6th Chief of Clanranald, behaved with such viciousness that his clansmen murdered him and put his uncle Alasdair in his place. When Alasdair died in 1530, his natural son, John of Moydart, succeeded him until

MacDonald of Clanranald

he was imprisoned by James V in 1540. This provided the opportunity for a faction to attempt to put the son of the 5th Chief in his place. But it was defeated in 1544 at the celebrated battle *Blar na Léine* (Field of Shirts), so called because the combatants abandoned their plaids in the heat, and fought only in their long linen shirts. When James V's widow Mary of Lorraine became Regent, she pardoned John of Moydart and he died Chief of Clanranald in 1584. By this time the Catholic Church had been abolished in Scotland, but in the relative immunity of the outer Hebrides the clan Ranald have retained their faith to the present day.

In these circumstances it was natural that they should have rallied to Montrose when he reached the Highlands with the commission of Charles I, and Catholic MacDonalds joined him to make war upon the Campbells and the Calvinists. Niall Mac Mhuirich chronicled their campaigns in Gaelic prose, while Iain *Lom* MacDonald, descendant of the first Donald of the Isles, celebrated it in the more modern verse of the day. John, 11th of Clanranald, lived to witness the defeat of Montrose and the triumph of Charles II's restoration before he died in 1670. His son John, the 12th Chief, who fought with him in the same wars, died in 1686, before the deposition of James VII. But Iain *Lom* the bard lived to taste the bitterness of the Calvinist Revolution, and to blame the Campbells for the massacre of Glencoe, although the real culprits were King William and Dalrymple of Stair.

Allan the 13th of Clanranald was killed fighting for James VIII in 1715, and the brother who succeeded him ended his days an exile at the court of St Germains. The 17th Chief barely escaped with his life when he fought for Prince Charles in the Forty-Five.

But worse was to follow when Ranald MacDonald succeeded in 1794 as a minor and an absentee. Although he inherited rents to the enormous amount of £25,000 a year from estates that his family had ruled for five hundred years, he dissipated his entire fortune in Regency London and Brighton. The miseries of his Hebridean clansmen, as his factors attempted to squeeze a last farthing from them to subsidize Clanranald's swanking and dissipation in the fashionable world, evidently meant nothing to him. Between 1828 and 1837 his people and their islands were sold to perhaps the most vicious landlords in the history of the Highland clearances. Their name was Gordon. While a cartoon preserves the idiotic Clanranald dancing in the first quadrille at Almack's, Margaret Fay Shaw has garnered the harvest of his people's surviving traditions in her *Folksongs and Folklore of South Uist*, republished in 1977.

MacDonell of Glengarry

The cadet branch of Clanranald which became established on the mainland of western Inverness-shire built for its stronghold the castle of Invergarry. The gaunt ruins still stand beside the waters of Loch Oich. Its owners have opted for the spelling, MacDonell, which is closer to the original Gaelic *MacDhomhnuill*. The patronymic of the chiefs, *Mac Mhic Alasdair*, derives from the 4th MacDonell of Glengarry, and it was Alasdair the 6th who married Margaret, co-heiress of Sir Alexander MacDonald of Lochalsh. This alliance later provided grounds for the claim that Glengarry was rightful chief of the whole Clan Donald, while its more immediate result was to cause prolonged bloodshed between MacDonells and MacKenzies over the debateable lands of Lochalsh. Angus, the offspring of this marriage, received a crown charter of confirmation for his lands of Glengarry in 1574, and they were erected into a barony in 1627 for his son Donald, the 8th Chief.

Angus the 9th of Glengarry expressed his gratitude to Charles I by fighting in the army of Montrose, and also for Charles II when he came to Scotland after his father's death. For this he was forfeited by Cromwell but created Lord MacDonell and Aros at the Restoration in 1660. When he died without heirs the chiefship passed to the junior branch of Scotus, which continued the royalist tradition of the clan. Alastair the 11th of Glengarry carried the royal standard of James VII at Killiecrankie in 1689, and of James VIII, the Old Pretender, at Sheriffmuir in 1715. Yet Field Marshal Wade was able to report after the Forty-Five that the 12th Chief of Glengarry could still raise five hundred armed clansmen.

Duncan the 14th was able to demonstrate the truth of Wade's

MacDonell of Glengarry

report, through William Pitt's plan for raising Highland regiments. The company he contributed in 1794—5 was recruited largely from the Glengarry estate itself. When this was disbanded in 1801 most of the men emigrated to Canada, where they founded the Gaelic-speaking settlement called Glengarry on the banks of the St Lawrence River. Today it is one of Ontario's counties. During the American war of 1812—15 the settlement raised a corps called the Glengarry Light Infantry which was praised for the excellence of its services.

The emigrants were spared an appalling experience, for Duncan of Glengarry's son was the notorious Alasdair, whose flamboyant Raeburn portrait and friendship with Walter Scott have given him a reputation abroad rather different from the one he earned himself in his own country. He rivals even Clanranald among the contemptible Highland chiefs who rewarded so ill the centuries of devotion which his clansmen had given to his family. While he was cutting his ridiculous Regency figure of a Highland Chief, destitution and emigration spread like an epidemic through his vast territories. His son, Aeneas, sold the encumbered estate and emigrated to Australia. A younger son of Duncan the 14th Chief, General Sir James MacDonell, was praised by Wellington for his conduct at Waterloo; and in 1838 he was appointed Governor-General of Canada, where the inhabitants of another Glengarry were privileged to welcome a more creditable representative of the house of *Mac Mhic Alasdair*.

147

MacDonald of Glencoe

After Clan Donald had been rewarded for their support of King Robert
Bruce with the forfeited lands of the MacDougalls of Lorne, a son of
Angus Òg of Islay settled in Lochaber. He was known as Iain *Abrach*,
and he died in 1338, before Iain of Islay was first styled Lord of the
Isles in 1354. The cadet branch of the MacDonalds of Glencoe, their
chiefs called Maclain after their progenitor, is thus an extremely early
one. But they held their lands of the Lordship, and when this was
abolished in 1493, they found themselves instead the feudal vassals
of the Stewarts of Appin. During the troubles that attended the
minority of Mary, Queen of Scots, an Earl of Argyll with a particularly
rapacious eye for MacDonald property secured the superiority of
Appin.

The fate of other clans in a similar predicament, during the next
century, contrasts notably with the survival of the MacDonalds in
Glencoe. Certainly they lived in a natural fortress: the Maclains built
no castle in Glencoe, nor needed to. These surroundings also bred an
exceptionally brawny race, as a traveller remarked at the time of the
massacre. 'I generally observed the men to be large-bodied, stout,
subtle, active, patient of cold and hunger.' When the Revolution of
1688 placed William of Orange on the throne, Maclain was an old man,
who had spent a lifetime on bad terms with his neighbour Sir John
Campbell of Glenorchy, 1st Earl of Breadalbane. In addition, the
Campbells had suffered for their Calvinist allegiance under the last

Stewart kings, while Glencoe was (and remains) a centre of Episcopalian worship. Religious as well as historical grounds dictated that the MacDonalds should be reluctant to forsake their allegiance to the deposed King James VII, while the Campbells inevitably supported King William.

In the circumstances they would have been wise to stand aside, and leave the persecution of their hereditary enemies to this odious King and his Scottish Secretary, Sir John Dalrymple of Stair. Breadalbane was a close associate of Dalrymple's, and must have known the extent of his private prejudices. When the chiefs were ordered to make their submission to the nearest civil authority before 1 January 1692 under pain of the utmost rigour of the law, Dalrymple wrote: 'If Maclain of Glencoe and that tribe can be well separated from the rest, it will be a proper vindication of the public justice to extirpate that sect of thieves.' It was the same argument in favour of genocide, including the old, women and children, that had been used a century earlier in the reign of James VI.

Maclain delayed until the last day of the old year before riding to nearby Fort William to take the oath of submission. The garrison commander there was an old man like himself, who had held civil as well as military authority in Cromwell's time. But he had not been invested with civil authority by the new regime, and so Maclain had to hurry south through snow storms, all the way to Inveraray. He did not arrive until 6 January, but his oath of submission was accepted.

So the people of Glencoe had no misgivings when a detachment of troops arrived to billet themselves in their houses. The soldiers were entertained hospitably for a fortnight until, in early morning darkness, the massacre began. The aged Chief was shot as he rose from his bed. His wife had the rings bitten from her fingers, and was left, stripped naked, to die in the snow a day later. But their two sons escaped, and so did about 150 men with their women and children, while only 38 people perished. Perhaps this was partly because the soldiers lacked enthusiasm for their task; partly because another detachment of troops did not arrive in time to block the bottom end of the glen.

Dalrymple was furious when he heard that so many had escaped: he wished to massacre all the Camerons and the MacDonalds of Glengarry as well. A public outcry of indignation naturally led to blame being fixed on the Campbells. The troops who carried it out were men of Argyll's regiment, commanded by Robert Campbell of Glenlyon, but in fact very few of the officers or men were Campbells. It was King William who had signed and counter-signed the order for the crime, though the Scottish Parliament exonerated him and placed the blame on Dalrymple. King William created him Earl of Stair, and he had his own revenge when he worked like a fanatic to destroy Scotland's Parliament forever in the Union of 1707.

MacDonald of Kingsburgh

The fame of the MacDonalds of Kingsburgh belongs to the father and son who were the last to enjoy this title. Alexander of Kingsburgh was factor to his Chief, Sir Alexander MacDonald of Sleat, whose wife Lady Margaret, daughter of the Earl of Eglinton, was such a well-loved figure in Skye. MacDonald of Sleat possessed a cousin Hugh, who held from him a tack (or lease) of Armadale in Skye. Hugh's wife belonged to the same kindred of Sleat.

But she had been married earlier to a MacDonald of the branch of Clanranald, a great-grandson of Allan, the 9th Chief of that name. Since 1704 her first husband's family had enjoyed the life-rent of Milton in South Uist, a property that her son took over in 1745, after his father's death. Here her daughter Flora had been born in 1722.

When Prince Charles landed in the Hebrides, both MacLeod of Dunvegan and Sir Alexander of Sleat refused to support him, while in the outer islands Clanranald succumbed in a personal meeting with the Prince, and sent 200 of his clansmen to join the 400 MacDonells from Glengarry and the 150 MacDonalds from Glencoe who assembled beneath the Jacobite standard in Glenfinnan. By the time Prince Charles had fled from Culloden with a huge price on his head, Hugh MacDonald of Armadale was a Hanoverian officer in the outer Hebrides. Flora was able to travel from Skye to visit her brother in South Uist with impunity. Thither the Prince also fled for safety, but after eight weeks there, Hugh the Hanoverian sent word to warn him that his position was becoming dangerous. His safest course, it was decided, would be to return to Skye disguised as Flora's servant, and from there seek the mainland again.

It would be hard to find, in the annals of any nation, a story to surpass the tale of courage and mutual trust shared by men and women of different political and religious allegiances, united in their scorn for the immense reward offered for the betrayal of the Prince. Flora conducted him straight to the Hanoverian headquarters at Sleat while it was occupied by soldiers. She mesmerised an officer with her charms in one room so that he did not observe the frantic scurryings of Lady Margaret, as she arranged the safe conveyance of the Prince. Lady Margaret took Alexander of Kingsburgh into her confidence, who undertook the capital risk of taking Flora and the Prince to his home for the night. Kingsburgh's wife taunted with badinage the soldiers who caught her red-handed, after the Prince had escaped from there to Raasay. None of these were Jacobites: they merely possessed the pride of their race. Nor did anyone betray the Prince at Portree, where he parted from Flora on his journey back to the mainland. Only one of them ever received a brief message of gratitude from him; for gratitude was not a characteristic of the Stewarts.

Flora was arrested at Armadale and imprisoned aboard two ships before being sent to London. Kingsburgh was taken from Armadale, first to Fort Augustus, then to Edinburgh, where he was kept prisoner a year until the amnesty. His son Allan was a lieutenant in one of his Chief of Sleat's companies. and when Flora had returned and he was twenty-eight years old she married him in 1750. They lived at Flodigarry until the death of Alexander, when they moved to Kingsburgh in 1772. The following year Dr Samuel Johnson visited them there with Boswell, and slept in the very bed in which the Prince had passed his last night in Skye. He found Flora 'a little woman of a mild and genteel appearance, mighty soft and well-bred.' Boswell described her husband as 'a large stately man, with a steady sensible countenance.'

In 1774 they left Kingsburgh for North Carolina during the largest wave of emigration from the Highlands that had ever occurred. They arrived on the eve of the outbreak of the American War of Independence. From New York, Allan of Kingsburgh's cousin Alexander sent a messenger urging him to raise the Highlanders to fight for George III. He did so, and was given the rank of Brigadier General by a Governor who could only find safety in a ship. At Moore's Creek the Highlanders were mown down in the first victory of the war, and Allan sent a prisoner to Halifax, Virginia. In 1779 Flora sailed home, to await her husband's return. One of their sons died of his wounds at Moore's Creek, another was lost at sea. When they were finally reunited in the Hebrides, they were too poor to afford a home of their own. But of their five sons, John MacDonald (1759–1831) became their pride and support, and an outstanding military engineer.

The MacDonald of Kingsburgh tartan is of particular interest. It is taken from a waistcoat that Alexander of Kingsburgh gave to Prince Charles while he was a fugitive.

MacDougall

The Viking raiders and settlers were distinguished in the Gaelic records as *Dubh Ghall* (Dark Foreigner) and *Finn Ghall* (Fair Foreigner). The first of these descriptive names was given to the eldest son of King Somerled, who was himself known by a Norse one: for *Summarliði* is Norse for Summer Sailor. Dougall, his son, had as his mother the daughter of Olaf, King of Man. He was thus the senior heir in Scotland of the Gaelic-Norse royal stock, and after the death of Somerled in 1164 he became senior King in old Dalriada. In 1244 the Scottish records refer to Duncan Mac Dougall of Argyll, and so the clan name was established by then.

The sub-kings who became transformed into chiefs built for themselves two great castles on the mainland shore of Loch Linnhe in Lorne. One was Dunstaffnage, the other Dunollie near Oban, whose ruins their descendants still possess to this day.

It was Ewen, son of Duncan MacDougall, who was forced to choose between his true overlord, the great King Haakon IV of Norway, and Alexander III, King of Scots, when Haakon brought his fleet through the western isles in 1263 to assert his sovereignty over them. Ewen of Argyll surrendered his islands to the Norwegian king and requested his permission to transfer his allegiance to Alexander. It proved to be a wise choice, for Haakon's fleet retired in disorder from Largs and he himself died in Orkney on the journey home. But Ewen's son Alasdair, 4th in descent from Dougall, was less fortunate in the choice he was called upon to make. He had married a sister of John Comyn, the most powerful man in Scotland, whose own son the Red Comyn stood next in line to the Scottish throne after the Balliols at the time when Bruce made his bid for it.

When Bruce slew the Red Comyn at the altar rails in Dumfries, the MacDougalls became involved in the blood-feud which ended in the total destruction of the Comyn power. But before this occurred, the MacDougalls very nearly captured Bruce in the narrow pass of Brander by Loch Awe; and it was then that Bruce lost the elaborate cloak-pin known as the Brooch of Lorne. When he had established himself as King, the MacDougalls lost forever the island kingdom which they had succeeded in preserving in Haakon's time. Then a MacDougall chief married Bruce's grand-daughter Joanna, and in 1344 David II reinstated him in the mainland lordship of Lorne. But the Bruces proved to be poor breeders of males. By 1388 the lordship had passed with an heiress to the new dynasty of Stewart that had won the crown itself by another Bruce marriage.

The chiefship thereupon passed to the descendants of the 4th Chief's brother, a line which had fortunately supported King Robert I and been rewarded with the custody of Dunollie Castle. During the brief reign of James VII it appeared possible that the 20th MacDougall of Dunollie might recover Lorne itself from the Campbells by royal charter. But after the Revolution of 1688 the tables were turned, and the MacDougalls were fortunate to be left in possession of Dunollie after taking part in the Jacobite rising of 1715.

MacDuff

Clan Duff was originally the royal Scoto-Pictish line of which Queen Gruoch (travestied by Shakespeare as Lady Macbeth) was the senior representative. After the death of her second husband King Macbeth—who also belonged to the house of Duff—her son by her first husband succeeded as King Lulach, but was murdered in his turn in 1058. Malcolm Canmore thus won the crown, and as much of the territory of southern Scotland as he had been able to conquer with English military help. Although he possessed a son by his first marriage within the Scottish royal house, it was his sons by his second marriage to the Saxon Princess Margaret who usurped the throne after him, again with English help.

But Margaret's eldest son, for whom she chose the very English name of Aethelred, was also by-passed by his younger brothers. The explanation may be that he had already made his marriage with the heiress of the senior line of the Scottish royal house, and preferred this legitimate heritage to the crime of usurping the crown of his elder half-brother. The heiress was a grand-daughter of Queen Gruoch and sister of King Maelsnechtai, who reigned in Moray where the arms of Canmore had not penetrated. Aethelred's name became transformed into the Gaelic form of *Aedh*, and with the earldom of Fife

MacDuff

he also succeeded to the position of hereditary Abbot of Abernethy, the ancient Pictish capital whose round tower is one of the finest surviving monuments of the Columban church. After his death in about 1128 the men of Moray made several unsuccessful attempts to gain the throne for his sons. But finally Clan Duff gave its allegiance to the usurping line of Queen Margaret, and were rewarded with unique privileges.

The Earl of Fife became the premier subject of the kingdom, bore the heraldic red lion rampant of the royal house, and enthroned the King of Scots on the stone of Scone at his coronation. Kinsmen of the Earl could escape the penalties for homicide by seeking sanctuary at the MacDuff cross near Abernethy, and making a fixed payment. The male line of Earls failed in 1353, and passed through an heiress until it reached the royal Stewart who was Regent during the captivity of James I in England. In 1425 the earldom passed to the crown.

Meanwhile, in the northern territories of Macbeth and Gruoch's kingdom, families of Clan Duff emerged in historical record, assuming a royal descent that could no longer be proved. Among these was David Duff of Muldavit in Banffshire in the year 1401; and William Duff of Braco, whose descendant was created Duke of Fife in 1889 when he married the daughter of Edward VII. Others of the clan have assumed the name of MacDuff, while the direct line of the ancient house has been continued in the family of Wemyss.

154

MacEwen

There are upwards of a dozen alternative spellings used by Clan Ewen, and several different theories of its origins and fortunes. Doubtless the MacEwens descended from the original Scots of Dalriada. But their earliest historical forbear is Ewen of Otter on the shores of Loch Fyne in Argyll, who flourished in about 1200. The 18th-century Statistical Account of the parish of Kilfinnan records: 'on a rocky point on the coast of Lochfine, about a mile below the church, is to be seen the vestige of a building called *Caesteal Mhic Eobhuin, i.e.* Mac Ewen's castle . . . This Mac Ewen was the chief of a clan, and proprietor of the northern division of the parish called Otter.' The manuscript genealogy compiled by a MacLachlan in about 1450 traces his descent from Anradan, the common ancestor of the MacLachlans and the MacNeills. The names of most of his successors as chiefs of Otter are on record until in 1432 the barony of Otter was granted to Sween MacEwen by James I, with remainder to the heir of Duncan Campbell of Loch Awe.

Thereafter Clan Ewen was without a Chief, without a single homeland, a stronghold or archives. The name turns up in Lochaber, in the Lennox and in Perthshire. Naturally it begins to turn up in the criminal records in particular, like that of other dispossessed clans. In 1576 two Cameron brothers are denounced for the murder of Donald Dow McKewin. In 1598 an indictment is drawn up against two hundred MacEwens, described as broken Highland men and trespassers, armed with bows, two-handed swords, steel bonnets, hackbuts and pistols, living by brigandage. They are listed with MacGregors, MacLachlans and MacNeills in 1602 as vassals of the Earl of Argyll, who is answerable for their behaviour. Ten years later several Mac-Ewens are fined for giving succour to the proscribed MacGregors. The clan was perhaps lucky to have escaped a similar fate.

But like the MacGregors, the MacEwens also made a contribution to Highland civilisation of which the Scottish government and universities knew nothing. They became bards to the Campbells of Argyll and of Breadalbane and to MacDougall of Dunollie. Amongst the fugitive relics of their art is the poem which Neil MacEwen composed in 1630 on the death of Sir Duncan Campbell of Glenorchy, his autograph copy being preserved by the house of Breadalbane. And John Campbell of Islay found in Cawdor Castle a genealogy dated 1779, which contained this explanation: 'In the following account we have had regard to the genealogical tree done by Neil MacEwen, as he received the same from Eachann MacEwen his father, as he had the same from Arthur MacEwen his grandfather, and their ancestors and predecessors, shennachies and pensioners to great families who, for many ages were employed to make up and keep such records in their accustomed way.'

There is no evidence as to whether these were the descendants of the chiefs of Otter, or what was the ancestry of the hundred and fifty MacEwens whom General Wade reported as having crossed from Skye to fight in the Jacobite uprising of 1715. Of the four MacEwens mentioned as having risen for Prince Charles in the Forty-Five, two came from Stirling, one from Perth and one from Dundee. They were already scattering beyond the Highlands. But one of the most distinguished of their name in this century, Sir Alexander MacEwen, the Scottish Nationalist, was Provost of Inverness, the Highland capital.

Macfarlane

Alwyn, Earl of Lennox at the end of the 12th century, had a younger son Gilchrist, upon whom his brother Earl Malduin bestowed the property of Arrochar by the side of Loch Long. Gilchrist's grandson Malduin was among the Gaelic supporters of Robert Bruce, and father of Parlan from whom the clan derived its name. *Iain Mac Pharlain*, the 7th Chief in descent from Gilchrist, received a confirmation of his title to Arrochar in 1420, and when Earl Duncan of Lennox was beheaded by James I in particularly revolting circumstances, the house of Macfarlane became the senior male representatives of the ancient earldom of Lennox, although this was taken over by the Stewarts.

The Macfarlanes remained loyal to the Stewarts, however, and in particular to their Lennox branch. Sir Iain the 11th Chief fell in the Lennox contingent at Flodden in 1513, leaving as his heir Andrew, who earned the reputation of a wizard. Duncan the 13th Chief fell fighting against the English at Pinkie in 1547, during the minority of Mary, Queen of Scots. His clan had been defined as 'men of the head of Lennox, that spake the Irish and the Anglo-Scottish tongues.' This was the time when Gaelic, the original language of the Scots, was being described as Irish, and the northern English tongue that was evolving in the Lowlands as 'Scots'.

Two contributory causes led the Macfarlanes to play a decisive part in the final downfall of Queen Mary. Duncan, who fell at Pinkie, was described as one of the first Gaelic chiefs to embrace the reformed religion, and his clan were also adherents of the house of Lennox. After the death of Mary's husband King Henry, Lord Darnley, his father, the Earl of Lennox, sided with the Queen's enemies. When the Queen escaped from captivity in Loch Leven Castle to make a last bid to recover her throne, the 14th Chief brought a force which tipped the scales against her in the rout of Langside in 1568. But his clan returned to their former loyalty to the crown when Walter the 16th Chief fought under Montrose in the cause of Charles I. His island stronghold of Inveruglas in Loch Lomond was destroyed by the Roundheads when Cromwell invaded Scotland. Thereafter the seat of the Macfarlanes became the house of Arrochar by Loch Long.

Here, at a time when so many mainland chiefs were becoming increasingly anglicised and detached from the cultural life and economic interests of their clansmen, the 20th Chief set a very remarkable example. Walter Macfarlane of that Ilk devoted his entire life to research into the history of his country, and into the preservation and transcribing of documents, particularly of church records. His accurate and thorough collections have proved invaluable. He is also remembered for an incident recorded by Boswell. 'My old friend, the Laird of Macfarlane, the great antiquary, took it highly amiss when General Wade called him Mr Macfarlane.' In England at that time to omit the 'Mr' would have been far too familiar, whereas, '"Mr Macfarlane," said he, "may with equal propriety be said to many; but I, and I only, am Macfarlane."'

Soon after this excellent Chief's death in 1767 without heirs his brother sold Arrochar. The direct male line of the chiefs expired with the death of William, the 25th, in 1886 without issue.

MacGillivray

The MacGillivrays were already one of the principal clans in old Dalriada when King Somerled drove out the Norsemen, and then died in battle in 1164, challenging the authority of the King of Scots, Malcolm IV. When Malcolm's nephew Alexander II subdued Argyll in 1222 the *Clann Mhic Gillebhràth* were evidently dispersed. While some of its members remained in Mull and Morven, tradition relates that Gillivray, progenitor of the clan which belonged to the Clan Chattan confederation, placed himself under the protection of the Mackintosh chiefs. By 1500 Duncan MacGillivray is found in Dunmaglas, whose churchyard still preserves the memorials of the chiefs.

Here in Strathnairn the MacGillivrays became one of the most prominent members of Clan Chattan until the Fifteen and the Forty-Five. As Episcopalians they possessed a natural concern to reverse the Calvinist Revolution settlement of 1688 which had resulted in the persecution of their religion. When the Mackintosh chief remained loyal to his Hanoverian commission in 1745 and his wife 'Colonel

MacGillivray

Anne' raised his clansmen instead for the Jacobite cause, it was Alexander the MacGillivray chief who fell at Culloden, near the well which still bears his name, leading the men of Clan Chattan. Twenty years later the Episcopal Bishop Forbes kept a diary which preserves many intimate details of the manner in which the heir of Dunmaglas and other MacGillivrays assisted him as he went about his pastoral duties on his pony. Incidentally, the Bishop remarks that the modern name Garron which is given to this indigenous Highland horse with its aboriginal eel-stripe was still used according to its original Gaelic meaning: for *Geàrr* is the verb, to cut. 'Mounted the Highland Garrons once more, for so they term Geldings in all the Highlands.'

Soon the mammoth emigrations across the Atlantic occurred, which the outbreak of the American War of Independence in 1775 only temporarily arrested. Among the most successful of the emigrants were the MacGillivrays who prospered in the Canadian fur trade. William MacGillivray, head of the North West Company, became a member of the Legislative Council for Lower Canada in time to combat the 5th Earl of Selkirk's grand design to settle the destitute Gaels of Ireland and the Scottish Highlands as farmers on Red River. He defeated Selkirk by means of murder, arson, perjury, theft and blackmail.

Meanwhile, in Strathnairn, Bishop Forbes addressed William of Dunmaglas as Captain MacGillivray, for his impoverishment in the aftermath of Culloden had induced him to join the army. In 1783 he died and was succeeded by his son John Lachlan, who was chief during the decades of the clearances and who at his death in 1852 bequeathed all the farms on his estate to his tenants. Thereafter the last known chief went to India and was last heard of in New Guinea. But his name is worthily represented in the northern Highlands by a cadet branch of his family. Donald MacGillivray of Calrossie's father built up the world-famous Calrossie herd of cattle, so helping to preserve the stock of the animal on which the prosperity of the Highlands depended for so many centuries before the introduction of sheep. Donald MacGillivray is one of the most distinguished exponents of pibroch in Scotland today.

MacGregor

The MacGregors are the most famous victims of the expansion of Clan Campbell in Gaelic Scotland. Although this gained its greatest momentum after the downfall of the Lords of the Isles, the misfortunes of the MacGregors began much earlier. They were neighbours of the MacNabs, and their Gaelic motto, *Is rioghal mo dhream* (My blood is royal), contains the claim that they shared the same royal origins. Like the MacNabs, they suffered misfortune during the Scottish wars of independence. Their chief, Iain MacGregor of Glenorchy, was captured by the English in 1296, and his property passed through a MacGregor heiress to the clan of her Campbell husband. But Gregor MacGregor, who was perhaps Iain of Glenorchy's nephew, set himself up as a leader of his clan, to hold their lands by the sword. So began Clan Gregor's long fight for survival as an independent tribe. The Campbells set up a rival line of MacGregor chiefs in 1519, and in 1552 they attempted to wipe out the true line. But although the legitimate Chief and his three sons were killed, a grandson survived until he too fell to the Campbells in 1604.

By then the entire clan had been outlawed and it had been made a capital offence to bear the name. The immediate cause of this proscription was the battle between the MacGregors and the Colquhouns which took place at Glenfruin in 1603. But like oppressed minorities in any age, the MacGregors were by now guilty of depredations and atrocities on an extensive scale. The penal laws against them were lifted briefly in the 17th century, but were not revoked until 1774. During the interval they were hunted with dogs like vermin. The direct male line of the chiefs had been extinguished in 1604, and when this office was revived, it was bestowed on Major-General Sir Evan MacGregor, as 19th Chief, whose family had previously adopted the name of Murray.

But by the time Sir Evan led his rehabilitated clan at the ceremonies that marked the visit of George IV to Edinburgh in 1822, its most bizarre member had already made his appearance there. Gregor MacGregor presented his credentials at the court of St James in 1820,

MacGregor

calling himself His Serene Highness Gregor I, Prince of Poyais. He was the grandson of Gregor the Handsome, who had served in the Black Watch soon after its formation. His Serene Highness had also served in the British Army, but in 1811 he had sailed to Venezuela in the very year in which that country led the other colonies of Latin America in proclaiming independence. Gregor received a commission from Simon Bolivar himself: and found a Colonel Campbell commanding a corps of riflemen. But Gregor became a General of Division, married Bolivar's niece, and was invested by him with the Order of Liberators. Then Gregor took to the sea, and captured one of the great fortresses of the Spanish Main with two small boats and 150 men. This was what led him to the Mosquito coast of what is now Nicaragua, where he created his imaginary kingdom of Poyais.

His military and naval victories in America were matched by the achievement of passing himself off as an independent sovereign, of a dynasty whose very name had so recently been outlawed in his own country. A former Lord Mayor of London sponsored a loan of £200,000. Scotsmen clamoured to emigrate to Poyais, exchanging their money for the worthless Poyais bank notes which Gregor manufactured in Edinburgh. Even after the first colonists had had to be rescued from the Mosquito coast, Gregor repeated his hoax in France. Finally he returned to Venezuela to spend the remainder of his days there, living on a hero's pension.

MacGregor (Rob Roy)

Rob Roy

When the Marquess of Argyll was executed after the restoration of Charles II in 1660 the penal acts against the MacGregors were repealed, but they were not restored to their former possessions. At this time Gregor MacGregor was the 15th Chief of the Children of the Mist. His younger brother Donald was married to Margaret Campbell of Gleneaves, and their younger son Robert was born in 1671 in the parish of Buchanan. He grew up to be immensely strong and was trained by his father in the skills of cattle raiding and the niceties of the protection racket. At the same time Rob Roy inherited the cultural tradition which had given Scotland Dean MacGregor of Lismore's priceless anthology of mediaeval Gaelic literature. Robert himself was well educated, and a good letter-writer: he was personally acquainted with his cousin Dr James Gregory, Professor of Medicine at

Aberdeen University and a member of what was to become perhaps the most outstanding intellectual dynasty of its time in the British Isles.

But the circumstances of Rob Roy's clan were to make his own career a sorry contrast, though it is more celebrated than the Book of the Dean of Lismore himself, or all the achievements of the Gregorys. In 1688 the revolution which placed William III on the throne also restored Argyll to his possessions. Rob Roy's father Donald was gazetted Lieutenant Colonel in the Jacobite forces in 1689 and leader of his clansmen, presumably because Gregor the Chief was too old. He died unmarried in 1693 when the penal acts against his clan were renewed, and Rob Roy became acting head of the clan as tutor to the young Chief. In 1712 a warrant was granted for his arrest on a charge of embezzlement, his chief creditor being the Duke of Montrose. Rob Roy wrote a letter to Atholl, explaining that he had offered Montrose payment in full but that Montrose had refused, his intention being to ruin him. So essential was it for a member of the proscribed clan to avoid arrest that he now went into hiding. His wife Mary was a daughter of MacGregor of Comar, and it is said to have been at this time that she composed the pipe tune 'Rob Roy's Lament.'

To none did the Jacobite rebellion of 1715 offer more attractive prospects. On 9 December Rob Roy proclaimed the Pretender among the Mores and Buchanans at Drymen, and early in the new year he seized Falkland Palace; but he did not march his clansmen to join the forces of the Earl of Mar at Perth. When his house in Breadalbane and his other properties were ravaged and burnt he seized Graham of Killearn while he was collecting the Duke of Montrose's rents, and compensated himself with these. Montrose captured Rob Roy but he escaped, and in 1717 surrendered to Atholl.

He recovered his freedom, perhaps through the intervention of Argyll, perhaps by the help of his clansmen, and continued his depredations against Montrose for years. He had adopted his mother's name of Campbell, and it was Argyll who arranged his final reconciliation with Montrose. In 1722 he sent a letter of submission to General Wade, the Hanoverian commander in the Highlands, only to be sent a prisoner to Newgate. In 1727 he was carried to Gravesend, handcuffed to Lord Ogilvie, to be transported with him to Barbados. But before his ship sailed he was pardoned, and so returned to end his days peacefully in Balquhidder. He died in 1734, a Catholic convert. Of his five sons, one was executed in 1754, one escaped his sentence to die penniless in France, and one was attainted for fighting in the Forty-Five, but pardoned.

The tartan that commemorates Rob Roy is the simplest there is, and the oldest known to have been worn by a MacGregor.

MacInnes

Mac Aonghuis is Gaelic for Son of Angus, and the original pronunciation of the name has led to its transformation into Aeneas.
(A more unfortunate parallel is the Norse Thorkil which became the
Gaelic Torcuil, and was transformed into Tarquin.) The Pictish King
Onnust who died in 761 possessed the same name that has become
anglicised as Ennis and MacInnes. It has no connection with the
name derived from the barony of Innes, though there are instances
of the name deriving from Angus.

The earliest reference to the sons of Angus is given in the 7th-
century *Senchus Fer nAlban* (History of the Men of Scotland).
Here we see the structure of society in Dalriada in the century
following the death of Saint Columba. The Scots from Ireland who
had settled here were divided into three 'kindreds', those of Gabrán,
Lorne and Angus. The kindred of Gabrán could muster 800 fighting
men; Lorne 700; while the *Cenél nOengusa* could raise 500 at a
hosting. The kindreds were organised in houses, of which that
of Gabrán possessed 560, Lorne 420, and Angus 430 although it
could not muster so many fighting men. But its naval commitment was
greater, since two seven-benched boats had to be contributed by
every twenty houses. The kindred of Angus possessed Islay, later to
be the seat of the Lordship of the Isles.

But although Angus was to become a favourite name of the
MacDonalds of Islay, concrete evidence is lacking of any connection

164

between them and MacInnes. Nor is there any record of the latter's descent from the kindred of Angus. The MacInneses are next found as original inhabitants of the mainland of Morvern, where they suffered severely, early in the 13th century, during the conquest of Argyll by Alexander II. From this period there is scarcely a Scottish clan whose history is more tenuous. Gaelic tradition gives their chief the title *Fear Cinn Lochalainn*, Chief of Kinlochaline, the massive castle whose ruins still stand upon their strategic rock in Morvern. Certainly a MacInnes was still in command here when the castle was captured and burnt in 1645 by the young MacDonald giant known as *Mac Colla Ciotach*, who served under Montrose. By this time the MacInneses had become dependents of the Campbells of Argyll, and consequently supporters of the Covenanters against Charles I. For the same reason they later supported the Hanoverians against the Jacobites, though another section of the fragmented clan joined Stewart of Ardsheal in the Jacobite interest, while a third had become hereditary bowmen to the Mackinnons in Skye.

Among those who emigrated, several achieved distinction in the colonial Highland world of Canada. Donald MacInnes, who was born in Oban in 1824, left Scotland in 1840 and settled finally in Hamilton where he became a successful merchant and ultimately a Senator. Thomas MacInnes was born in Nova Scotia in 1840, and he too became a Senator after a career as a physician and a Member of the Canadian House of Commons. His son Thomas joined the Yukon gold rush and ended his life at Vancouver, an author and a poet. Another of their fellow clansmen, Rennie MacInnes, became Bishop of Jerusalem in 1914. But they have also achieved distinction in the lands in which the kindred of Angus settled so long ago. Duncan MacInnes was appointed Dean of Argyll and the Isles, and then in 1953 Bishop of Moray, Ross and Caithness until his death in 1970.

Macintyre

It is generally accepted that this name derives from the Gaelic *Mac an t-Saoir*, meaning son of the carpenter: a meaning that would account for its occurrence in so many different parts of the Highlands. But it is associated particularly with Lorne in northern Argyllshire, where the Macintyres of Glenoe were hereditary foresters to the Stewarts of Lorne. With the rise of the Campbells of Glenorchy from which the houses of Argyll and Breadalbane sprang, the Macintyres of Glenoe became tenants of Breadalbane until they emigrated to America in 1806.

But a sept of Glenoe settled at *Camus na h-Eiridh*, probably during the 15th century, and the late Alastair Macintyre, the Scottish BBC broadcaster, was recognised as 16th Chieftain of *Camus na h-Eiridh*, oldest of the clan's cadet branches. Another distinguished broadcaster is Ian McIntyre, head of the BBC's Radio 3 since 1978. Neither is there any novelty in the association between this name and eloquence.

Macintyre, and Glenorchy

In 1496 the Mackintosh chief took a Macintyre bard under his protection; in the field of music, so closely associated with poetry in Gaelic society, families of Macintyres became hereditary pipers both to MacDonald of Clanranald and to the Menzies chiefs. The most famous name of all belongs to one who followed the profession of the hereditary foresters of Lorne. Duncan *Bàn* Macintyre (1724–1812) was born in Glenorchy, and spent much of his life as forester first to the Earl of Breadalbane, then to the Duke of Argyll. Thus, when much of the rest of Britain was becoming transformed from an agricultural to an industrial society, Duncan *Bàn* was living still in the pre-agricultural setting of man, the hunter. And his Gaelic poetry overflows with the knowledge and love of nature, of the characteristics of animals and of plants, of the intricacies and excitements of the hunt, that characterised his disintegrating society.

Later in life Duncan *Bàn* went to Edinburgh, where he became a member of the city guard and wrote poetry which reveals his intellectual shortcomings in a world that was foreign to him. But he received the privilege, rare for a Gaelic bard in his time, of publication during his own lifetime, and of a prominent memorial in Edinburgh's churchyard of the Greyfriars. Meanwhile the great sweep of Ben Dorain is not more beautiful than his song in praise of his favourite mountain, nor will his last farewell to the hills ever be forgotten.

Mackay

The Mackay country was the most remote from the seat of government of any part of the Scottish mainland. It extended from Cape Wrath along the north coast to the Caithness border, and varied between sixteen and twenty miles in depth, its southern frontiers defended by bleak uplands and splendid mountains. In 1427 it was estimated that the Chief of Mackay possessed 4,000 fighting men with whom to defend this province.

It was called Strathnaver, after the largest river that flows through it. Both Gaelic and Norse derivations have been offered for this name, but it is more likely that it has survived from some earlier language. The Gaelic still spoken in Strathnaver has many affinities closer to the Munster Gaelic of southern Ireland than to any Scottish dialect. The patronymic *Aodh* dates back to the earliest pre-Christian Irish folk tales and is not easily rendered in English spelling. In its genitive form, *Mac Aoidh*, Son of Aodh, it is pronounced in Strathnaver in a way best represented by the modern Irish spelling, Magee.

Until the 17th century every known marriage of a Chief of Mackay was with a member of the Scottish Gaelic aristocracy: and one of them was with a sister of the Lord of the Isles who led his Highland host to Harlaw in 1411. A hundred years later a clerk (as he described himself) of the northern Highlands wrote a vivid description of his society, by then labelled 'Irish' in the Lowlands. 'The great courtiers of Scotland repute the foresaid Irish lords as wild, rude, and barbarous people, brought up (as they say) without learning and nurture; yet they pass them a great deal in faith, honesty, in policy and wit, in good order and civility.' One of those great courtiers, Adam Gordon, had just seized the neighbouring earldom of Sutherland, and Strathnaver was the next Gordon target. In 1588, by violence, fraud and the abuse of royal authority, the first Mackay Chief was reduced to the status of feudal vassal to a Gordon Earl. His great body of clansmen was at once conscripted to assault the next Gordon target—the Sinclair earldom of Caithness.

But Donald, Chief of Mackay, found other service for his clansmen when in 1626 he took a regiment of three thousand men to fight on the Protestant side in the Thirty Years' War. At Stettin the earliest portraits of Mackays in Highland dress were published in 1631: and in 1637 Robert Monro published his unique chronicle, *Monro His Expedition with the Worthy Scots Regiment (Called MacKeyes Regiment)*, 'the memory whereof shall never be forgotten, but shall live in spite of time.'

This military tradition was continued by Hugh Mackay of the cadet house of Scourie, who served with the Scots Brigade in Holland. He joined William of Orange at the Revolution of 1688, and commanded the forces which fought against Bonnie Dundee at Killiecrankie in 1689. There the Jacobite leader was killed, while General Mackay fell in action soon afterwards.

Donald, Chief of Mackay had been raised to the peerage as Lord Reay in 1628, and throughout the 18th century the Hanoverian Reay country remained unmolested. Its ancient way of life was preserved forever in the poetry of Rob Donn Mackay (1714–1778), the most graphic of all Gaelic poets in his detailed delineation of social relationships, everyday occupations and human aspirations. In his songs and his satires, Rob Donn is the only Gaelic poet comparable to his contemporary Robert Burns. The world so soon to be destroyed in the Sutherland Clearances of the early 19th century is commemorated in a language that fewer and fewer are able to understand. But his poetry has been presented in English translation in Ian Grimble's *The World of Rob Donn* (1979).

At first, the evictions of the Mackay country were confined to the valleys of Kildonan and the Naver valley already owned by the house of Sutherland. But in 1829 the 7th Lord Reay sold the remaining clan lands in his possession, the vast tracts of the far north-west in which Rob Donn had lived. In 1830 the cadet branch of Strath Halladale also sold out to the Sutherlands, and the entire Mackay country now lay at their mercy. The direct line of the Mackay chiefs died out in 1875, when their title passed to a branch of the family already enobled in the Netherlands. Hugh, 14th Lord Reay (b. 1937), Baron Mackay van Ophemert in the Netherlands, is the present Chief of Mackay.

MacKenzie

The first of this clan to stride into the centre of the stage of Highland history was named Alasdair. He did so as late as the 15th century, although in less than two centuries thereafter his descendants were to possess territories that stretched from the outer Hebrides in the west to the Black Isle in the east. Alasdair MacKenzie was one of those summoned to meet James I in 1427 and he lived until the murder of James III in 1488. In the interval he was perhaps the most significant chief to support the Crown against the Lord of the Isles, and for this he received the titles to his lands so often withheld from the ancient inhabitants of the Highlands. These lands included Kintail in Wester Ross, for long distinguished as Kintail Mackenzie to distinguish it from the other long salt-water inlet on the north coast, now called the Kyle of Tongue, but once known as Kintail Mackay. Alasdair's son Kenneth of Kintail continued the work of consolidation until he died in 1492 and was buried in Beauly Priory. There his stone effigy is still to be seen.

Kenneth's son Iain was one of those who escaped with his life from the field of Flodden in 1513, when he brought a contingent of his clansmen to fight there under James IV. He again survived the defeat of Pinkie in 1547, and lived until after the return of Mary, Queen of Scots to her kingdom in 1561. His grandson Colin remained loyal to Queen Mary but evaded the hazards of James VI's minority, and it was during this king's reign that the MacKenzies repeated their

tactics of joining the forces of the south against their Gaelic neighbours, with even more spectacular success. This time the victims
were the MacLeods of Lewis. They had survived James VI's orders
to Gordon of Huntly to exterminate them: they beat off the Fife
Adventurers. But these sold their interest in Lewis to Colin's son
Kenneth of Kintail, and while MacLeod of Lewis himself continued
his ten years' imprisonment in Edinburgh, the MacKenzies moved
into his island realm. Their chief was created Lord MacKenzie of
Kintail, his son, Earl of Seaforth. The Black Isle estates were erected
into a separate county and earldom of Cromartie. Lochalsh was
wrested from the Glengarry MacDonells. The 2nd Earl of Seaforth
became Charles II's secretary of state for Scotland. It is an exceptional
record for a dynasty of Gaelic chiefs of no particular consequence in
ancient days.

The clan's luck turned when the 4th Earl remained loyal to James
VII at the Revolution of 1688, to die in exile. It is to his time that the
traditional Gaelic prophecies attributed to the Brahan seer, *Coinneach
Odhar*, are attributed. The greatest mystery concerning these is that
some of the most intricate of them were actually in print before they
were fulfilled. Another is that there is no historical record of the seer's
execution in the period during which he is supposed to have lived.
It was in 1578 that orders were issued for the apprehension of
'Kennoch Owir, principal or leader in the art of magic.' There was no
Earl of Seaforth at that date.

The 5th Earl was attainted after the 1715 rebellion. It was then that
the MacKenzies' last song of triumph was composed, one of the
finest rants in the language. It is called *Caber Féidh*, which means
Deer Antler, the badge of the MacKenzies; and the verses ridicule
the surrounding clans which had fled before it. But from now on the
prophecies of the Brahan seer concerning its downfall were fulfilled,
and it was left to the MacKenzies to win eminence in a new field.
Another Kenneth MacKenzie became one of the bards of the constel-
lation of 18th-century Highland poets, noteworthy in this context for
his panegyric on Highland dress. John MacKenzie's *The Beauties of
Gaelic Poetry* was the finest anthology that had ever been compiled
until his time. In his other literary and historical work he was rivalled
by W. C. MacKenzie, historian of the Highlands and the Hebrides:
and the 19th century also produced Alexander MacKenzie of
Inverness, the pioneer chronicler of the Highland clearances. Sir
George MacKenzie's study of the agriculture of the former MacKenzie
province of Ross and Cromarty, published in 1813, was followed by
the manuscript volumes of Dr John MacKenzie's Highland memories,
which inspired his nephew Osgood MacKenzie of Inverewe to form
the gardens there which now belong to the National Trust, and to
commemorate its past in his book *A Hundred Years in the Highlands*.
In this century the island of Lewis has reared the scholar Dr Annie
MacKenzie, who provided the model edition of that astringent and
dateless poet of the 17th century, John MacDonald, known as Iain
Lom.

Mackinlay

Unlike MacInnes, but like Mackay, the English form of Mackinlay has had a K inserted where it does not belong. For it derives from *Mac Fhionnlaigh*, Son of Finlay. This is the style of the Farquharson chiefs, yet curiously the clan of Finlay *Mór* do not use this form of surname in the braes of Mar. It is only among those of his descendants who emigrated to the Lowlands that the names of Finlay, Findlayson and Mackinlay have come into currency. In Lochalsh and Kintail the surname of *MacFhionnlaigh* in Gaelic and Finlayson in English derive also from the parent stem of the Farquharsons of Braemar.

But the principal stock of this name belongs to the Lennox. According to the earliest account of them, given in 1723 by Buchanan of Auchmar, they sprang from a son of Buchanan of Drumikill of the name of Finlay. Those who emigrated to Ireland sometimes altered the spelling to MacGinley, while among those who crossed the Atlantic was the M'Kinley after whom the mountain in Alaska was named.

Mackinnon

The name borne by Clan Fingon had once been that of princes of the royal house of Kenneth Mac Alpin. By the 13th century it appears amongst the founder's kin of Iona, and by the middle of the 14th Fingon son of Niall Mackinnon and brother of Gillebride the Mackinnon Chief, was Abbot of Iona. So when the Chief of Clan Mackinnon entered into a bond with Finlay MacNab in 1606, and again with James MacGregor in 1671, and both of these documents referred to the royal origins which the parties to them shared, their long memories were perhaps not playing them false. Abbot Fingon followed the ancient custom of the Celtic church and of the dynasties which had kept its shrines for so long by marrying and leaving a family. His grandson Fingon likewise left a family, though he was accused of having helped to endow it out of the property of the monastery of

Iona. Its last abbot was Iain Mackinnon who died in 1500, and whose effigy still survives in Iona Cathedral. His father Lachlan Mackinnon added a Celtic cross to the island's splendid collection.

Meanwhile the chiefs had become the hereditary custodians of the standards of weights and measures in the Lordship of the Isles. In the late 16th century, long after the lordship had been abolished, a report stated that the Mackinnon chiefs had been appointed 'to be judge and decide all questions and debates that happen to fall between parties through playing at cards or dice or such other practice.' A hazardous office.

Originally the Mackinnons enjoyed extensive lands in Mull, beneath whose mountains Iona lies. But they lost a great part of these to the Macleans, although the chiefs retained their castle of Dunara. They were compensated by the Strathairdale district of Skye from which subsequent chiefs took their formal designation. In this island they became hereditary standard-bearers to the MacDonalds of Sleat, heirs to the chiefship of Clan Donald. Their principal strongholds here were Dunakin (Haakon's Fort) beside the narrows through which the great Norwegian King had sailed in 1263 to Largs: and another at Dunringill.

The 28th Chief, Sir Lachlan Mackinnon, was knighted by Charles II on the fatal field of Worcester in 1651, before Cromwell destroyed the Scottish army and the king fled back to the Continent. The clan's loyalty to the Stewarts remained unshaken by the Revolution of 1688. It rose in the 1715 rebellion and again in 1745. Lord President Forbes estimated that its effective fighting strength was then two hundred men. After Culloden its aged Chief was carried a prisoner to Tilbury Fort at the mouth of the Thames, but eventually was released on account of his age and ill health. The Attorney-General impressed upon him the extent of the King's clemency, and Mackinnon still possessed the spirit to reply: 'Had I the King in my power, as I am in his, I would return him the compliment by sending him back to his country.'

He died in 1756, and in 1765 his son Charles was forced to part with the twenty-six mile long valley of Strathairdale. The last of the Mackinnon lands went under the hammer in 1791. John, son of Charles, last of the direct line of the Chiefs of Clan Fingon, inherited nothing except his ancient office and died in poverty.

However, the heirs to the chiefship restored their fortunes in the West Indies, though this did not restore them to their ancestral acres. Alasdair Mackinnon of Mackinnon (b. 1926) lives in Taunton.

Mackintosh

Toiseach is Gaelic for a Chief or Headman. A *Mac an Toiseich* might therefore be the son of any such functionary, and in fact there are Mackintoshes who claim diverse origins. But the Mackintosh who became Chief of the Cat Confederation, Clan Chattan, claimed descent from the royal house of Duff. Shaw, second son of the 3rd Earl of Fife, was appointed Constable of Inverness Castle in 1163, with a grant of land in the valley of the Findhorn river. He became known as *Mac an Toiseich*, and his son Shaw Mackintosh was appointed crown chamberlain in the north with a charter of confirmation for his lands from William the Lion. He died in 1210. The 4th Mackintosh of this line obtained a lease of Rothiemurchus, where his son Farquhar Mackintosh was living when he raised the men of Badenoch for Alexander III to repel the invasion of King Haakon of Norway. It was during this 6th Mackintosh's chiefship that the MacGillivrays put themselves under his protection and became members of the Clan Chattan.

The skill with which the Mackintosh chiefs steered themselves through the hazards of history was displayed early, in the wars of independence. Although Edward I of England himself came in strength as far north as Moray, and the Bruce's most powerful opponents, the Comyns, dominated the territories of Clan Chattan, the 6th Mackintosh supported the Bruce cause against them. The 7th was able to acquire the barony of Moy where his successor lives to this day. The 10th Mackintosh made as astute a choice as the 6th had done when the Lord of the Isles brought his army to Harlaw in 1411: he brought his clan to fight with the forces of the crown. In 1428 he was appointed Constable of Inverness by James I.

But despite their record, the Mackintoshes fell victim to Stewart policies towards the Highlands. In 1496 the 11th Mackintosh was ordered by James IV to hand Inverness Castle to a Gordon. The 12th was seized in one of the royal kidnapping operations and imprisoned in the castles of Edinburgh, Stirling and Dunbar from 1497 until 1513. As in the Lordship of the Isles, the removal of the apex of local authority merely led to anarchy and violence, such as the Campbells and Gordons made such an art of fomenting and exploiting. The 14th Mackintosh succeeded in obtaining a charter to his lands from James V in 1523 but his successor was murdered in the kitchens of Gordon of Huntly in 1544, and his property forfeited on a trumped-up charge, when the King was dead and a Hamilton held the Regency. Such were the vicissitudes of central government politics at this time, however, that the 16th Mackintosh was able to secure an Act of Parliament reversing the forfeiture in 1550, and ten years later he was invested with the stewardship of Lochaber. In 1562 he had the satisfaction of fighting in the army of Queen Mary against Gordon of Huntly at Corrichie, where the Earl died on the field while his most evil relative was taken to Aberdeen to be executed.

Sir Lachlan Mackintosh succeeded his grandfather as 17th Chief in 1606. James VI ordered that he should be sent to Oxford or Cambridge —in pursuance of his policy of anglicising Highland chiefs and destroying Gaelic culture rather than fostering it. Thereafter the clan supported Charles I in the Civil War and rose for the house of Stewart in the 1715 rebellion. But by the time of the Forty-Five the 22nd Chief was a Captain in the Black Watch, and remained loyal to his commission. It was left to his young wife, described in admiration as Colonel Anne, to raise four hundred of his clansmen for Prince Charles Edward. The 23rd Chief continued in the Hanoverian tradition when he fought for George III in 1776 at the battle of Brooklyn and was taken prisoner. He left no heir, and the chiefship passed first to a Jamaica merchant, then to a shipowner on the Canadian lakes from whom the present Chief descends.

The late Vice-Admiral Lachlan Mackintosh of Mackintosh (1896–1957), 29th Chief, was succeeded by his son Lieut. Commander Lachlan Mackintosh (b. 1928), who lives still in the ancestral lands of Moy in Inverness-shire.

MacLachlan

This is one of the clans which descends according to tradition, fortified by a Gaelic manuscript of 1450, from the oldest traceable family in Europe. The line of Lachlan passed, according to this tradition, through the historical O'Neill kings from Niall of the Nine Hostages, who was High King of Ireland in 400. Aedh, younger grandson of King Flaithbertach (who went on a pilgrimage to Rome in 1030), married a Scottish princess who was the heiress of Cowal and Knapdale. In about 1238 their descendant in these properties, Gilpatrick son of Gilchrist, witnessed a charter by which one of their cousins increased the endowments of Paisley Abbey. Gilpatrick was the father of Lachlan *Mór* after whom the clan takes its name, although it descends in the male line from the royal house of O'Neill. And not only the clan. Lachlan Water and Lachlan Bay, the village of Stralachlan, and the barony of Strathlachlan with its Castle Lachlan commemorate the founder almost to excess.

In 1292 King John Balliol erected Argyll into a sheriffdom, and Gillescop MacLachlan was one of the twelve principal barons of whose lands it was composed. It is interesting that the Chief's family should have continued to favour the same form of name, and that the descendant of the Devotees of Christ and Saint Patrick should have been baptised a Devotee of the Bishop. His son received the same name, and happily for his clan he gave his support to Robert Bruce and attended the King's first Parliament at St Andrews in 1308. In 1314

Gillescop MacLachlan the younger made a grant to the preaching friars of Glasgow. This care for the Church was seemly in a family which belonged to the same house of O'Neill as Saint Columba himself, and it was maintained over a long period. In 1456 Donald of Castle Lachlan confirmed his family's grant to Paisley Abbey.

Just as the MacLachlans had prospered through their support of Robert Bruce, so they continued to flourish by collaborating and marrying with the clan that rose to supremecy in Argyll—the Campbells. In 1536 Lachlan MacLachlan was prominent among the party of the Earl of Argyll which visited France at the marriage of James V to Madeleine of Valois. By the time the Chief's estates were enumerated in a statute of 1633, they contained over thirty farms in Strathlachlan and the neighbourhood of Loch Fyne, together with the living and patronage of the church of Kilmory. They were erected into a free barony in 1680, before the supreme hazard of the 1688 Revolution.

The MacLachlans remained loyal to the Stewarts and probably fought at Killiecrankie in 1689, where the Jacobite leader Graham of Claverhouse was killed. They supported the old Chevalier in the rising of 1715, and Lachlan MacLachlan, the 17th Chief in descent from Lachlan *Mór*, raised his clan for Prince Charles in 1745. The Rev. John MacLachlan of Kilchoan, who was Chaplain-General to the Jacobite forces, wrote of his Chief at Culloden: 'the said Colonel being the last that received orders from the Prince on the field of battle, he was shot by a cannon ball as he was advancing on horseback to lead on his regiment, which was drawn up between the Mackintoshes and the Stewarts of Appin.' Castle Lachlan on Loch Fyne was bombarded from the sea into a ruin. But its bereaved and homeless occupants were more fortunate than many. The Chief had been killed before he could be attainted, and the long-standing friendship of the Campbells did the rest. Through the intercession of the Duke of Argyll, the 18th Chief received a title to his lands. A new Castle Lachlan was built, in which Marjorie MacLachlan of MacLachlan, the 24th Chief, lives today.

MacLaren

There is much that remains shadowy and speculative about the origins of *Clann Labhran*. If they take their name from a 13th-century Abbot Lawrence of Achtow in Balquhidder, their early conflicts with the MacGregors and Buchanans are explicable, but not their massacre of Buchanans in Strathyre in the 12th century. Descent from a mediaeval Abbot in Strathearn suggests a branch of the Celtic dynasty of earls who succeeded the Pictish kings of the Dark Ages there. Yet it was on grounds of descent from owners of the island of Tiree that John MacLaurin, Lord Dreghorn, son of Professor Colin MacLaurin, established his claim in 1781 to the chiefship of the MacLaren clan. The rallying cry of the clan is *Creag an Tuirc*, which means Boar's Rock, and this rock stands near Achtow and Achleskine in Balquhidder —a far cry from Tiree. When the line of Lord Dreghorn came to an end the clan remained without a chief until, only a few years ago, the

MacLaren

representative of the Achleskine branch was recognised as MacLaren of MacLaren. These circumstances do not inspire confidence that much is known for certain about the identity of the MacLaren chiefs during the period when their office played a meaningful part in Highland life.

During the 15th century one of the Stewart lords of Lorne married a daughter of MacLaren of Ardveche, and their son Dougal was the progenitor of the Stewarts of Appin. The line of Ardveche itself continued until 1888, but it does not appear to have been considered as the house of the MacLaren chiefs.

MacLarens were emigrating to serve as soldiers in France and Italy before the end of the 15th century. When the Chief of Mackay took his clansmen to do the same over a century later, he stated that it was because conditions had been made impossible for him at home. Was it the same with the MacLarens? They were overrun twice by the landless MacGregors in 1542 and 1558, and described as a broken clan. By the time of the Thirty Years' War they were enlisting in the Swedish service in which Mackay's regiment fought. The modern Swedish writer Carl G. Laurin is one of many who commemorates their names. The insecurity caused by the policy of successive Stewart sovereigns and the actions of their Campbell and Gordon lieutenants were especially severe in the area in which the MacLarens lived.

Maclaine of Lochbuie

Nothing is known with certainty of this clan before its settlement in Mull, although it is evidently of the original stock of the Scots of Dalriada. It takes its name from the 13th-century *Gill'Eathain na Tuaigh*, Gillean of the Battle-axe. The two principal branches of the Maclaines of Lochbuie and the Macleans of Duart descend from the brothers Hector and Lachlan, who first received these properties from John of Islay, 1st Lord of the Isles, in the mid-14th century. Which of the brothers was the elder was still a matter of litigation in the 19th century.

Hector of Lochbuie's son Charles was the ancestor of the *Siol Tearlaich*, or Descendants of Charles, the Macleans of the North who became members of the Clan Chattan confederation. *Murchadh Ruadh*, Murdoch Redhead, succeeded to Lochbuie, to which his successor Iain *Òg* received a charter from James IV after the Lordship of the Isles had been annexed to the Crown. In about 1494 he was followed by his son *Murchadh Geàrr*, Stunted Murdoch, in circumstances long remembered in fireside tradition.

It was told that Iain *Òg*'s elder son Ewen rose against him and was killed in the insurrection. Maclean of Duart shut away the now childless chief of Lochbuie on a small island, with only an ugly crone to attend him. She however gave birth to Stunted Murdoch, who escaped to Ireland, while his uncle seized the estate. *Murchadh Geàrr* returned, recovered his inheritance by force of arms, obtained his legitimisation in 1538, and is the ancestor of the present chief of Lochbuie.

The Maclaines of Lochbuie fought for Charles I in the army of Montrose, with all the more alacrity because Lochbuie and his entire family had recently been converted to the Catholic faith by the Irish Franciscan missionary, Cornelius Ward. Lochbuie himself sent an account of his conversion to the Pope. Hector of Lochbuie led 300 of his men in the victorious charge of Dundee at Killiecrankie in 1689. Thereafter they escaped the ruin that overtook so many Jacobites, as Boswell and Johnson discovered during their Hebridean journey in 1773. Dr Johnson describes how they landed in Mull, to be 'entertained for the night by Mr Maclean, a Minister that lives upon the coast, whose elegance of conversation, and strength of judgment, would make him conspicuous in places of greater celebrity. Next day we dined with Dr Maclean, another physician, and then travelled on to the house of a very powerful Laird, Maclean of Lochbuy; for in this country every man's name is Maclean.' By this time the castle had been abandoned. 'Lochbuy has, like other insular Chieftains, quitted the castle that sheltered his ancestors, and lives near it, in a mansion not very spacious or splendid.' Its owner receives equally faint praise. 'We found a true Highland Laird, rough and haughty, and tenacious of his dignity.'

By the following century the estate was burdened with debt. But Donald the 20th of Lochbuie, who was born in 1816, went to Java as a merchant and made the fortune which enabled him to clear it of its encumbrances. In the time of his grandson Kenneth, however, the ancient castle was impounded by an Englishman, and Gillean the 23rd of Lochbuie has not recovered it.

Maclean of Duart

Whether or not Lachlan was older than his brother Hector, it is the line of Duart that was accepted as chief of the whole name of Maclean. Lachlan himself married a daughter of John of the Isles, and the Castle of Duart that was bestowed on him with extensive lands in Mull first appears in record in 1390. John of the Isles also made Lachlan chamberlain of his house. When the lordship was abolished, Hector of Duart received a confirmation of his titles from the crown in 1495, and they were erected into the barony of Duart in favour of his son Lachlan.

Several Campbell marriages took place in the following century, but they did little to promote amity with the power that was advancing towards the seat of the dispossessed MacDonalds. Indeed, Hector's son Lachlan went so far as to maroon his wife—a sister of the Earl of Argyll himself—on a tidal rock in the Sound of Mull still known as the

Lady Rock. Assuming her drowned, he reported her death to the Campbells. But she had been rescued by passing fishermen, as a result of which her husband was stabbed to death in Edinburgh in 1523 by her brother Campbell of Cawdor.

Later in the 16th century an even more ruffianly chief of Duart, Sir Lachlan *Mór*, pursued the career which began the downfall of the MacDonalds of Islay whom his house had hitherto supported, and led to the takeover of Duart itself by the Campbells. He was for good measure an Elizabethan agent. Lachlan *Mór*'s megalomania led inexorably to the foreclosure of the lands of Mull by the house of Argyll. When he was killed fighting in 1598 his sons avenged him by a massacre of the people of Islay which lasted for three days. These were the sons whom Cornelius Ward failed to convert at the time when Maclaine of Lochbuie became a Catholic.

One of them, Sir Lachlan, was created a baronet by Charles I, for whom he took up arms. Argyll captured him in 1641, and released him only when he had given bonds for his family's debts and arrears of feu duty. Sir Lachlan joined Montrose, when Argyll invaded and ravaged his lands, though Castle Duart was not surrendered until after Montrose's defeat. When Sir Lachlan died in 1649 his sons were minors, of whom Sir Hector nevertheless fought and died for Charles II at Inverkeithing in 1651, leaving his four-year-old brother Allan as heir. The estate was saved by Argyll's execution in 1661 after the Restoration, but only for a while. By the time Sir Allan died in 1674, leaving another infant heir, the brood of Lachlan *Mór* had come home to roost. The action begun by Argyll in 1672 for payment was followed by letters authorising ejection and arrest. In 1674 letters of treason were issued, then of fire and sword. By 1679 the Campbells had gained possession of Duart and extensive areas of the estate while the chief went into exile. After the Revolution of 1688 Argyll obtained the whole of the Duart estate without further difficulty. Out of exile came Sir Hector Maclean of Duart in 1745, to be captured, carried prisoner to London, and released to die in Italy without issue.

Yet the story has a happy ending. The ruins of Castle Duart were recovered in 1911 and repaired. In the following year Sir Fitzroy Maclean, 10th Baronet and 26th Chief of the clan, was restored to his ancient seat with fitting ceremony. His grandson, Lord Maclean of Duart, was Chief Scout of the Commonwealth from 1959 until 1975.

Maclean

Hunting Maclean

When Hector of Duart was killed at the battle of Harlaw in 1411, the chiefship descended to his son Lachlan, two of whose sons illustrate the way in which the clan expanded through the islands and the mainland. While Lachlan's eldest son inherited Duart, Donald defeated the MacMasters of Ardgour and established the dynasty which has remained there ever since. It is represented today by Catriona Maclean, the Maid of Ardgour, while Sir Fitzroy Maclean represents the cadet branch in which alone the male line still continues. Between 1943 and 1945 he was the Brigadier who commanded the British mission to the Jugoslav partisans.

Another of Lachlan's sons was Iain *Garbh*, who established the line of the Macleans of the island of Coll with its formidable castle by the shore. This was already abandoned in favour of a Georgian house nearby when Johnson visited Coll in 1773: and by this time its owner possessed most of the great mountainous island of Rum also, as well as large tracts of Mull. So Johnson and Boswell spent 'the first day and night with Captain Maclean, a gentleman who has lived some time in the East Indies; but having dethroned no Nabob, is not too rich to settle in his own country.' In 1848 the last Maclean of Coll sold his patrimony and emigrated to South Africa, leaving the Georgian house to become a ruin also.

Throughout the Maclean lands the bards left their record of the effects on people's lives of events over which they had little or no control, and especially of the misfortunes of the 17th century. The Rev. John Beaton composed a poem on the deplorable condition of Mull. His successor, the Rev. John Maclean, first Calvinist minister of Kilninian after the Revolution of 1688, reveals himself in his Gaelic verse as a Jacobite at heart despite his religion, and a loyal clansman.

But it is in this century that the Macleans have produced a Gaelic poet whose utterance will outlast the death of his language as surely as the Declaration of Arbroath has outlived the Abbey's massive walls. Sorley Maclean was born in 1911 in the island of Raasay, and probably descends from Iain, son of Maclean of Boreray in Uist, whose descendants reached Raasay by way of Skye. In his family and among his forbears are poets and pipers. Of his remarkable brothers, Calum Iain Maclean was an outstanding collector and editor of Gaelic oral tradition until his untimely death; and John Maclean, for long the principal of Oban High School, is distinguished by his translations into Gaelic from classical literature. Sorley Maclean himself spent the greater part of his professional career as head of Plockton School in Wester Ross, and has now moved into the home of a great-great-grandfather, John Stewart, who composed poetry before him.

It was in 1943 that his collection *Dain do Eimhir* was published, an event as significant in Gaelic literature as the publication of T. S. Eliot's *Waste Land* in English. For over a quarter of a century since then, the influence of Sorley Maclean has dominated Gaelic poetry. It may be considered that the quality of Gaelic poetry was never higher than now, when the numbers who can understand it are so rapidly diminishing, and the debt to Maclean's inspiration should not be underestimated. Latterly, he has issued English versions of some of his poems, and Iain Crichton Smith has just published a volume of his own English translations from Sorley Maclean's *Dain do Eimhir*.

MacLeod of Lewis

MacLeod of Lewis and Raasay, Dress

Although Leod is now pronounced in English to rhyme with cloud, its Gaelic pronunciation still approximates to that of the Norse name *Liotr*. The clan takes its name from Leod, son of Olaf the Black, King of Man and the north isles, who was himself a member of the dynasty of Godred Crovan, King of Dublin, Man and the Hebrides. King Godred was among those defeated by Harold of England at Stamford Bridge in 1066, when King Harald Haardrade of Norway abandoned the ship in which he carried the sacred relic he had brought back from Constantinople. Sir Iain Moncreiffe, the Highland historian, considers that this may be how the fairy flag of MacLeod came into the possession of Leod's descendants. For it is a silk fabric about a thousand years old, of eastern Mediterranean origin.

Olaf the Black gave Leod lands in the long island of Lewis and

Harris, and these passed to his son Torcuil (a curruption of the Norse name Thorkil), ancestor of the MacLeods of Lewis. Torcuil's brother Tormod (a name later transformed into Norman) acquired lands in Skye which passed to the house of Leod by marriage with the daughter and heiress of the Norse steward of that island. Thus, in the 13th century, the clan was divided into its two great branches of the *Siol Torcuil* and the *Siol Tormoid*.

After the failure of the great King Haakon IV of Norway in 1263 to maintain his sovereignty over the western isles, they were ceded to Scotland. But the MacLeods do not appear to have received any title to their possessions either from Alexander III, who defeated King Haakon, or from Robert Bruce who finally won his crown. It was in the reign of the Bruce's son David II that the MacLeods received their first surviving royal charter, by which time power in the Hebrides had passed to the house of MacDonald. David II's grant, however, concerned the mainland. It confirmed to Torcuil, 4th MacLeod Chief of Lewis, the lands and Castle of Assynt in Sutherland which had evidently been acquired by marriage. Ruaraidh the 5th Chief bestowed these upon his second son Norman, and so founded the sept of the MacLeods of Assynt who are still to be found in Sutherland today. Its senior line ended in shame. On the eve of Charles I's Civil War Neil of Assynt, who signed himself Neilson, still lived in Ardvreck Castle, whose ruins now crumble on their peninsula in Loch Assynt. But he was paralysed by debt and by terror of the rapacious Gordons. When Montrose fled from his defeat at Carbisdale with a price on his head in 1650 he fell into Neilson's hands, who surrendered him to his death in Edinburgh. It was said that he never received more of the reward than some sour meal, as Iain *Lom* MacDonald mentioned in his furious denunciation. 'Neilson from dreary Assynt, if I caught you in my net I would give evidence to compass your condemnation, and I would not save you from the gallows. The death shroud be about you, despicable one, for you have sinfully sold the truth for Leith meal, most of which had gone sour.' Neil MacLeod did not save his property by betraying Montrose.

In the 16th century, another cadet branch of Lewis obtained the island of Raasay beside Skye, and it was these who constituted the senior male line of the MacLeods of Lewis after the MacKenzies of Cromarty had succeeded in gaining possession of the Lewis properties early in the 17th century through the claims of a bogus heiress. But Raasay was sold in 1846 and the 14th chieftain lives today in Tasmania. And although the MacKenzies have lost their ill-gotten acquisitions in Lewis, the present Earl of Cromartie lives in Castle Leod in Strathpeffer and among his titles is that of Lord MacLeod.

With the downfall of the MacLeods of Lewis the chiefship passed to the line of Dunvegan. It is held today by John MacLeod of MacLeod (b. 1935) after passing through his mother and grandmother from Sir Reginald MacLeod, the 27th Chief who did so much to restore the estate.

MacLeod of MacLeod

While so many Highland strongholds lie in ruins today, Dunvegan Castle in Skye, the seat of the chiefs of *Siol Tormoid*, has been occupied by them for twenty generations during seven centuries. It is therefore of some interest to notice what its muniments do and do not include. There are no title deeds from the King of Scots to whom the islands were ceded in 1266 by the Norwegians under the Treaty of Perth, none from King Robert Bruce whom the MacLeods supported, a charter for Glenelg on the mainland only from his son David II, none that survive from the days of the Lordship of the Isles, whose vassals the MacLeods found themselves to be by the stroke of a distant pen. After the fall of the Lordship in 1498 MacLeod of Dunvegan at last received a charter from the crown, but not for all the possessions that were rightfully his. So when successive Stewart sovereigns summoned the Highland chiefs to show the titles to their lands, what did they expect them to exhibit when even the Lords of Dunvegan had been denied proper titles? It was the appalling ineptitude of the central government that compelled clans to fight for their home-acre, just as the MacLeods in Skye had to fight a losing battle against the MacDonalds of Sleat for their lands of Trotternish.

But in the time of troubles occasioned by the dismantling of the Lordships, the punitive policies of James IV and James V, and the powers given to the Campbells and the Gordons, Dunvegan was extremely fortunate in the calibre of its 8th Chief. He was known as

Alasdair Crotach (Hump-backed Alexander) as the result of an injury. Although he supported the claimants to the Lordship after its abolition, he succeeded in extricating himself when James V made his expedition to the Hebrides, seizing and imprisoning chiefs on his journey. He even secured a charter to the disputed lands of Trotternish in 1542, the year of James V's death. But it is in the cultural field that *Alasdair Crotach* is to be remembered especially. He rebuilt the church of Rodel in Harris, the finest that remains in the outer Hebrides, where his tomb is an outstanding example of the monumental sculpture of the period. He built the Fairy Tower at Dunvegan, its finest building, and he is said to have been the first Chief to encourage piping there. In a society which has been judged largely by the criminal records (often faked) of a distant government that knew nothing of its arts or literature, Dunvegan was to blossom as a centre of these arts after the patronage of the Lordship was destroyed. Here the Beatons came with their ancient learning. Here the new music of pibroch was developed by the MacCrimmons. Here the most famous Gaelic harper, Roderick Morrison, found his audience.

This achievement is associated particularly with Sir Roderick MacLeod of MacLeod the 15th Chief, known as *Ruaraidh Mór*. He died in 1626 and is immortalised by Patrick *Mór* MacCrimmon's lament. By then the Franciscan missionary Cornelius Ward had visited Skye, received *Ruaraidh Mór's* encouragement to proselytize, and reported to Rome that he was 'a very lordly ruler' and a devout Catholic. It is thought that Mary MacLeod was by then a girl of ten, already in his household at Dunvegan. The simple, lovely language of her poetry has preserved the freshest picture that remains of the society whose passing the Blind Harper, Roderick Morrison, was to lament.

The MacLeods supported Charles I in the Civil War, and their contingent of about 700 men was annihilated at Worcester, fighting for Charles II in 1651. Stewart ingratitude, and conversion to Calvinism, combined to hold the MacLeods aloof from the Jacobite risings, so that Boswell and Johnson found the old patriarchal society still intact here when the 22nd Chief entertained them at Dunvegan in 1773.

MacLeod

In the parish of Assynt, where the MacLeod castle of Ardvreck was crumbling into ruin beside its loch, there was born in 1780 perhaps the most remarkable product of Calvinism in Scottish history. At this time the creed which had been ordained by Scotland's Parliament in 1560 was still being carried to the more remote parts of the Highlands, by men frequently described as *Ministeirean Làidir*—Strong-armed Ministers. Never was there a stronger than Norman MacLeod, who returned from university as a divinity student to preach in his native parish, fell foul of the minister there, and embarked on the career of a latter-day Moses. In 1817 he embarked with the flock whom he had mesmerised by his preaching, to establish a community of the Elect in the new world. They landed in Pictou, Nova Scotia, where the Assynt emigrants lived for several years, ruled with a tyranny to which they willingly submitted under their chosen pastor. But they began to hanker for greener pastures. So they built a ship called *The Ark*, large enough to carry Norman's family and all who wished to accompany them, and sailed towards the Gulf of Mexico. Soon they were driven off course by a storm, and so came to rest in 1820 at St Ann's, Cape Breton. Here once again the Old Testament prophet established his dictatorship, acting as teacher, judge and fiery expounder of the errors of all who did not agree with his doctrines. When his son David sailed to Australia and wrote home, extolling its merits, the seventy-one-year-old patriarch decided to move again. Another boat was built for all who wished to go and (most significant of all), a second ship carried an additional 747 people who found they could not live without their minister.

Norman MacLeod left for Australia in 1851, but he did not remain there long. Tempted by the reports from New Zealand, particularly of its similarity to Scotland, he sailed with his flock to Waipu in 1854. He was still riding on horseback to preach in the farthest corners of his parish at the age of eighty-two.

By this time another clansman had earned equal fame by his uncompromising fortitude. Donald MacLeod was born at Rossal in Strathnaver, and was a youth serving his apprenticeship to his father as a stone-mason when Patrick Sellar arrived in 1814 to destroy his village and empty the entire strath. Flouting all the powers that attempted to silence him, Donald MacLeod published the details of the Sutherland clearances that were finally gathered into his book *Gloomy Memories*. It was published in Canada where its author ended his days, and despite the attempts to discredit its evidence, it is now accepted as the truth. But the portrait that has been published of Donald MacLeod is quite bogus.

Perhaps the most outstanding of all Scotland's dynasties of churchmen in modern times is that of Dr Norman MacLeod. He was born in the manse of Morvern in Argyll in 1783, and in addition to his eminent services in the ministry he issued the Gaelic writings that provided the anthology *Caraid nan Gaidheal*. Once, this book was to be found with the Bible in every Highland home, the beauty of its prose and the humour and humanity of its contents flowing naturally out of the rich oral tradition that flourished at this time. Dr MacLeod died in 1862 but his descendants continued his work: most notably Dr George MacLeod, who was born in 1895 and in 1937 became Leader of the Iona Community. This is engaged in restoring the buildings of Scotland's most sacred site and fulfilling the prophecy that before the world comes to an end Iona will be as it was. When Dr MacLeod succeeded as 4th baronet he did not use this title, but in 1967 he accepted a life peerage, so that the voice of his Church might be heard in the House of Lords.

Macmillan

Macmillan

In Gaelic literature a Macmillan is referred to as *Maolanach* (a tonsured person), or as *MacGhillemhaoil* (son of the devotee of the tonsured one). The tonsure of the Celtic church consisted in shaving the hair from the front half of the head, and there can be little doubt that the clan descends from some unremembered dynast of the early church in Dalriada. Its chiefs acquired territories in Knapdale, in the heart of this area, through a MacNeill heiress: and they are commemorated there by the Macmillan tower of Castle Sween, the oldest stone-built castle in Scotland, and by the elaborately engraved cross in Kilmory churchyard, upwards of twelve feet high. On it is inscribed *'Haec est crux Alexandri Macmillan'*. Possibly the Highland chief hunting the deer on one side of it is Macmillan himself; as probably, the claymore beneath the crucifix on the reverse side is his. But his descendants lost the lands of Knap, which became a bone of contention between MacNeills and Campbells, and were purchased in 1775 by Sir Archibald Campbell of Inverneil.

But long before this disintegration occurred, the earliest known sept of the Macmillans had become settled in Lochaber. Its cadet chiefs descended from Iain, eldest son of Malcolm *Mór*, the 1st of Knap. In Lochaber they soon became involved in the troubles which followed the failure of the Lord of the Isles at Harlaw in 1411. During that period of insecurity MacDonalds, Camerons, Mackintoshes and many lesser clans shifted their allegiance uneasily between the Lordship and the

Hunting Macmillan

Crown, seeking safety or gain where they thought it might be found. In 1431 Mackintosh bestowed Murlagan upon the Macmillans and they became dependants of Clan Chattan and dwellers upon the western shores of Loch Arkaig. The learned Chief of Macfarlane recorded that Charles Macmillan bound himself and his posterity as 'hereditary servants' to the Mackintosh who died in 1457. This Charles was the ancestor of the Inverness Macmillans, and younger son of Ewen the 1st of Murlagan. So the Lochaber clan proliferated, as Mackintosh tenants living in the heart of Cameron country. In the 17th century the chief of Murlagan refused to support Cameron of Lochiel against the Mackintoshes. Lochiel borrowed money from Campbell of Argyll to purchase the title to the lands which the Macmillans occupied from Mackintosh. When the Gentle Lochiel called upon Iain the 9th of Murlagan to fight for Prince Charles in 1745, he refused. But tradition says it was Murlagan's two sons who carried the wounded Lochiel from Culloden field, and Prince Charles made his last stand at their home by Loch Arkaig.

It was none other than Donald, grandson of the Gentle Lochiel, who cleared the Macmillans as well as his own clansmen with such ruthlessness from their ancestral homes. It was regarded as a peculiar act of perfidy that this was done by a resident chief, rather than by Lowland factors or foreign speculators. The story is told in *Bygone Lochaber* (1971) by the Gaelic scholar the Rev. Somerled Macmillan.

MacNab

MacNab means in Gaelic Son of the Abbot, and those who bear it descend from the hereditary secular abbots of St Fillan's near Loch Earn. Fillan himself was a 7th-century prince of the house of Dalriada who may himself have been their progenitor. When the Celtic church was dismantled, the MacNabs continued to hold their property as the barony of Glendochart until they had the misfortune to fight on the wrong side in the wars of independence that finally won Robert Bruce the Scottish crown. But the MacNabs survived the destruction of their writs and houses, and in 1336 their Chief received a charter from David II for part of their former possessions in Glendochart.

Since then their fortunes have varied exceedingly. In 1594 they were listed among the 'broken clans' of the Highlands, and in 1612 the sons of Finlay their Chief carried out a raid which reflects the lawlessness of those times. The neighbouring MacNeishes had waylaid a consignment of whisky on its way to MacNab. As soon as the news was brought to him, his sons set out in the stormy winter's night, carrying a boat through the hills to Loch Earn, where they rowed it to the island stronghold of the MacNeishes. There they cut off the head of the chief and brought it home to their father. Finlay MacNab's son Iain, the hero of this exploit, died fighting for Charles II at Worcester in 1651. The MacNabs were dispossessed of their lands by the Campbells. But at the Restoration in 1660 the Chief of the Campbells was executed and the property of the MacNabs restored.

The manner in which it was finally lost is one of the most bizarre in clan history. Francis MacNab, who succeeded as 16th Chief at the end of the 18th century, inherited the mansions of Achlyne and Kinnel, land that stretched from Menteith to Loch Tay, and through his mother the additional property of Arnprior. By the time he died in 1816 he had squandered the greater part of his patrimony, left the MacNab country littered with his bastards, but failed to beget a legitimate heir. The chiefship consequently passed to his nephew Archibald, who had hitherto spent most of his life in dissipations in London and Paris. Archibald settled at Kinnel as 13th Chief until 1820, when he bolted to evade his creditors, leaving his wife and eight children behind.

His MacNab factor provided him with the means to sail to Canada, where several hundred of his clansmen had already settled. He was welcomed with a public dinner at Montreal, such was the novelty of a real Highland Chief; and his social rank, and the polish he had acquired in London and Paris, enabled him to insinuate himself with the offshoots of the British aristocracy who then enjoyed the perquisites of colonial office. By this means MacNab obtained a territorial grant in 1824 which enabled him to operate the feudal system for the last time in the history of the British Empire. Nothing could illustrate better the loyalty of the Gaels to their chiefs than what followed. Despite all that had happened at home, twenty-one families there signed his bonds in their blind trust, and sailed to become his vassals. They tamely surrendered their bonds on their arrival, although these were their only security. By 1830 he had over sixty families in thrall, and although by this time they were sickened by his cruelty and vindictiveness, they had no copy of the original bond to consult in defence of their rights. The 13th MacNab cohabited with a sluttish housekeeper, and his clansmen were not edified when she bore their chief a son.

It was two Buchanan brothers from his own neighbourhood in Scotland who succeeded in exposing the system by which he had exploited his fellow-countrymen for so long. In 1843 he was convicted on criminal charges and totally discredited by the clansmen who, twenty years earlier, had wept with gratitude for his presence among them. The newspapers investigated every detail of his career. When he won a libel action against them, the jury assessed the damages for demolishing the character of the MacNab of MacNab at £5. He slunk home, to be presented with a house in Orkney to live in, by the wife he had deserted. He died in 1860 and for long there was little eagerness to fill the title of Chief of MacNab. His more worthy cousin Sir Allan MacNab (1798–1862) became Prime Minister of Canada.

And in 1864 there was born to Alexander MacNab in New Zealand and his wife Janet McQueen a son Robert. He entered Parliament in 1893 and became Minister of Justice and Marine during the First World War. He is chiefly remembered as one of New Zealand's earliest and most distinguished historians.

James MacNab of MacNab (b. 1926) is the present Chief.

MacNaughton

Nechtan is a name of the Pictish kings. It is commemorated by the victory which Brude, King of the Picts, won in 685 at Nechtansmere against the invading English from Northumbria. By the 12th century Clan Nechtan were the proprietors of Strath Tay and in the following one they had added possessions in Argyll. Here Gilchrist MacNaughton bestowed a church at the head of Loch Fyne on the abbey of Inchaffray in about 1246, and was granted by Alexander III the castle and island of Fraoch Eilean in Loch Awe in 1267. Gilchrist son of Malcolm, the second Chief in historical record, was evidently one of the magnates of that ancient Gaelic society. In addition to his castle in Loch Awe he possessed Dunderave on Loch Fyne, the castle of Dubh Loch in Glenshira and Dunnaghton in Strathspey. He was one of the twelve great men whose lands were formed into the new sheriffdom of Argyll in 1292. Like their kinsmen the MacDougalls of Lorne, and like the Comyns in the north, the MacNaughtons under Donald their Chief opposed Robert Bruce. After he had become King, many of their lands in Argyll were forfeited and granted to the Campbells.

But when Donald's son Duncan became Chief he gave his support to the Bruce's son David II, during the troubled years in which Edward III of England supported the senior claims of Edward Balliol to the Scottish throne. As a reward King David granted to Duncan's son Alexander extensive lands which helped to restore the family fortunes.

At almost the end of the 14th century Colin Campbell of Loch Awe made grants to Maurice MacNaughton there which were confirmed by the Stewart sovereign, Robert III. So the clan was once again prosperous by the time its Chief Alexander was knighted by James IV and perished with his sovereign in 1513 at Flodden.

The MacNaughtons continued loyal to the Stewart kings, both during the wars of Charles I, and at the Revolution of 1688 which turned James VII off his throne. In 1689 Alexander the Chief fought under Graham of Claverhouse at Killiecrankie and in 1691 his estates were forfeited. His son John was the last Chief of the direct line, and he might have salvaged his fortunes when he arranged to marry the second daughter of Sir James Campbell of Ardkinglas. But he allowed himself to be too lavishly entertained by his prospective father-in-law, who then succeeded in marrying him to his elder daughter. MacNaughton fled to Ireland with the daughter of his choice, while his father-in-law secured his conviction for incest and was rewarded with what remained of the MacNaughton property.

The chiefship remained dormant until the 19th century when a remarkable demonstration was made by about four hundred members of the clan. They found that the chiefship had descended through a younger son of Sir Alexander, killed at Flodden, who had emigrated to Antrim in Ireland in about 1580. The representative of this line was then Edmund MacNaghten, after whose death his brother Sir Francis MacNaghten of Dunderave, 1st baronet, was recognised as Chief of the clan. The line of chiefs of this immemorially ancient tribe has therefore continued in the male line since the beginning of historical record, and is now represented by Sir Francis of Dunderave, 8th baronet.

MacNeill of Colonsay

This is one of the clans which descends, like the Lamonts, MacLachlans and MacSweens, from Niall of the Nine Hostages, the earliest historical High King of Ireland. King Aodh O'Neill (1030–33), possessed a son, Anrothan, who married a princess of Dalriada, and from these sprang the house of Neil's son Torquil of Taynish, who was Keeper of Castle Sween in Knapdale in 1449. By this time the

MacNeill of Colonsay

MacNeills also held the island of Gigha off the coast of Kintyre, and the senior branch also established themselves in the islands of Colonsay and Oronsay beyond the Firth of Lorne. In 1530 the Privy Council described Torquil MacNeill of Gigha as 'Chief and principal of the clan and surname of MacNeills'. So when Gigha passed to the Campbells in 1554, Colonsay became the seat of the chiefs. But as the power of the Campbells increased at the expense of their nearer neighbours, so the effectiveness of the house of Colonsay continued to decline, while the Macneils of more distant Barra remained relatively immune. The passing of the chiefship from Colonsay to Barra in these circumstances is an interesting illustration of the manner in which the office was regarded at the time.

However, Hector MacNeill of Taynish recovered Gigha from Campbell of Cawdor in 1590, and it was sold to MacNeill of Colonsay in 1780. This was a period of island prosperity under an enlightened chief, who introduced a new pattern of crofting and new houses with chimney stacks. His son Alexander sold Colonsay to his brother, the famous Lord Justice General who was consequently able to adopt the title of Lord Colonsay when he was raised to the peerage in 1867. But finally the island was sold, and after the death of Alexander MacNeill, its last owner, the chiefship passed to his son of the same name, whose home is in New Zealand.

Macneil of Barra

In 1427 Gilleonan Macneil received a charter to the island of Barra, and to Boisdale in neighbouring South Uist, from the Lord of the Isles; and tradition recalled that his father *Ruaraidh* (in English, Rory) was one of thirty-three Ruaraidhs who had held Barra before him. Sir Iain Moncreiffe deduces from this and other evidence that the Macneils of Barra had acquired their inheritance from an heiress of the ancient house of *MacRuaraidh*, descendants of the sea-kings of the Isles. After the downfall of the Lordship, they were confirmed in possession by crown charter in 1495, after which a succession of *Ruaraidh* chiefs of Barra proceeded to give much evidence of Viking ancestry.

In 1625 the Irish Catholic missionary Cornelius Ward came to Barra, and found the effigy of Saint Barr still venerated in his roofless church. He baptised two sons of the Chief and many more, before travelling on to the islands of Clanranald. The island remains Catholic to this day. But in 1745 it also contained the 'devil of a Minister' as Duncan Cameron of Barra called him, who 'despatched away expresses with informations against us' when the Prince reached Barra. 'But as the good luck was, he was not believed.' The Minister concerned was the grandfather of Lord Macaulay. Although MacNeil of Barra did not join the rebellion, he was nevertheless taken captive after it, and suffered the same disgraceful treatment in the hulks at Tilbury as those who had.

MacPhee

Today this name is written in Gaelic *Mac a'Phi,* which gives the English phonetic spelling Macafie, sometimes shortened to Macfie or MacPhee. But probably MacDuffie is nearer to its original form, which appears to have been *Mac Dhuibh Shìth,* Son of the Dark Fairy. So the name of the Lector of Iona is given in 1164, and so the Chief of the MacPhees of Colonsay is designated in a charter of 1463. The Dean of the Isles referred in 1549 to 'McDufisithe of Collinsay.'

The Dark Fairy is evocative of the dark stranger who must be the first to cross the threshold at the new year, bringing food and drink as symbols of good fortune as the leanest season of the year approaches. The identity of this stranger is as mysterious as the meaning of the term Hogmanay. But in many countries the most aboriginal stock, often a defeated remnant living in remote places, came to be looked upon as a fairy folk. It is hardly surprising that legend should have given the sons of the Dark Fairy, living in small islands, descent from a supernatural creature of the sea.

Among the islands from Faroe to the south of Ireland, the story was told of the seal-woman who lured a mortal by her seal-singing, which closely resembled a plaintive woman's voice. In many of these versions the mortal prevents his seal-bride from returning to the sea by hiding her seal-skin trousers. When she finds them she abandons her mortal family, but provides them ever after with a regular supply of fish. The seal-wife has taken over the role of the dark stranger of Hogmanay.

When John Leyden visited the western isles in 1800 he was told the story of a Gaelic ballad about the mermaid of Colonsay, which he turned into an English ballad. But he seems to have misheard the name of the mortal of Colonsay with whom she fell in love, for he gives it as MacPhail.

The MacPhees of Colonsay were hereditary keepers of the records of the Lords of the Isles, which have vanished almost without trace. A solitary mediaeval Gaelic charter attests that the administration of the Lordship was conducted in the vernacular as well as in Latin. After the Lordship was abolished in 1493 the MacPhees remained loyal to the forfeited MacDonalds and shared their downfall. In 1609 there was still a MacPhee of Colonsay to be tricked amongst the other chiefs into signing the infamous Statutes of Iona. But in 1623 Malcolm of Colonsay was slain under a pile of seaweed where he was hiding, and the island passed into other hands. Some of his clansmen settled in the Cameron country on the mainland, while those who still remain on the islands have only succeeded in doing so by holding out for centuries under the precarious tenure of crofters.

So many of this broken clan became completely rootless that the very name of MacPhee is today equated with the profession of the itinerant tin-smiths known as tinkers. And since the tinkers have occupied something like the position of the *Dubh Sìthe* of immemorial antiquity, a historical cycle has come full circle.

MacPherson

Just as the Calvinist ministry tended to become hereditary in certain families after the Reformation, so the Celtic forms of religious organisation, planted in Scotland a thousand years earlier, preserved the hereditary principle long after the celibacy of the priesthood ought to have put an end to it. Hence the names MacTaggart (Son of the Priest), MacNab (Son of the Abbot) and MacPherson (Son of the Parson). In each case it was possible for MacTaggarts, MacNabs and Mac-Phersons to descend from different priests, abbots and parsons. But the great Badenoch clan which for so long contested the primacy of Clan Chattan descended, according to tradition, from the hereditary parsons of Kingussie, of whom one was described as Duncan Parson in 1438 and his descendants as MacPhersons. On the other hand they were also described as chiefs of Clan Mhuirich since they claimed descent from Muireadhach, Prior to Kingussie in 1173. This is an earlier *Muireadhach* than the bard who came from Ireland to the Lennox and founded the MacMuirich clan, whose name became transformed finally to Currie. So the MacPhersons have no historical connection with the island MacMhuirichs.

The exact nature of the descent which they shared with the Mackintoshes from the ancestor Gille Chattan is also uncertain, and was a fatal source of strife within Clan Chattan. For an increasing external menace made internal unity essential. The Comyns were the overlords of this province until their destruction by King Robert Bruce. After them came the Stewarts, among them the barbarous Wolf of Badenoch. Finally the jackal Gordons of Huntly moved in with vice-regal powers from the Crown. In 1490 Bean MacPherson signed a bond of 'Duncan Mackintosh, Captain of Clan Chattan', thus recognising him as Chief. In 1609 Andrew MacPherson of Cluny and five others of his name signed a document which again virtually recognised Mackintosh as the Clan Chattan Chief. But they gave him little loyalty during the interval. In 1528 James V issued a characteristic Stewart royal directive to wipe out the Mackintoshes, leaving 'no creature living of that clan except priests, women and bairns.' The prescribed methods of execution were 'slaughter, burning, drowning, and other ways', and the Gordon agents were poised to carry them out and to take over the property. It is significant that the MacPhersons were not involved: although it was a tradition of the two oldest MacPherson houses of Pitmean and Invereshie that Duncan Parson had been a Mackintosh.

The Gordons of Huntly fed the MacPherson claim to the chiefship of Clan Chattan in an attempt to set them against the Mackintoshes, to the destruction of both. It was exactly the policy their Sutherland branch was then pursuing for the mutual destruction of the Mackays and Sinclairs. The conflict flared until 1672. Andrew of Cluny (who had signed the significant bond of manrent in 1609) was succeeded by his son Colonel Ewen, who led the Badenoch men in the army of Montrose. When his son Andrew of Cluny died in his prime in 1666 the eloquent Sir Aeneas MacPherson of Invereshie lamented: 'he was an Absolom for beauty, a Joseph for continence, a Tully for eloquence and a Jonathan for friendship.' In 1672 his brother Duncan lost the case before the Privy Council, and was pronounced to be Chief of Mac-Pherson while Mackintosh was 'the only and true representer of the ancient and honourable family of the Clan Chattan.'

Sir Aeneas MacPherson of Invereshie, who was born in the troubled year 1644, is the earliest considerable writer about the affairs of his clan. He presented a *Loyal Dissuasive* to his Chief, Duncan of Cluny, and left many other papers concerning the affairs of Clan Chattan. His letters to Gordon of Huntly, now 1st Duke of Gordon, whom he terms 'the patron turned persecutor', contains the wrath of centuries. The father of Sir Aeneas had died of wounds when he was a baby, fighting under Montrose at Tibbermore; and although Aeneas himself became a lawyer, his later life was as adventurous as his father's had been. At the Revolution in 1688 he became a Jacobite agent, using his father's name for the *alias* of Williamson. He was arrested and sent a prisoner to Edinburgh in 1690. Here his fellow-agent Nevil Payne had been tortured by the servants of the new Secretary of State, Dalrymple of Stair, stage-manager of the Glencoe massacre. Once again Sir Aeneas employed his pen for the indictment against the use of torture which he sent to the dreadful Dalrymple. He was freed, arrested again, once more freed, and then imprisoned a third time in

(*Above*) MacPherson; (*below*) Hunting MacPherson

increasingly harsh and filthy conditions. Finally he received a sentence of banishment, and so came to the exiled court at St Germains until he was able to return under Queen Anne's indemnity in 1702. He died in 1705, shortly before the Union of the two kingdoms.

His Jacobite career is overshadowed by that of Ewen of Cluny, who succeeded his father as Chief of MacPherson in 1746 and was one of the most spectacular clan leaders to fight in the forces of Prince Charles Edward. While the house of Cluny was burnt to the ground and the estates forfeited, Cluny MacPherson lived in hiding for nine years, supported in safety by his clansmen despite the colossal reward on his head. Finally he escaped to France in 1755, and the forfeited estates were restored to his son in 1784 and the seat of Cluny rebuilt.

It was at this time that the literary achievement of Sir Aeneas of Invereshie was overshadowed by that of another cadet, who had been a mere child at the time of Culloden. James MacPherson was brought up at Balavil near Ruthven in Inverness-shire, and after leaving university he taught in the school of his native parish, and then became a private tutor. First he published original poetry in English, and when it received no attention he issued what purported to be translations from Gaelic poetry composed by Ossian, son of Fingal, in extreme antiquity. His epic of *Fingal*, which appeared in 1761 caused a greater stir than any volume of poetry ever published in Britain had ever done. In 1763 he added an even longer epic called *Temora*. Almost incredibly, it was for a time generally accepted that they were translations from Gaelic originals of the 3rd century. They were even considered to outshine Homer, although MacPherson's inflated and turgid style of poetic English prose has made sad work of the mediaeval Gaelic ballads and traditional tales from which he stole his basic themes. However, his hoax helped to turn the eyes of the outside world at last upon Scotland's neglected Gaelic heritage, and to save the manuscript of Dean MacGregor of Lismore, even if it did not save the libraries of the Beatons or the MacMhuirichs.

A remarkable contribution to the genuine tradition has since been preserved by John Lorne Campbell's systematic recording of the repertoire of John MacPherson (1876–1955) of the island of Barra. In his *Tales of Barra Told by the Coddy* he gives a unique record of the art of a bilingual Hebridean, telling both different, and in one case the same story, through the very different media of Gaelic and English. Alas, by the time 'Ossian' MacPherson was driven to producing his epic originals for publication, his Gaelic had grown so rusty that the bogus originals (never completed) are no better than his bogus translations. Their author lies in the poet's corner of Westminster Abbey: but the Coddy's tales will live longer.

Lieut. Colonel William MacPherson of Cluny and Blairgowrie (b. 1926) succeeded his father Brigadier Alan MacPherson as the clan Chief in 1969.

Macquarrie

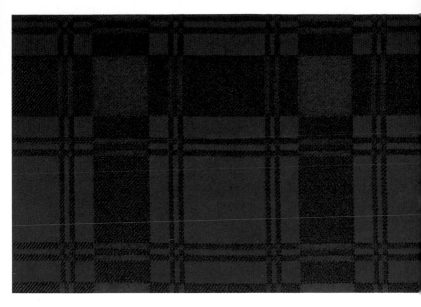

Like the names More and Campbell, this derives from a Gaelic term of description. *Guaire*, meaning noble, is the root of the clan called Macguire, Macguaire, Macquarrie and Macquarie. According to tradition, Guaire was the brother of Fingon, from whom the Mackinnon chiefs descend, and the Macquarrie chiefs had their seat in Ulva, which lies off the far larger island of Mull. The first who survives in historical records is Iain of Ulva, who witnessed a charter of the Lord of the Isles in 1463 and died about ten years later. In the perfidious expedition of 1609, when James VI summoned Highland chiefs to attend the sermon of a bishop, had them kidnapped, and compelled them to sign the Statutes of Iona, Macquarrie of Ulva was among the magnates of the Isles who submitted to this latest stroke of Stewart trickery. After the downfall of the Lordship of the Isles the Macquarries had attached themselves to the Macleans of Duart, then dominant in Mull. This alliance led to the disaster of 1651, when the Chief of Ulva perished with so many of his men, fighting for Charles II at Inverkeithing, whither they had accompanied the Macleans.

When Johnson and Boswell visited Ulva in 1773, Johnson found 'an Island of no great extent, rough and barren, inhabited by the *Macquarrys;* a clan not powerful nor numerous, but of antiquity, which most other families are content to reverence.' They stayed with the Chief, Lachlan Macquarrie, five years before he sold his property. Boswell observed: 'M'Quarrie's house was mean; but we were agreeably surprised with the appearance of the master, whom we found to be intelligent, polite, and much a man of the world.' The visitors were equally impressed by the adjacent island of Staffa that he owned, later to become so famous for the strange rock formation of Fingal's cave and the music which Mendelssohn wrote for it.

The descendants of the last laird of Ulva distinguished themselves in the army and in India; but the most famous of all was his cousin Lachlan Macquarie (1762–1824). Born in Ulva, he rose to the rank of Major-General and then returned to buy himself an estate in Mull. After Captain Bligh had been dismissed from the post of Governor of New South Wales, with the assistance of John MacArthur, General Macquarie was appointed to succeed him. Although MacArthur soon became his arch-enemy, Macquarie was not prevented from performing immense services to Australia. He restored order, promoted education, road-building and exploration, and introduced stern Sabbatarian rules. This ugly feature of Calvinism was perhaps excuseable as an aid to promoting an orderly society that was largely composed of transported convicts. In his efforts to build a better world for them when they were emancipated, Governor Macquarie earned well the title that he shares with his rival MacArthur, as a Father of Australia.

Macqueen

Clan Donald believed that they were of the *Siol Cuinn*, the Kindred of the famous King Conn of the Hundred Battles in Ireland. The Macqueens or MacSweens they held to be of the same kindred, taking their different patronymic from Sweyn, the Norse name from which the modern Danish Svend derives. When the 10th Mackintosh Chief married a Clanranald bride, a number of Macqueens accompanied her, and their descendants settled in Strathdearn and multiplied in the Findhorn Valley. So a branch of Macqueens became members of the Clan Chattan. They were known as Clan Revan after the original escort of the Clanranald bride, and their chiefs were styled Macqueens of Corribrough. As late as 1778 Lord MacDonald of Sleat wrote to Corribrough offering a commission to his son in these terms: 'It does me great honour to have the sons of chieftains in the regiment, and as the Macqueens have been invariably attached to our family, to whom we believe we owe our existence, I am proud of the nomination.' The family of Corribrough has since emigrated and the Chief of Clan Revan lives in New Zealand.

In the Hebrides the MacSweens are numerous in Scalpay to this day, where they have for long enjoyed a reputation as outstanding seamen. In Skye the Macqueens held the lands of Garafad for many generations, and it was the fourth generation of Macqueen Ministers of Snizort who accompanied Johnson and Boswell on their visit to the island. The Rev. Donald Macqueen was then described as the most intelligent man in Skye and Johnson confirmed: 'This is a critical man, sir. There must be great vigour of mind to make him cultivate learning

Macqueen

so much in the isle of Skye, where he might do without it.' Unfortunately
Macqueen suspended his critical faculties over the bogus Ossianic
poetry of James MacPherson, which earned Johnson's ridicule.
But when Macqueen took Johnson to see the ruins of the temple of
the goddess Anaitis, neither of them knew that in fact the place-name
Annat invariably indicates an early Christian site.

It was from this time that the massive exodus of Macqueens and
other Hebrideans across the Atlantic occurred. During the distress of
the following decades, Scotland's monster was Robert Macqueen,
Lord Braxfield, the 'hanging judge'. It is only fair to Clan Revan and the
Macqueens of Skye to mention that he came from Lanarkshire.

MacRae

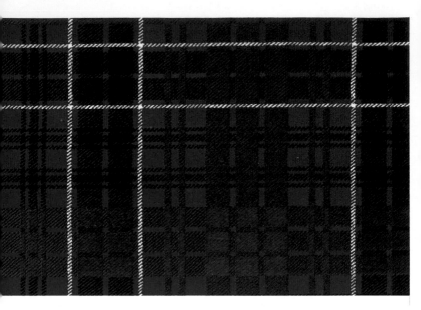

MacRath means in Gaelic Son of Grace, and of its many English spellings the Irish form Magrath is the one that best preserves its original pronunciation. The most famous Highland branch is that of Kintail in Wester Ross, which was erected as a barony for the Chief of the MacKenzies in 1508. Kintail's stronghold stands on Eilean Donan in Loch Duich, named after the saint of the Celtic church who was martyred on the island of Eigg and commemorated also in Kildonan in Sutherland. This castle was held for them by the MacRaes, who became known as 'MacKenzie's shirt of mail'. In 1539, when the MacDonalds recognised Donald, Chief of Sleat in Skye, as Lord of the Isles, and attempted to revive the forfeited lordship in his name, they invested Eilean Donan. But Duncan MacRae shot the Chief of Sleat with an arrow from the castle battlements, and he perished of the wound. Some years later Duncan MacRae, Chamberlain of Eilean Donan, was granted the estate of Inverinate. Meanwhile a MacKenzie became the first Lord of Parliament from the ranks of the Gaelic chiefs, and his clan extended their powers into the MacLeod lands of Lewis. From these new properties the MacKenzie chiefs derived their new title of Earls of Seaforth, while the MacRaes enjoyed the offices of Chamberlain of Kintail and of Constable of Eilean Donan Castle, together with the hatred of the MacLeods whom they had helped to dispossess.

After the Reformation the MacRaes added to their warlike reputation in the fields of religion and literature. The Rev. Farquhar MacRae of Inverinate (1580–1662) combined his office as Chamberlain at Eilean Donan with a ministry in Kintail that lasted for over forty years. One of his sons was the Rev. John MacRae (1614–1673) of Dingwall, while his grandson Duncan MacRae of Inverinate was the compiler of the precious Gaelic anthology known as the Fernaig Manuscript. Duncan was born in about 1640 and educated at Edinburgh University, and like his brother John he became a composer of Gaelic poetry. He married one of the daughters and co-heiresses of John MacLeod of the island of Raasay, but the well-merited hatred of the MacLeods for a MacRae deprived him of this inheritance. His wife was a party to the transaction which passed Raasay to a MacLeod cousin. Nevertheless, Duncan was known as *Donnchadh nam Piòs*, from the magnificence of his silver table service.

1688 was the year in which his wife was served co-heiress of Raasay, and it is the date on the first page of the Fernaig Manuscript. It is also the date of the Calvinist Revolution which placed William of Orange on the throne, and led to the persecution of Episcopalians. The most notorious victims were the Episcopalian MacDonalds of Glencoe; the most regrettable, that ornament of Gaelic civilisation, John Beaton. But Duncan MacRae of Inverinate was another devout Episcopalian, and an example of the cultured aristocracy of the Highlands which, during the next century, was to be destroyed.

It was in 1774, while this process was at its meridian, that John MacRae emigrated from Kintail to America just in time to fight on the wrong side in the War of Independence, and to die during his imprisonment. But before he did so, he composed the Gaelic songs in America which were carried back across the Atlantic and preserved by oral tradition in Kintail. Among them is one of the most beautiful of Scotland's lullabies, and the poetry tells of nostalgia for the past, the perils of the present, and the hope for a new generation in the future. These songs of *Iain Mac Mhurchaidh*, as he is known, have been preserved by the great singer J. C. M. Campbell, whose mother was a MacRae, and who grew up near to Eilean Donan in Kintail.

Malcolm

Maol is Gaelic for shaven-head, and thus a term for a monk. As a prefix, in personal names it acquired the meaning of a devotee of a man of God, like that other term for a youth or servant, *Gille*. The first syllables of Malcolm (Servant of Colm) and Gillanders (Servant of Andrew) are virtually interchangeable although the original meaning of each is different. The connection between Malcolm and MacCallum is less close, although these are sometimes shown as alternative names for the same clan. There is an essential difference between a Devotee of Callum (or Colm) and a Son of Callum.

Neither is there historical evidence that the MacCallum country of Lorne in Argyll was filled with people who used the two names indiscriminately. It is to be expected that such an ancient Gaelic

Malcolm

name as Colm should be found in the areas of original Gaelic settlement. As early as the 14th century the Malcolm form of it appears in parts of Dunbartonshire and Stirlingshire. But it was not until late in the 18th century that the Chief of the MacCallums, Alexander of Poltalloch, took the strange step of altering his name to Malcolm as though the two were indeed interchangeable. His successor, Sir Ian Malcolm of Poltalloch, added a further eccentricity by adjudicating the correct sett of the MacCallum tartan while continuing to use a name which cannot upon any evidence be said to belong to that clan, and which in addition possesses a different tartan.

Among the original Malcolms who moved south to settle in Dumfries-shire, the most distinguished was General Sir John Malcolm, whose hill-top memorial dominates the border where the road crosses it between Carlisle and Langholm. Malcolm was one of the men of the borders who went to India to serve, like Gilbert Elliot of Minto and John Leyden, when so many others went to exploit. He was British Resident at the court of Mysore in 1808 when Leyden, the poet from Teviotdale, came to visit the soldier from Eskdale, and these two proconsuls in a distant land exchanged complimentary verses. In 1800 Malcolm went to Persia, the first representative of a British government since the reign of Charles II, and subsequently published his invaluable *History of Persia*.

The present Chief is Robin Malcolm of Poltalloch (b. 1934).

Matheson

This name derives from the Gaelic *Mac Mhathain*, and the clan descends traditionally from a 12th-century Gilleoin, reputed to have been a scion of the ancient royal house of Lorne. They held their lands of the mediaeval earls of Ross, and *Cormac Mac Mhathain*, later designated the 2nd Matheson Chief, fought under his earl in the final conflict against the Norsemen which culminated in the defeat of Haakon IV of Norway at Largs in 1263. The Matheson territories in Wester Ross lay close to the straits through which he sailed to that encounter, and which are called to this day Kyleakin *(Caol Haakoin —* the Straits of Haakon). The Saga of Haakon makes grisly mention of the devastations of Cormac in the Hebridean islands that were still under Norse control.

Once the rule of the western isles had come under the Lordship of the MacDonalds, the Mathesons became their supporters, particularly when the earldom of Ross was added to their principality. Mathesons fought for Donald of the Isles at Harlaw in 1411, where Alasdair their Chief was made a prisoner. From now on the fortunes of the Lordship waned, and with them those of the Mathesons who remained loyal to it. Two other clans were expanding to fill the power vacuum, the MacLeods of Lewis in the islands to the west, and the MacKenzies of the mainland to the east. The Mathesons found themselves squeezed between their more powerful neighbours. One of them did succeed in obtaining a footing in the organisations of church and state which sometimes secured protection in the dark corners of the kingdom. Dougal *mac Ruadhri* Matheson was prior of Beauly on the borders of Ross between 1498 and 1514: and he sat in Parliament in 1504 when Ross was erected into a separate sheriffdom. But more characteristically, the Chief *Iain Dubh* died in defence of Eilean Donan Castle in Wester Ross in 1539. Formerly the Mathesons had been allies of the Mac-Donalds, constantly harried by the MacKenzies despite a claim of kinship between them. On this occasion they were supporting the MacKenzies against the MacDonalds of Sleat.

Branches of the Mathesons spread to the Hebrides and to the north of Scotland, and it was among these that the clan produced a Gaelic poet of particular interest in the 18th century. Donald Matheson (1719–1782) farmed in Kildonan, a strath lying within the Gordon earldom of Sutherland, where he was respected as a religious poet of the new Calvinist dispensation in those parts. In 1766 the earldom passed to a baby girl who was brought up in Edinburgh while her vast estates were administered by her lawyers and agents. In 1773 an emigrant called Hugh Matheson, almost certainly a kinsman of the bard, described the tyranny which these men exercised. 'The price of cattle has been of late so low, and that of bread so high, that the factor who was also a drover would give no more than a boll of meal for a cow, and obliged the tenants to give him their cattle at his own price.' From the extortion of these underlings on the make, the precursors of the notorious Patrick Sellar, Donald Matheson pointed the way of escape to a new promised land – Carolina.

I am seeing the shadow
Of things that occurred long ago
When the children of Israel
Were in distress in Egypt.
He took them with a strong hand
Away from Pharaoh himself,
When Pharaoh hastened after them.
The landlords are enslaving
People at this time,
Oppressing and evicting them
To the land that will bring prosperity to our children.
Oh praise be forever
To Him of highest glory,
Who opened a way out there
And prepared sustenance for them.

Those who did not follow Donald Matheson's advice to emulate the children of Israel had the thatched roofs burnt over their heads in the Kildonan clearances a generation after his death. And it was probably from the Sutherland evictions that Sir James Matheson went forth to found his great commercial empire in the Far East, and returned to buy much of the island of Lewis, with its former castle of the MacLeods at Stornoway. The woodland of imported trees that he planted there is not the least remarkable of his monuments.

Maxwell

Maccus son of Undweyn witnessed an inquisition of David I, and also a charter to Melrose of 1153. It appears to have been he who gave his name to Maccuswell, a pool of the Tweed near Kelso bridge, and also to Maccustoun. *Wael* is old English for a pool, but there is disagreement as to whether Maccus was of English or Norwegian descent. His eldest son was Herbert of Maccuswell, and some time before 1159 he bestowed its church upon Kelso Abbey. His son, Sir John, was royal Chamberlain in about 1231—3 and it is said to have been he who acquired Caerlaverock Castle in Nithsdale. He died in 1241 and was buried in Melrose, to be succeeded by his brother Aymer as Chamberlain before he became Justiciar of Galloway in 1264. Aymer's son, Sir Herbert of Maxwell, was one of the magnates who recognised Margaret of Norway as Queen of Scots after the death of Alexander III in 1286, and John Balliol after her death. His grandson, Sir Eustace, was holding Caerlaverock for Edward I in 1312, but he dismantled its fortifications in the interests of Robert Bruce, and was one of those who signed the Declaration of Arbroath in 1320, informing the Pope that his country would have no other king but Robert. Later he supported the king *de jure*, Edward Balliol, but returned to his allegiance to the Bruces. After his death in 1342 his brother and heir, Sir John, accompanied Bruce's son David II to the field of Neville's Cross, where he was captured and sent prisoner to the Tower of London. Here he probably died.

His successor, Herbert Maxwell, was knighted when James I returned from his long captivity in England in 1424, and became a Lord of Parliament in the reign of James II. The Maxwells were appointed Wardens of the Marches, and John, 4th Lord Maxwell was imprisoned by James IV for lawlessness on the Border, until he 'paid a great composition for himself and all those who were with him'. But he died with his King at Flodden in 1513. The 5th Lord was nominated Regent while James V was away in France in 1536 and 1537 choosing a wife, and as Great Admiral of Scotland he escorted Scotland's greatest Queen, Mary of Lorraine, to his country in 1538. His eventful life included capture at Solway Moss in 1542, when he was released on promising to further the designs of Henry VIII of England. But evidently he gave the English king little satisfaction, for he was kidnapped and taken back to London. This time he was freed only after promising to surrender Caerlaverock Castle to the English. He died in 1546, shortly before England's dreadful king.

The 8th Lord was created Earl of Morton after the execution of the Douglas Earl in 1581, and it was to compensate his family after this title had been restored to the Douglases that Robert Maxwell was created Earl of Nithsdale in the next century. The 5th Earl was sentenced to death in Westminster Hall for his part in the 1715 rebellion, and was rescued by his devoted wife on the eve of his execution. She rushed to London and went repeatedly in and out of his prison with her attendants, until the guards were thoroughly confused. Finally Nithsdale left, disguised as one of the women, while his wife remained behind. Later, she departed with loud farewells to an empty room. The pair lived in poverty at the Chevalier's court in Rome until the Earl's death in 1744.

The second son of the 1st Lord Maxwell was father of Edward, who received a charter to the barony of Monreith in 1482. His descendant William was created a baronet in 1681, and was the ancestor of Sir Herbert Maxwell (1845–1937) the politician and historian. Sir Herbert's youngest son was Gavin Maxwell (1914–1969) the student of animals and primitive peoples, and author of books of outstanding English prose and universal popularity.

Menzies

Hunting Menzies

This name was brought from Mesnières in Normandy to England, where it was transformed into Manners, the surname of the dukes of Rutland. During the more gradual process of Normanisation which took place in Scotland under the descendants of Malcolm Canmore and Queen Margaret, a branch of this family moved into Lothian, and from thence into the Highlands. This was achieved by royal patronage after Sir Robert de Meyneris had risen at the court of Alexander II until he became by 1249 Chamberlain of Scotland. So it came about that the earliest surviving charter of the ancient Highland family of Moncreiffe was not a grant of lands to this first representative of an Anglo-Norman family in Scottish records, but the other way round. The lands concerned were those of Culdares in Glenlyon, now spelt Culdair: and so by the mid-13th century the Menzies family became established within the earldom of Atholl. In 1296 Sir Alexander Menzies, son of Sir Robert the Chamberlain, was granted Aberfeldybeg in Strath Tay, where so many of his name remain to this day. At the same time he was granted the property of Weem, although it was not until nearly two centuries later that his descendant built Weem Castle which the Clan Menzies Society is now restoring.

The Chamberlain's grandson carried his family's spectacular success to even greater heights when he supported Robert Bruce who rewarded the Chamberlain's grandson, also named Sir Robert Menzies, with the MacNab lordship. By the time of King Robert

Black and White Menzies

Bruce's death the vast Menzies possessions extended west from Aberfeldy almost as far as Loch Lomond.

They had reached their limit, although in 1423 a David Menzies became Governor of Orkney and Shetland when these islands still belonged to the crown of Norway. In 1510 Sir Robert Menzies, senior descendant of the Chamberlain, received a charter from James IV which erected his properties into the barony of Menzies. The newly-built castle of Weem was at the same time renamed Castle Menzies. The Chief of what was by now a Gaelic-speaking clan became known as *Am Mèinnearach,* meaning The Menzies. In 1665 his descendant Sir Alexander Menzies of Menzies was created a baronet, and this title survived until the death without heirs of the 8th baronet in 1910.

A kinsman of the first baronet, named Colonel James Menzies, held the ancient estate of Culdares in Glenlyon, and it was here that a member of his house introduced the larch from the Tyrol in 1737, which now flourishes throughout the Highlands. The Culdares branch is also extinct in the male line, and *Am Mèinnearach* descends today from its heiress. Another extinct branch which has left a most distinctive memorial to Scotland is that of Pitfoddels, which was established in the 14th century. It was the last Menzies of Pitfoddels who founded in the valley of the Dee the Catholic College of Blairs, which trains candidates for the priesthood.

Moncreiffe

Around Perth lies the centre of the old Pictish kingdom, the crowning place and moot hill of Scone, the site of the royal palace of Forteviot, the Celtic religious centre of Abernethy, later occupied by Augustinian monks. The fertile valleys in which these places lie are overlooked by a hill called *Monadh Craoibhe,* Gaelic for Tree Hill. If the Pictish fort on its summit is older than Forteviot, if the tree was the Druids' sacred bough, then the name of Moncreiffe indeed overlooks those of Abernethy and Scone. Since the introduction of heraldry the Moncreiffes have always borne the red lion rampant of the Scoto-Pictish kings in their arms, and their badge is a wreath of oak leaves and acorns. Sir Iain Moncreiffe of that Ilk, the distinguished Highland historian and genealogist, has accordingly ordained these as the colours of the Moncreiffe tartan, here reproduced for the first time. Sir Iain conjectures that his line descends through a female stem from the Celtic royal dynasty.

As in the case of several names of equal antiquity, there is a long gap in time before it appears in the records of the new establishment. But when Sir Mathew of Moncreiffe was brother-in-law of one of the Regents of Scotland he obtained a charter of confirmation from the Crown in 1248 for his lands of Moncreiffe, and another charter for his Highland lands near Loch Tay from Sir Robert de Meyneris, who became Chamberlain of Scotland and founder of the Highland clan of Menzies. The first cadet branch was founded soon afterwards.

In 1312 Sir John Moncreiffe of that Ilk bestowed Easter Moncreiffe upon his younger son Mathew. A tower house was built here, but it has crumbled into ruin, while the historian who descends from this branch lives in the house that was built nearby in 1599 to replace it.

Like the Brodies of Brodie, the Moncreiffes have remained in possession of their patrimony for an extraordinary length of time. In both cases this is partly to be explained by the fact that they did not often play the fullest part in Scotland's history that their position might have given them the opportunity to do. Not for them the kaleidoscopic fortunes of the Boyds or the Douglases. But a laird of Moncreiffe was Chamberlain to the young King James III in 1464, while both Sir John of that Ilk and John of Easter Moncreiffe were killed in 1513 with James IV at Flodden. A Moncreiffe took part in the murder of Rizzio in 1566. In 1592 Easter Moncreiffe was erected into a free barony.

The family was raised to the baronetage in 1626. But Sir John Moncreiff the 2nd baronet being childless, he sold the barony of Moncreiffe to his kinsman Thomas, who was himself created a baronet in 1685. It was Sir Thomas who engaged Sir William Bruce, the outstanding architect in the classical style, to design the new house of Moncreiffe which replaced the old castle. This house, built by the architect of Holyroodhouse, Kinross and Hopetoun, was burned down in 1957 in a fire which killed the 23rd laird and 10th baronet. He has been succeeded by Sir Iain Moncreiffe, Albany Herald, as Chief of the name, who lives at Easter Moncreiffe. But his son Merlin having succeeded his mother as 24th Earl of Erroll, his younger son Peregrine is heir to the chiefship, though not to the baronetcy.

Meanwhile the descendants of the line of the older baronetcy have preserved the spelling Moncreiff. Of these, Sir James the 11th baronet was appointed Lord Justice Clerk in 1869 and created Lord Moncreiff. The same family produced two other judges as well as the present Episcopal bishop of Glasgow. The 5th Lord Moncreiff lives still in the ancestral castle of Tulliebole in Kinross.

A third spelling distinguishes the cadet branch which descends from a younger son of the 10th laird of Moncreiffe. It includes the Moncrieffs of Brandiran and of Kinmonth, as well as the Scott Moncrieefs.

Abroad, Moncreiffes encountered hazards which they generally avoided at home. One of them took part in the conspiracy of 1574 to restore the deposed King Eric XIV of Sweden, and perished in the attempt. Three branches were ennobled in France but one ended in a distinguished scholar, another on the field of battle, while the Marquis de Moncrif was executed during the French Revolution.

Montgomery

It is a curiosity of our history that the only county name to be transported from Normandy belonged originally to a castle in the parish of
Lisieux, and became planted in Wales. The first person on record as
having brought it to Scotland was Robert of Montgomery, who
obtained a grant to lands in Renfrewshire and witnessed charters
between 1165 and 1177. It was his descendant who captured Harry
Hotspur at the battle of Otterburn in 1338, after Douglas had been
killed and buried by the braken bush. So the ballad tells:

> The Percy and Montgomery met,
> That either of other were fain;
> They swapped swords, and they twa swat,
> And aye the blood ran down between.

'Now yield thee, yield thee, Percy,' he said,
'Or else I vow I'll lay thee low.'
'To whom must I yield,' quoth Earl Percy,
'Now that I see it must be so?'

Hotspur had to build the castle of Polnoon as his ransom; and by marrying the heiress of Sir Hugh Eglinton, John Montgomery also acquired the baronies of Eglinton and Ardrossan. Their grandson Alexander was created 1st Lord Montgomerie in 1449, and became a member of the King's Council and ambassador to England.

Hugh the 3rd Lord was amongst those who fought against James III at Sauchieburn in 1488, where the King lost his life. He received the island of Arran with the custody of Brodick Castle, and in 1508 was created 1st Earl of Eglinton. The 3rd Earl remained a devout Catholic at the Reformation and was among those who fought for Queen Mary in her final defeat at Langside. He was declared guilty of treason by Parliament and warded in Doune Castle. As soon as he was released he attempted to secure toleration for Catholics in those harsh days of Calvinism triumphant. But the tables were turned when the 3rd Earl's daughter Margaret married Robert Seton, 1st Earl of Winton, and their son Alexander succeeded as 6th Earl of Eglinton. For he was a staunch Presbyterian, who fought with the Covenanters in the wars of Charles I. He also supported Charles II as a Covenanted King, and in 1659 he was imprisoned by General Monk after the death of Cromwell, lest he should take up arms again in the royalist cause. He must have laughed when, in the following year, Monk himself marched to London with his Coldstream Guards and placed Charles II on the throne there.

Alexander Montgomerie, the court poet of the reign of James VI, was a second son of Hugh of Hessilhead Castle in Ayrshire, a kinsman of the Eglintons. By 1577 he was in the suite of the Regent Morton, and James VI gave him a pension. But somehow he fell into disgrace, and left Scotland in 1586. He was deprived of his pension, and imprisoned on the Continent.

His allegorical poem 'The Cherrie and the Slae' appeared in 1597, while his flyting in the traditional manner with Sir Patrick Hume of Polwarth was published in 1621, some ten years after his death, as *Flyting betwixt Montgomerie and Polwart*. The famous song, 'Declare, ye banks of Helicon', is now considered a rather doubtful attribution to Alexander Montgomerie.

Archibald, 18th Earl of Eglinton (b. 1939) is the Chief of the Montgomerys and lives at Skelmorlie castle in Ayrshire.

More

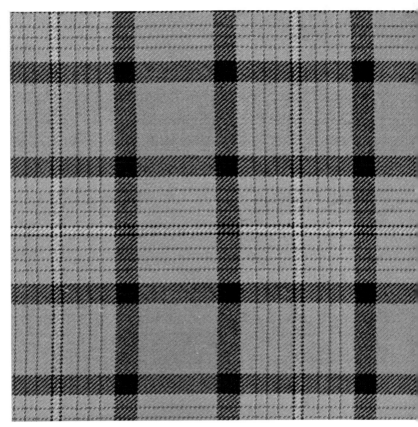

Muir

This is a somewhat puzzling example of a name which appears to have two quite different alternative meanings. The English one would indicate residence beside a moor or heath, while the Gaelic one is a descriptive suffix following a personal name. When Thomas de la More acted as executor to the will of Devorguilla, mother of King John Balliol, in 1291, it might appear that his name contains the English territorial meaning. But Norman bowdlerisation is at least as probable in this case; and this shows very clearly in another example of 1296. When Donald, son of Michael More in the wholly Gaelic province of the Lennox, rendered homage, his name was written Dovenal le fiz Michel More de Levenaghes. Here the name has been left without the insertion of *de* or *de la*, in its proper role as an adjective, which follows the noun in Gaelic. *Mór* simply means Big; and may be compared with *Òg* (Young) and *Beag* (Small) which have provided the Scottish surnames Oag and Begg.

The commonest descriptive title given to a man, in the oldest surviving tongue of the country, is naturally one of the most widely dispersed that one is likely to find. In the case of families connected with the immigrant Anglo-Norman aristocracy, it is natural to find the prestigious *de*, with its suggestion of a property origin. Yet it could be a mere slip of a Norman pen that has preserved the names of de la More jurors at Conyngham in 1296, while the knight who witnessed charters of King Robert Bruce was designated simply Adam More. Robertus More was a burgess of Aberdeen in 1317, and in the following century the name is found in countries in which the Norse tongue was still spoken—Orkney and Shetland.

In 1347 Elizabeth, daughter of Sir Adam Mure of Rowallan, married King Robert II. The prosperity of the Mures of Rowallan survived that of the royal Stewarts, only to die out in the male line in 1700. A variant of their spelling of the name was borne by the poet Edwin Muir (1887–1959), who belonged to the little island of Wyre in Orkney: and he shared this spelling with the two distinguished brothers, John Muir the Sanskrit scholar and Sir William Muir the biographer of Mohammed. General Sir John Moore gave immortality to a spelling more common in Ireland, by his heroic retreat to Corunna during the Napoleonic wars.

It has been suggested that such variants are peculiar to particular localities: that Moar belongs to the northern isles, and Moir to Aberdeen. The study of a single pedigree proves that even if this happens to be the case today, it is without historical significance. In the parish of Drymen, a Gaelic area in which Buchanan chiefs had been parish clerks, the register used the so-called Aberdonian spelling when John Moir married Margaret Mclew in 1724. Their son, born in 1730, was likewise called John Moir, but his son William, born in 1758, was given the so-called Shetland spelling Moar in the record of his marriage in 1786. His wife had the local Gaelic name of Elizabeth Buchanan, and he followed the immemorial occupation of farming. The Drymen register called him William More when their son was born. In the manner characteristic of this period their son John More (1788–1868) entered the service of religion, and became the Anti-Burgher minister at Cairneyhill in Fife. When he married Jean, daughter of the theological Professor George Paxton, the Edinburgh register reverted to the 'Aberdonian' spelling, Moir. Thereafter, as the minister's descendants moved into new professions, ever farther from a Gaelic background that was in any case evaporating behind them, their name ceased to deviate from the More spelling. His son James, born in 1834, became a doctor of medicine in Wigtownshire. His grandson John, born in 1862, followed the same profession in England. His great-grandson, Lieut. Colonel James More C.I.E., D.S.O. (1883–1959) was Political Agent in Kuwait, and the Colonel's son John More, born in 1931, is the distinguished Scottish artist.

Morrison

Morrison represents three quite different names that have all come to be spelt in the same way. The Morrisons of the central Highlands are originally Sons of Maurice, and have no connection with the Hebridean clan. Even in the islands there are two distinct derivations. One branch of the Morrisons descends from the O'Muircheasain bards who come from northern Ireland to Harris in the outer Hebrides, while the true clan patronymic is *Mac Ghille Mhuire* – Son of the Virgin Mary's Servant. It belongs to the north of the island of Lewis, that area of intensive settlement by the Norsemen a thousand years ago. Subsequently its people reverted entirely to the Gaelic language and culture.

The Morrisons were heirs to this double heritage. A legend tells that they were first shipwrecked on these coasts; so that their clan badge is driftwood. Clan genealogies trace their descent from Somerled, the King of the Isles who died in 1164 and probably descended himself from the Celto-Norse kings of Ireland. According to this tradition, Ceadhain Mac Mhuirich of the tree of Somerled changed his name when he married the Morrison heiress in Lewis in the 14th century. Tradition and legend may err in their details, but there can be no doubt that historical fact is embedded in them.

The Morrison chiefs once held the hereditary Celtic office of judge in Lewis. Its Gaelic name was *Britheamh,* which became anglicised to Brieve; though both terms derive from the Latin of the Christian Church. Probably the arbitrations of the Morrison brieves were based partly on the Celtic Brehon laws, of which many ancient codes survive, partly on the rules of the Norse deemsters. This alternative title is based on the Germanic word Doom, meaning Judgment. Because the Scandinavians remained illiterate for so many centuries longer than the Celtic peoples, it is natural that the Gaelic title should suggest an adjudication in writing, the Norse one a spoken judgment.

The first historical reference to a brieve using the surname of Morrison and described as holding the hereditary office of deemster occurs in the 16th century, when the assault upon the whole structure of Gaelic society in Scotland by the central government was entering a critical phase. His name was Uisdean, generally barbarised to Hucheon. In 1601, when the brieve Iain *Dubh* Morrison was killed, the jurisdiction of his family had probably come to an end. In 1605 the head of the Gordons accepted the invitation of James VI, now resident in London, to embark on a campaign of conquest and extermination in the Hebrides. 'His Lordship offers to take in hand the service of settling the North Isles . . . and to put an end to that service by extirpation of the barbarous people of the Isles within a year.' Such was the time of troubles in which the Morrisons ceased to act as brieves in Lewis. It was said that their authority had once extended from the Butt of Lewis as far east as Caithness. Certainly large numbers of the clan settled on the mainland beyond the north Minch, where their neighbours were the Mackays. It is perhaps on account of this that the Morrison tartan is that of the Mackays, with a red line added to it. But this is not in itself evidence of long association. The Mackay sett is of unknown antiquity, while the Morrison one is comparatively recent in its present form.

One of the most memorable Morrisons of Lewis is Ruaraidh (or Roderick in its anglicised form), who was born there in about 1660. He is remembered as *An Clarsair Dall*, the Blind Harper, and in fact he holds the highest place in the traditions of his country of anyone who played the clarsach. Unfortunately it is only his poetry which survives, and it cannot be said for certain to what extent the airs associated with it are of his own composition. The most famous is his *'Oran Mór Mhic Leoid',* surely one of the most beautiful of Gaelic laments. In it he not only mourned the death of his patron at Dunvegan, but also the passing of the old Celtic culture there under his anglicised successor. The blind harper lived to see the Stewarts deposed, but died in about 1712, before the Hanoverian succession.

The present Chief of clan Morrison, Iain Morrison (b. 1938), is a physician like his father before him.

Munro

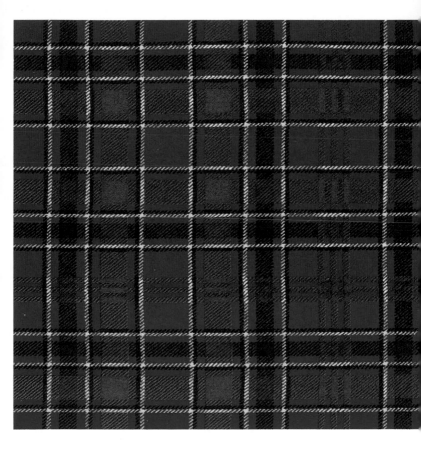

The ancient territory of this clan slopes from the high massif of Ben Wyvis, down to the shores of the Cromarty Firth and the fertile farmlands of Easter Ross. The area is rich in Pictish remains. Had the records of the Lordship of the Isles survived, the relationship of the Munros to the Gaelic west might be easier to define. Suffice to say that the origin of their name is a matter of speculation, that they held their lands of the earls of Ross until it was forfeited from the Lord of the Isles, and that afterwards they held directly from the crown.

It is a piece of 15th-century Munro pipe-music that might be called the earliest embryo of pibroch. Its name is *'Blar bealach nam brog'*, which means The Field of Shoe-pass—in the sense of a battlefield. But unlike the MacCrimmons to the west of them or the Mackays to their north, the Munros made little further contribution to this art.

It was as early Gaelic promotors of the Reformation in the extreme north of Scotland that they made their most profound mark in those days. Alexander Munro of Kiltearn (c.1605–1653) conducted his ministry in the most distant corner of Scotland, at Durness beside Cape Wrath, and his signature appears on documents as a justice of the peace throughout the decade of the 1630s. But above all, he was the first man to remedy the fact that there was still no Bible in the vernacular, although the Catholic Church had been abolished by Act of Parliament as long before as 1560. Alexander committed the Bible story to Gaelic poetry for the benefit of his parishioners.

> The wonder of the works of the Creator
> Made by Him at the beginning of time;
> This is an epistle each man may read,
> The might of God, written in the universe.

Nor was the Rev. Alexander alone. Two other Munro ministers were enrolled as justices of the peace in the sheriffdom of Sutherland and two in Caithness at the same time as himself. And in 1637 there was published in London a work no less unique than the Gaelic compositions of Alexander Munro.

The Chief of the Mackay country in which Alexander served sailed with a regiment in 1626 to fight in the Thirty Years' War. With the Mackay regiment sailed Robert Munro of Foulis, the clan Chief, and also a cadet of the Obsdale branch who spelt his name Robert Monro, and who rose to the rank of General. It was he who published his account of the fortunes of the Mackay regiment in 1637; a record which has no parallel in Europe in the annals of that terrible war. 'If you ask why I wrote these observations,' Monro explained, 'it was because I loved my comrades; if why I published them, know it was for my friends.'

There was yet another Robert Munro, a descendant through younger sons of the 10th Chief of Foulis, who was Commissary of Caithness and who died in 1633. Four of his sons fought against Cromwell at Worcester in 1651, of whom William and three other Munros were transported to New England after the royalist defeat. The descendants of the 10th Chief multiplied fast in the land to which their ancestor had been sent a prisoner, and it fell to one of them to make a symbolic gesture of retribution. Ebenezer Munro (1752–1825) was a member of the body of Lexington minute-men who turned out on 19 April 1775, and he claimed to have fired the first shot in the American War of Independence that day. But the Munros had long demonstrated in their country of origin that the pen is mightier than the sword, and they were soon to do so in the country of their adoption. James Munro was President of the United States between 1817 and 1825, and it was by a stroke of the pen that he warned European nations not to molest his country's shores.

Captain Patrick Munro of Foulis (b. 1912) is the clan Chief.

Murray

Murray of Tullibardine

The usurpation of Malcolm Canmore's sons by his second wife, the English Queen Margaret, was for long resisted in the north of Scotland. Her youngest son David I gave feudal powers in the conquered province of Moray to Freskin, son of Ollec, whose grandson assumed the name of William of Moray. The late Lord Lyon, Sir Thomas Innes, suggests that Freskin was probably Pictish: but Sir Iain Moncreiffe inclines with more likelihood to the possibility that he was Flemish. While the senior line of Freskin became Earls of Sutherland, another had become Lords of Bothwell in Lanarkshire by marriage with an Oliphant heiress by 1253. Sir Walter the 1st Lord was a Regent of Scotland in 1255, and later in that century the magnificent stone castle of Bothwell was constructed. Edward I of England kept it strongly garrisoned in 1296 when he was seeking the submission of

Scotland. Sir Andrew, its 3rd Lord, was kept a prisoner in the Tower of London where he died, leaving his son Andrew Murray the head of his name in Scotland. Here Murray captured the castles of Urquhart and Aberdeen, and gradually extended his conquests south until he joined forces with William Wallace. In 1297 the two resistance leaders defeated the English army at Stirling Bridge, and were able to invite a foreign power to resume trade with their country, 'because the kingdom of Scotland, thanks be to God, has been recovered by war from the power of the English'. But Murray had been wounded in the battle and he died soon afterwards, leaving Wallace without his ablest colleague.

Andrew Murray's son of the same name succeeded as the 4th Lord of Bothwell and was Regent of Scotland when he was killed in battle against the English at Halidon Hill in 1333. By 1360 the lordship and its great castle had been carried by marriage to the mighty house of Douglas. The Murrays had multiplied by this time throughout Scotland, from Sutherland to the Borders, and they had already acquired other properties by the same process that had deprived them of Bothwell. In about 1320 Sir John Moray (his branch still prefer this spelling) obtained Abercairney with the hand of a daughter of the 7th Earl of Strathearn. Another Strathearn marriage brought Sir William Murray the property of Tullibardine, which was erected into a barony in 1443. A century later this branch was judged by the Lord Lyon to be the Chiefs of the clan, which was accepted by cadet houses of Murray all over Scotland, in the bands of association which they subscribed in 1586 and 1598. Sir John Murray, whose chiefship was recognised in this way was created Earl of Tullibardine in 1606, and the 2nd Earl married the Stewart heiress of Atholl. So the Murray chiefs became in the fullness of time dukes of Atholl.

Among the younger sons of the house of Tullibardine who established separate dynasties, Sir William Murray, who died in about 1511, is especially noteworthy. His descendants played a part in the mysterious Gowrie conspiracy of 1600 when James VI (as he alleged) was rescued from an attempt to murder or kidnap him. Sir David Murray was rewarded with the abbey properties of Scone which had belonged to the earls of Gowrie since the Reformation. The family rose to the rank of Viscount Stormont, and then Earl of Mansfield, and built Scone Palace, in which they live still. Another younger son of Tullibardine was Patrick Murray who died in 1476 and founded the house of Ochtertyre. It was raised to a baronetcy in 1673, and the 2nd baronet joined the 1715 rebellion. But the 3rd baronet held a government commission by the time of the Forty-Five, and although he suffered capture at the hands of the Jacobites at Prestonpans, it proved to be the lesser of two evils. Sir William Murray, the 11th baronet, still lives at Ochtertyre today.

Murray of Atholl

When *Am Moireach Mór* married the Atholl heiress, his family acquired vast territories and his clan became a power to rival Clan Campbell itself. They became Earls of Atholl in 1629 and Marquesses in 1676. This was the period during which the house of Argyll was in eclipse, and it remained to be seen whether the tables would be turned when Argyll returned in triumph at the Revolution of 1688. Queen Anne made Atholl a duke in 1703, and he was able to call out 4000 armed Athollmen in an attempt to oppose the Union of 1707. Fortunately for his house he did not support the Jacobite rebellions.

However, his eldest son, the Marquess of Tullibardine, led a contingent of Murrays to the standard of Prince Charles, and his younger son, Lord George Murray, became the leading general of the Jacobite army. Lord George had already served under his brother at Sheriffmuir in 1715, and after escaping abroad he returned to take part in the revolt of 1719, when he was wounded in Glenshiel. Once again he survived, to serve with distinction under the King of Sardinia until he was pardoned and returned home. It was observed by Johnstone after the Forty-Five that 'had Prince Charles slept during the whole of the expedition, and allowed Lord George Murray to act for him according to his own judgment, he would have found the crown of Great Britain on his head when he awoke.' On the other hand it was Murray who insisted upon the retreat from Derby, against the wishes of Prince Charles, and this decision was fatal. In such an enterprise there could be no retreat, and whatever the military odds, it is possible that the Hanoverian King might have fled while Prince Charles entered his capital in triumph. During the retreat Murray actually beseiged his own father's castle in Blair Atholl, which was occupied by Hanoverian troops. After Culloden he escaped to the Continent, and was received with honour and gratitude by the Pretender in Rome. But the Bonnie Prince, who could exercise so much charm over those whom he wished to serve him, never forgave Murray, and treated him after his defeat in a most scurrilous manner.

Another who played an outstanding part in the Jacobite tragedy was John Murray of Broughton. He descended from a second son of Murray of Philiphaugh in the time of James IV, whose great-grandson became proprietor of Broughton and was knighted by Charles I. John was born in the year of the 1715 and went to France in the year before the Forty-Five, when he tried to dissuade Prince Charles from his attempt. But when it was determined, he landed with Charles in Moidart in the office of his secretary. After Culloden he buried great sums of gold beside Loch Arkaig, and was soon afterwards captured and taken to London, ill and exhausted. Here he was persuaded to save his life by turning king's evidence. Although he probably contributed to the conviction of none save the scoundrel Lord Lovat, he was execrated as 'Mr Evidence Murray'. He lived on in the anonymity of London, composing his valuable *Memorials* as his apologia, and there died in 1777. The story of the Murray's many-sided and dominant role in those events is incomplete without Murray of Broughton.

The present Chief is George Iain Murray, 10th Duke of Atholl (b. 1931).

Napier

This name was given to the court official in charge of the royal napery or linen. The earliest reference to it in Scotland occurs in about 1290, when John Naper received a charter from Malcolm, Earl of Lennox. Probably it was the same Naper of the county of Dunbarton who did homage in 1296. The name became dynastic as well as functional when Alexander Napier made his fortune in the wool trade, and through his financial dealings with James I. He obtained a charter to the lands of Merchiston in 1436 and became Provost of Edinburgh in the following year. His son, Sir Alexander, was appointed a member of the household of James I's widow Joan Beaufort. After she had re-married, to Sir James Stewart, the Black Knight of Lorne, Sir Alexander was wounded while helping to rescue them, after the Livingstone faction had captured them at Stirling. James II rewarded him with Livingstone property and appointed him to the Livingstone office of Comptroller of the Household. He was one of the commissioners who negotiated the Danish marriage of James III, which brought Orkney and Shetland to the Scottish crown, and in 1472 he was in Bruges, 'taking up finance' and buying armour for the king. When he was appointed Master of the Household, he provided 'travelling gear' for the pilgrimage to Whithorn in 1473 with which the king and queen celebrated the birth of the future James IV. It is curious how the family which was to produce the greatest mathematical genius in Scottish history retained the functions proper to their name.

John the 3rd of Merchiston was killed at Sauchieburn in 1488 in the entourage of James III: his grandson was killed at Flodden in 1513, his great-grandson at Pinkie in 1547. After that, the family returned to the financial sphere in which it had gained such eminence. Sir Archibald the 7th of Merchiston (1534–1608) was made Master of the Mint at a time when it fell to him to treat with the English concerning the currency at the union of the crowns. He travelled to London for this purpose in 1604, where his financial knowledge caused astonishment. All his life he was active in the affairs of mining for the metals from which the currency was minted.

Such was the father of John Napier of Merchiston (1550–1617), the inventor of logarithms. He was also an advanced agriculturalist. He experimented with manures, and invented a hydraulic screw and revolving axle to clear coal-pits of water. He designed military weapons. He composed anti-Catholic treatises. In 1614 his treatise on logarithms, which opened a new epoch in the history of science, was published.

He had trained his son in the study of agricultural improvement. But he was the brother-in-law of Montrose and he supported him until his death in 1645, the great year of his victories. So did his son John, who became the 2nd Lord Napier and died in exile in 1658. Thereafter the family achieved phenomenal distinction as soldiers. During the Napoleonic wars there were no less than five Napiers who became generals, besides a Field Marshal and an Admiral. One of these, General Sir William Napier, was the historian of the Peninsular war, while his younger contemporary, Mark Napier, will always be remembered as the biographer of Montrose.

Nicolson

Tradition, reinforced by the Gaelic genealogy of 1450, gives one branch the Nicolsons or MacNicols an extremely ancient origin in the lands between Assynt and Durness on the north coast. Their ownership, however, passed to the MacLeods of Lewis with a MacNicol heiress. Another tradition gives a different branch an equally ancient past in the Hebrides, where MacNicol of Portree was said to have been one of the sixteen members of the Council of the Lordship of the Isles before it was abolished in 1493. Here the earliest historical references to the name begin in Skye in 1507, and the Nicolsons of Scorrybreck become established from that time as a line of chiefs.

One of the most notable of these was Donald of Scorrybreck, who became Episcopalian parson of Kilmuir after the Restoration of 1660 and continued in his office until well after the Revolution of 1688. It was not until 1696, in fact, that he retired rather than conform to the new Calvinist order. His career was paralleled by that of Thomas Nicolson, who was converted to the Catholic Church in 1682 and was already working in the Scottish mission in 1688. He was imprisoned, but then allowed to leave the country. In 1695 he was

Nicolson

appointed Scotland's first Vicar Apostolic, and although he was arrested on landing in the country, he was again released. So he was able to make the tour of 1700 which enabled him to write such a valuable account of life in the Hebrides at that time.

It was the turn of a Presbyterian when Donald MacNicol from Argyll made his precious collection of Ossianic ballads, before his appointment in 1766 as Minister of Lismore. A few years later Samuel Johnson made his Hebridean tour, and although he was correct in his judgment of MacPherson's bogus *Ossian*, he also made approbrious comments on Gaelic literature which incensed MacNicol. The result was his *Remarks on Dr Samuel Johnson's Journey to the Hebrides.* This tradition has been kept alive since by Alexander Nicolson, who was born in Skye in 1827 and compiled a collection of Gaelic proverbs which is a treasury of ancient wisdom and manners. A hundred years later another Alexander Nicolson published a *History of Skye* which integrates the traditional poetry of the island with exceptional skill.

The last chief of Scorrybreck emigrated to Australia, where the Chief of the Hebridean clan of MacNicol, Ian Nicolson (b. 1921), lives in New South Wales.

Ogilvie

Ogilvie in Angus derives from the British or Pictish word *Ocel Fa*, meaning high plain. It was in this Pictish province that the English from Northumbria were defeated in 685 at Nechtansmere by King Brude, and their advance into Scotland permanently halted. In about 937 died Dubhucan, Mormaer of Angus, and after the time of troubles which replaced the legitimate royal dynasty with Queen Margaret's usurping sons, a Dubhucan appears in the records again, this time probably bearing the new title of Earl of Angus. He was succeeded in 1144 by Gillebride, Earl of Angus, founder of the Ogilvie clan, and quite possibly the descendant of the ancient house of Angus. Gillebride's name became Normanised as Gilbert: in 1177 he settled the estate of Ogilvie on his son Gilbert.

Their descendants became hereditary sheriffs of Angus during the 14th century, and a Sheriff Ogilvie was killed at the battle of Harlaw in 1411. It was his son Sir Walter who became Lord High Treasurer, built the tower of Airlie, and married the heiress of Lintrathen. He died in 1440 and his grandson was created Lord Ogilvie of Airlie in 1491. When the 8th Lord was created Earl of Airlie in 1639, this was recognised as the line of the chiefs of Ogilvie. Of the many junior branches there was one which descended from the Treasurer's younger son Walter, and which acquired the properties of Findlater, within the sphere of influence of the Gordons of Huntly. How narrowly the Ogilvies of Findlater escaped the fate of the earls of

Sutherland at the hands of the Gordons is related in the latter's story. In 1638 James Ogilvie was created Earl of Findlater, and the earldom of Seafield was added as a reward for supporting the treaty of Union in 1707.

The castle of the Chief, 'The Bonnie Hoose o' Airlie', was destroyed in 1640 in one of the blackest crimes of the Campbells. The 1st Earl was with Charles I at York at the outset of the Civil War when Argyll used his position as a Covenanting leader to pursue his private vendetta against his absent neighbour.

> The Lady looked ower her window sae hie,
> An' O, but she grat sairly,
> To see Argyll an' a' his men
> Come to plunder the bonnie hoose o' Airlie.

The ballad is right in stating that Argyll himself was present: but in fact the Countess of Airlie was not. The atrocities are attested by the indemnity which Argyll obtained from the revolutionary Parliament for crimes including murder and torture. The 2nd Earl was captured at Montrose's defeat in 1645 at Philiphaugh and condemned to death. But he escaped from his prison on the eve of his execution, dressed in his sister's clothes, and his descendant had an equally lucky escape in the Forty-Five. The young son of the 4th Earl raised his clan in the Jacobite cause, and succeeded in escaping to France. But he was able to return under a pardon in 1783.

Oliphant

The Oliphants derive from a Norman family living in Northamptonshire at the time when they were particular friends of England's premier baron, before he became David I, King of Scots. David Holifard saved David's life at the rout of Winchester in 1141, and was rewarded by a grant of land in Scotland. By 1296, when William Olifat was among the Scottish prisoners held at Rochester, the name was presumably pronounced like that. So it is not surprising that it was sometimes changed to Oliver. In 1300 William Holifarth held lands of the abbey of Arbroath, and it was a century later that a branch of the family sprang to prominence in national affairs. Sir John Oliphant of Aberdalgie died in 1446, and his son Sir Lawrence became a peer in the Parliament of 1467, a member of the commission which concluded the treaty of Nottingham with England in 1484, ambassador to France in 1491, and Keeper of Edinburgh Castle two years later. His grandson was killed at Flodden in 1513, his great-grandson taken prisoner at Solway Moss in 1542, and ransomed.

The 4th Lord Oliphant was one of those who sat on the assize which acquitted Bothwell of the murder of Darnley. He afterwards signed the band for Bothwell's marriage with the Queen, attended the wedding, and fought for her at her final defeat at Langside in 1568. Nemesis followed. His heir took part in the Ruthven raid and was sentenced to banishment in 1584 by James VI. The ship in which he sailed was never seen again, though conflicting reports were received

Oliphant

that he had been hanged from its mast by the Dutch, and that he had been sold into Turkish slavery. The son who succeeded as 5th Lord was as quarrelsome as his father, and dissipated the entire estates of his family except for Gask, which had already passed to a cadet branch. He also tried to transmit his title to his only daughter: but in this he failed. Charles I bestowed it on his cousin Patrick, the nearest male heir. Disaster soon struck again. The 9th Lord took part in the Killiecrankie campaign after the Revolution of 1688 and was imprisoned in Perth until 1691. He joined the Jacobites again in 1715.

The house of Gask also supported the Jacobites, both in 1715 and in 1745, when the house was looted by Cumberland's troops and its documents removed. But when it was sold, friends purchased it and gave it back to its previous owners. Such was the family background of Carolina Oliphant, who was born at Gask in 1766 and became one of Scotland's outstanding poetesses. While her father's family failed to recover the peerage of Oliphant, her husband's title of Nairne was restored. So it is as Lady Nairne that 'the flower of Strathearn' is remembered today. Her humorous ballads rival those of Burns himself. 'The Ploughman' was an instant success, and so was 'Caller Herrin'' when she composed it for Nathaniel Gow, and 'The Laird o' Cockpen'. But it is as a Jacobite poet, author of 'Charlie is my Darling' and 'Will ye no come back again', that she is remembered best.

Ramsay

This is a Lothian name, first recorded when Simon of Ramsay was witness to a charter in favour of the monks of Holyrood some time before 1178. William of Ramsay witnessed a charter to the church of Coldingham in 1196, and by the following century a dynasty of this name begins to emerge. Sir Nessus of Ramsay was a frequent witness in disputes and in 1217 he put his seal to a charter of Alexander II. Nicholas, perhaps his brother, was witness to a charter in favour of the monks of Lindores. William Ramsey of Dalhousie, the first to be so designated, a member of the council of magnates of the realm in 1255, was perhaps another brother. Sir Nessus had two sons named Peter and Patrick. William of Dalhousie was succeeded by another of the same name who was among the signatories of the Ragman Roll in 1296, when the notables of Scotland swore allegiance to Edward I of England. But he became a devoted adherant of Robert Bruce and one of the parties to the Declaration of Arbroath in 1320.

Its undertaking to maintain a Bruce on the throne at all costs was honoured by Sir Alexander Ramsay of Dalhousie during the troubles of King Robert's son David II. When Black Agnes, Countess of Dunbar, was holding her stronghold against the English, it was Ramsay who finally brought her reinforcements from the sea and so raised the seige of Dunbar. In song and story it is said that he led guerilla bands on English raids from the caves of Hawthornden. But when the King appointed him Constable of the great castle of Roxburgh, Ramsay incurred the envy of Sir William Douglas, the Knight of Liddesdale. In 1342 his rival seized him and shut him up in Hermitage Castle, where Ramsay is said to have been starved to death. But his descendants multiplied and flourished until their senior representative, Sir George Ramsay, became Lord Ramsay of Dalhousie in 1618, and his son Earl of Dalhousie in 1633.

It was at this time that David Ramsay, a mercenary soldier from Fife who took part in the Thirty Years' War in Europe, became involved in one of the most mysterious intrigues of Charles I's reign. Sir Donald Mackay, 1st Lord Reay, had raised a Mackay regiment to fight in this war, and on the Continent he found what he fancied to be evidence of treason on the part of Ramsay against his sovereign. The King revived the antique procedure of a court of chivalry for the last time in our history, which in 1632 ordered trial by combat between Ramsay and Mackay. King Charles stopped it, paid for Ramsay to be sent abroad, and warned his cousin Hamilton 'not to have to do with such a pest as he is'. Hamilton nevertheless advanced him to a colonelcy: and it remains an open question whether either Hamilton or Charles himself were planning to raise an army under cover of the European war for use in Britain, using Ramsay as their agent.

The subsequent military record of the Ramsays was more creditable; indeed it has been outstanding. George, third son of the 2nd Earl, entered the Dutch service and fought for the Dutch King at Killiecrankie in 1689. He was made a lieutenant-general and Scottish Commander-in-Chief by Queen Anne in 1702. The 3rd Earl died a brigadier in Spain in 1710, the 6th and 7th rose to the rank of lieutenant-colonel, the 9th was present at Waterloo with the rank of major-general. Most outstanding of all, the 10th became Governor-General of India in 1848 at the age of thirty-four and returned in 1856 on the eve of the Mutiny, having presided over the annexation of the Punjab, Lower Burma and Oudh. When he died, leaving only daughters, the earldom passed through cadet lines which continued this military tradition, and added high naval rank as well.

Robertson

The senior branch of the kindred of Saint Columba in Scotland were the hereditary abbots of Dunkeld, of whom Duncan was killed in battle in 964. His successor Abbot Crinan married a member of the royal house, and his younger son was father of Madadh, Earl of Atholl, from whom the Robertsons descend. Earl Henry had a son, Conan of Glenerochie, and it was Duncan the 5th of Glenerochie who first gave his name to Clan *Donnchaidh*. He led his clan in the army of Bruce at Bannockburn, and their lands were erected into the barony of Struan for his grandson Robert in 1451. So the clan acquired its second surname of Robertson, though some of its members took the names MacConachie, Donachie or Duncan.

It was the first Robert of Struan who captured the murderers of

Robertson

James I in 1437. Thereafter Clan *Donnchaidh* remained loyal to the Stewarts despite the fact that the Stewart earls of Atholl stripped them of half their lands of Struan. They fought under Montrose for Charles I, and Alasdair the 17th of Struan supported Bonnie Dundee in the cause of James VII. He was a gifted poet, and was still a young man, studying for the church, when his succession to the chiefship and the Revolution of 1688 caused him to exchange the sword for the pen. He was forfeited, but pardoned after Queen Anne succeeded to the throne. When she was succeeded by the house of Hanover he took up arms again, both in 1715 and in 1745. But although the chiefs of Struan were dispossessed they lived on by Loch Rannoch until the last of their estates were sold in the present century. Langton Robertson, 26th of Struan and Chief of Clan Donnchaidh, lives at Kingston in Jamaica, but his son represents him at gatherings of the clan society.

Rose

Rose

Although the difference between Rose and Ross is a single letter in English and a mere accent in Gaelic, they are nevertheless of quite separate origins. The lordship of Ros near Caen in Normandy belonged to William the Conqueror's half-brother Odo, Bishop of Bayeux, who received the lands of Kent after the Conquest. Many young knights of Ros accompanied Bishop Odo to England, of whom three received manors in Kent from him. As these extended into other parts of England, they maintained a tight-knit family connection with the Boscos and the Bissets to whom they had been related in Normandy. This provides the over-riding assumption that the Hugh Rose who had obtained the estate of Kilravock in Scotland by 1282 descended from one of the Norman protégés of Bishop Odo, for he gained it with the hand of the heiress Mary Bosco.

Hugh of Kilravock is one of the few significant Scottish barons who does not appear in the Ragman Roll of 1296 as having submitted to Edward I of England; and his son Sir William captured Invernairn Castle for Bruce after his succession in 1306. The episode is related by Blind Harry. Hugh the 4th of Kilravock married the daughter of Sir Robert Chisholm, Constable of Urquhart Castle on Loch Ness, and received with her hand the lands of Strathnairn. Hugh the 5th lost the family charters at Elgin in 1390 when the Cathedral was burned.

But from this time onwards the records of the Roses are among the most complete in Scottish family history, preserving a fascinating

238

Hunting Rose

picture of local life as it revolved round the characteristic tower-house. Hew Rose, Minister of Nairn, first told it in the history he began writing in 1633, and in 1753 the Minister of Elgin, Lachlan Shaw, continued it. The Spalding Club published these histories in 1848 with a wealth of documents from the Kilravock charter room.

Hugh the 7th Laird built or restored the castle after his succession in 1454. This was when the feud with the Urquharts of Cromarty reached its climax, provoked by the attempt of the parents to arrange a double marriage to which all four of the intended spouses objected. In 1492 Hugh the 7th took advantage of a commission from Gordon of Huntly aimed against the MacKenzies to invade Cromarty. 600 cattle, 100 horses, 1000 sheep, 400 goats and 200 swine were lifted from that fertile province, apart from provisions. The feud ended when Alexander Urquhart's daughter Agnes married Hugh the 9th laird.

It was at this time that Campbell of Argyll used falsehood, deception, and the difficulties of the Roses to carry off the heiress of neighbouring Cawdor and so secure this inheritance. Her mother was Isobel Rose, and the child was intended for Kilravock's own grandson. This grandson inherited Kilravock in the troubled year 1544 and proved to be one of the most remarkable men in his house. Everybody trusted him, from Mary of Lorraine the Regent to his smallest tenant, as his correspondence shows. Queen Mary visited him in 1562, and her son James VI in 1598.

Ross

Like the lands beyond the Kyle of Sutherland to the north, the promontory of Easter Ross has not only given its name to a mediaeval earldom and a modern county, but also to a clan. The Kyle divides territories which preserve their Norse name of South Land from one that is called by the Gaelic name for a promontory: *Ros*. And for centuries the ancient racial enmity was continued by the clans living on either side of the firth.

The chiefship of a clan Ross originates in 1215, when *Fearchar Mac an t-Sagairt* (Farquhar the Priest's Son) assisted Alexander II against the heirs of the old Celtic dynasty that had been disinherited by the usurpation of the sons of Malcolm III and his second wife Queen Margaret. The part that Farquhar played was an exceptional one. He took the side of the Normanising King in the south, right in the heart of old Scotland, where resistance in the name of the legitimate line was strongest. Yet Farquhar was probably heir to the O'Beolains, hereditary Abbots of Applecross and descendants of the Irish King Niall of the Nine Hostages. Farquhar was now given the Norman order of knighthood and, a few years later, the earldom of Ross. In 1372 it passed to an heiress, while the chiefship became vested in the girl's uncle, Hugh Ross of Balnagown.

At Tain in Easter Ross stood the shrine of the Celtic Saint Duthac, which acquired extraordinary celebrity, until by the Middle Ages it had become a place of sanctuary. The wife of King Robert Bruce once tried in vain to find safety there, and in the 15th century James IV made annual pilgrimages to Tain. Today the shrine is only a battered ruin, a victim of the enemies of Clan Ross beyond the Kyle long before the Calvinists could lay hands on it. But two mediaeval churches in Tain, the sacred relics of Saint Duthac, and the abbey of Fearn remained for the reformers to deface and destroy. At Applecross there was a fine collection of Celtic church sculpture for them to smash to pieces. A relic of the Norsemen fared better. They had placed their law-making centre in Ross-shire, commemorated by the name Dingwall. Although Tain fought for centuries to maintain its position as the capital of Ross, Dingwall is today the county town.

The heritage of Clan Ross, Pictish, Gaelic, Norse and southern Scottish, has been diverse and rich—as might be expected in a fertile peninsula backed by the great mountains of the Celtic west, and facing the busy traffic of the Moray Firth and the North Sea. One strand of their heritage gave Scotland an outstanding composer of love-poetry in the short-lived schoolmaster of Gairloch, William Ross (1762–1790). While he was composing the Gaelic songs that are still sung throughout Scotland, his contemporary, Colonel George Ross, was placing his signature to the American Declaration of Independence, and his brother John was fighting and dying to give effect to its brave words. And it was the widow of John Ross who designed the first flag of the United States, in the form of stars and stripes.

Ruthven

The Ruthvens are said to have had a Norse origin. They take their name from the lands north of Loch Rannoch in Perthshire, those dun uplands amongst the Grampians called in Gaelic *Ruadhainn*. Here the ruins of the barracks still stand in which the garrison troops of the 18th century lived in one of the most unfriendly stations to which they could have been sent. Here the Struan chiefs of Clan Donnchaidh lived on into the 19th century, when the barracks had been converted into a residence, the surrounding glens now emptied of the people who had once been such a worry to distant governments.

By this time the Ruthven chiefs had come and gone with equal clamour. They increased their consequence early by marriage to a Cameron heiress and in 1487 Sir William of Ruthven was raised to the peerage. It was the beginning of a saga worthy of their Viking origins. Patrick, 3rd Lord Ruthven, was an unedifying ringleader of the self-styled Lords of the Congregation of Jesus Christ who deposed the Queen Regent Mary of Lorraine in 1559, and hounded her to her death. As he had treated the mother, so he treated the daughter. In 1566 he was the leader of those who burst into Mary, Queen of Scots' supper room in Holyrood Palace and murdered her servant Rizzio before her eyes. He was dressed in armour and was said to have man-handled the Queen, and to have been the assassin who

Ruthven

plunged Darnley's own dagger into Rizzio, in whose corpse it was later found. When Mary succeeded in detaching the fickle Darnley from the conspirators, Ruthven fled to England, and he died in the same year.

His son was a chip off the old block. Created Earl of Gowrie while James VI was still a youth, he headed the conspirators who seized the King in Gowrie's house in 1581, and took over the government in his name. But this time the Ruthvens had met a sovereign who was a match for them. First he escaped from their clutches and beheaded the Earl. Lastly he accused the 3rd Earl and his brother Alexander of an attempt to murder him when he rode to visit them from Falkland in 1600. Both men were killed during the alleged rescue of the King, and the name, arms and peerages of Ruthven extinguished. The secret of the Gowrie conspiracy has never been solved: James VI knew how to frame people, and the Ruthvens had a record as assassins.

After over three centuries of amendment the earldom of Gowrie has been restored to the Ruthvens. Alexander the 2nd Earl (b. 1939) is Chief of this name.

Scott

Scott belongs to the same branch of names as Inglis and Wallace (or Welsh). Uchtred *'filius Scoti'* was living in 1130 and his descendant Sir Richard 'le Scot' obtained large estates in Lanarkshire by marriage with an heiress, and lived through the wars of independence to die in 1320. There is nothing to suggest that he descended from the original Scots of Dalriada. His successor, Sir Walter Scott, received a charter to the barony of Kirkud from Robert II in 1389 and was killed at Homildon Hill in 1402. Sir Walter's son, Robert, obtained part of the lands of Branxholm, whose castle is still the seat of his senior descendant. Robert's son, Sir Walter of Branxholm, obtained the remainder of those lands after he had helped to suppress the Douglas family in 1455. Branxholm was erected into a barony in 1488, in the time of Sir Walter's son David, lord of Buccleuch.

David's great-grandson Sir Walter of Buccleuch was knighted at Flodden, but when the baby Mary, Queen of Scots became sovereign he appears to have formed the disreputable plan to kidnap her and hand her over to Henry VIII. The Duke of Suffolk reported: Buccleuch's offer to deliver the young Queen seems an unlikely matter and not with the King's honour to be practised in such sort.' Scott was appointed Warden of the Middle Marches, fought at Pinkie in 1547, married the widow of George Turnbull of Bedrule amongst a succession of wives, and was murdered in Edinburgh High Street in 1552. He was succeeded by his grandson Sir Walter, described as 'a man of rare qualities', whose son of the same name carried on a predatory war against the English and rescued the Armstrong leader Kinmont Willie from Carlisle when he was imprisoned there. In 1606 he was created 1st Lord Scott of Buccleuch, and his son was made Earl of Buccleuch in 1619. But after the 2nd Earl died in 1651 his daughter Anne became his sole heiress. She married the Duke of Monmouth, eldest bastard son of Charles II. He was created Duke of Buccleuch, a title which survived his attainder and execution. The 3rd Duke became 5th Duke of Queensberry, inheriting the Douglas palace of Drumlanrig, and added to his colossal fortune by marrying the heiress of the Duke of Montagu.

Sir Richard le Scot who died in 1320 possessed a junior grandson, Walter of Synton. The Synton line became extinct in 1721, but it had produced the cadet branch of Harden in 1535, to which Auld Wat was served heir in 1563. He married Mary Scott, 'the flower of Yarrow', and from this pair two remarkable branches sprang. In 1677 Walter of Harden married Helen Hepburne, and their descendant married Diana, Baroness Polwarth in 1754. The Hepburne-Scotts of Polwarth thus retain their descent in the male line.

The 8th Lord Polwarth married a grand-daughter of the Earl of Aberdeen who became Prime Minister, and whose whole life proclaimed the strength of his social conscience. Their son, the 9th Lord Polwarth, married a great-grand-daughter of Sir Thomas Fowell Buxton, the philanthropist upon whom Wilberforce had laid his mantle in the House of Commons. Such was the family background of one of Scotland's most outstanding humanitarians and prison reformers. His grandsons are the theological Professor Robin Barbour of Aberdeen University and Lord Polwarth, Minister of State for Scotland.

Greatest of all the Harden branch was Sir Walter Scott (1771–1832), 1st baronet of Abbotsford. Beginning as a student of historical documents and a collector of the oral tradition of the Borders, he became first Britain's most popular poet, then Europe's most influential novelist. He made his country a place of pilgrimage from all parts of the world, and when the publishing firm with which he was associated went bankrupt, he chronicled the tragedy of his career in a diary which is perhaps the supreme masterpiece of all his prolific writings.

'I see before me a long, tedious and dark path, but it leads to stainless reputation. If I die in the harrows, as is very likely, I shall die in honour.' Thus Scott wrote himself into the grave to honour his obligations.

Seton

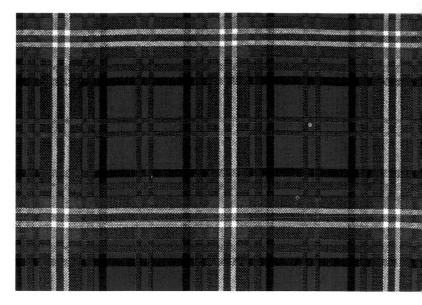

The village of Sai near Exmes in Normandy had given its name to Seton in Scotland by the time Alexander of Seton witnessed a charter of David I in about 1150. John of Seton appears as a witness to an Annandale charter early in the following century. At the end of the century the name perished heroically in circumstances that remind us how fortuitous was the survival of the dynasties of Bruce and Stewart. For Sir Christopher, son of Sir Alexander of Seton, married the Bruce's sister Christina. He was present at the coronation which took place at Scone in March 1306, and saved the new King's life when he was unhorsed at Methven in June. But he was captured, taken to London, and there hanged, drawn and quartered.

From a doubtful genealogy Sir Alexander of Seton emerges as Governor of Berwick between 1328 and 1333, and Lord of Seton. He was succeeded by his grand-daughter Margaret Seton, who married Alan of Winton in about 1347. Their son was Sir William of Seton from whom descended George, created 1st Lord Seton in 1449. Meanwhile Alexander, second son of Sir William of Seton, married Elizabeth, heiress of Sir Adam Gordon. Their son Sir Alexander became 1st Earl of Huntly and died in 1470, having founded the house which also acquired the earldom of Sutherland and kept the surname of Gordon in both titles.

George, 5th Lord Seton supported Queen Mary of Lorraine against the Lords of the Congegation and was appointed Master of the

Household when her daughter Mary, Queen of Scots returned to her kingdom. Mary and Bothwell spent some days at Seton after Darnley's murder, and here their marriage contract was signed. Lord Seton was one of those who waited for Mary on the banks of Loch Leven when she escaped from captivity in 1568, and he fled to Flanders after the defeat of Langside. Here he drove a four-horse waggon for his livelihood, and remained active on Mary's behalf until his death in 1583. It is noteworthy that James VI showed great favour to the sons of this man who had shown such loyalty to his mother and grandmother. The eldest was created 1st Earl of Winton, while another was appointed Chancellor of Scotland in 1606 and created 1st Earl of Dunfermline. The 4th Earl of Dunfermline was forfeited after the Revolution of 1688 but his younger brother William founded the junior branch which produced Lord Pitmedden the judge (?1639–1719). The life-peerage died with him, but he was created a baronet. Evidently he had a taste for the macabre, for he contributed a *Treatise of Mutilation and Demembration and their Punishments* to the 1699 edition of Sir George MacKenzie's *Laws and Customs*.

The family has been copiously served by its own historians. There is George Seton, whose *A History of the Family of Seton during eight Centuries*, published in 1896, was amplified (where amplification was not easy) by Robert Seton in *An Old Family, or The Setons of Scotland and America* in 1899. More succinctly, the loyalty of the 5th Lord to Queen Mary is commemorated by the inclusion of Mary Seton in the song of the Queen's Maries.

Shaw

This name may derive from two entirely different sources. The Middle Irish *Sidheach,* meaning a wolf, gave rise to the old Gaelic personal name *Sithech.* It was first recorded in one of the Gaelic marginal entries of the Book of Deer, written in the 12th century. In about 1178 a Culdee (*Céli Dé*) of Muthill in Perthshire, called *Sitheach,* witnessed a charter of the Bishop of Dunblane. Between 1455 and 1469 there occur several references to three individuals acting as royal couriers. The corrupt forms in which their names are recorded, such as Scheo, Schetho and Schethoc, mark the transition to the clan name Shaw which finally emerges in the Clan Chattan confederation. There are others. In 1234 *'Fercardus filius Sethi'* witnessed an agreement, and elsewhere he was called *'Fercardus senescallus de Badenoch'.* A charter of Alexander of Islay, Earl of Ross, mentioned *'Scayth filius Ferchardi'* in 1338.

James Shaw of Rothiemurchus was killed at the battle of Harlaw in 1411 and his son Alasdair had to recover his patrimony from the Comyns, which he had succeeded in doing by 1464. But although the Shaws were still a significant element of Clan Chattan by the time of the Jacobite rebellions, they had lost their hold on Rothiemurchus long before then, and had scattered widely throughout the Highlands.

Shaw

There was a farmer in Rothiemurchus in the 17th century called Donald Shaw, who produced a son, Lachlan, in 1692. Lachlan became schoolmaster in Abernethy before taking a charge as minister first at Kingussie, then Cawdor, then in Elgin, where he died in 1777. In the course of his long lifetime he made himself the outstanding local historian of Moray, and published studies of uncommon value.

The other source of the name is a Lowland placename of the south-west. In 1284 John 'de Schau' witnessed a document which bestowed lands on the monks of Paisley, and there are several similar examples of this kind. In 1296 various men of Shaw in Lanarkshire rendered homage at the time of the Ragman Roll. In 1331, on the other side of Lowland Scotland, a John of Shaw became a burgess of Dundee. Among the many Shaws of Ayrshire the remarkable sons of Charles Shaw, clerk of the county of Ayr, deserve mention. One was John (1792–1827) the brilliant and short-lived surgeon and anatomist. Alexander, his younger brother, also became a surgeon and was the author of respectable medical treatises. Patrick composed Scottish law reports of considerable usefulness, while Sir Charles was knighted as a general, but fell below the family standard in his rambling and egotistical memoirs. At the time when Lachlan Shaw, of entirely different origins, was a minister in Elgin, the grandfather of these men became Moderator of the General Assembly in 1775, and earned his place in the poetry of Burns.

Sinclair

The name derives from Saint-Clair-sur-Elle in Normandy, and was established in Scotland when Henry de St Clair was granted lands in Lothian in 1162. His descendant Sir William became guardian to Alexander III's heir and was granted the barony of Rosslyn in 1280. Alexander's heir died; the King himself fell over a cliff and was killed in 1286; his infant grandchild, the Maid of Norway, perished during the sea journey to her kingdom. When Robert Bruce finally restored the independence of the kingdom at Bannockburn, Sir Henry Sinclair of Rosslyn fought with him upon that field.

It was Sir Henry's son who married Isabel, co-heiress of the earldom of Orkney, and their son who became premier Earl of Norway by right of his inheritance. It altogether eclipsed Sinclair's status in the Scottish Lowlands. The Orkney dynasty descended from the noble house of Møre in Norway, and had intermarried with the royal house of Scotland. Thorfinn the Mighty belonged to its dynasty, and the builders of Kirkwall Cathedral. In 1379 this became Henry Sinclair's inheritance. His grandson William was the last Norwegian earl, and in 1455 he became the first to hold Caithness as a Scottish earldom. It was also he who rivalled his ancestors by building that other wonder of Scottish mediaeval architecture, Rosslyn Chapel.

Nothing could present a greater contrast than the castle which the earls of Caithness built for themselves a mile north of Wick. The fortress of Girnigo is perched on a precipitous rock promontory, approached by a narrow causeway. It appears impregnable, and it needed to be, because by the 16th century the predatory Gordons had penetrated to the far north. Here the 5th Earl of Caithness (1566–1643) fought his long rearguard action against them until he was forced to flee, leaving Girnigo and all its muniments to that destroyer and fabricator of historical evidence, Sir Robert Gordon of Gordonstoun. In happier days the Earl had built a more modern mansion opposite Girnigo; inspired, perhaps, by the Stewart palace of Kirkwall that he had captured on the King's instructions. At any rate, he was the first to leave his comment on this fine example of Scottish renaissance building. 'I assure your lordship it is one of the greatest houses in Britain,' he wrote in his elegant hand. His own castles were to share its fate, though the Gordons failed to get possession of his earldom. The ruins of Girnigo belong still to the 20th Sinclair Earl.

The Sinclair connection with Norway ended dramatically. In 1607 James VI permitted his subjects to serve as mercenary soldiers in Sweden. One of those who raised a contingent in Caithness was Colonel George Sinclair, and in 1612 he attempted to reach Sweden by the shortest route, sailing to Norway and marching his men through Gudbrandsdal. But while his men passed through the narrow defiles, Norwegian peasants waited above with rocks and stones, which they released in an avalanche upon the Scottish soldiers. A monument still marks the spot where they perished, 'smashed to pieces like potters' vessels by the country people', as the inscription runs. It is the subject of a Norwegian ballad, and of the dance tune that Grieg used with such dramatic effect in one of his suites.

Since then it is the Sinclairs of Ulbster who have given greatest distinction to the name—an illegitimate branch descending from the 4th Earl. Sir John of Ulbster (1754–1835) was one of the most advanced pioneers of scientific agriculture in British history. It was he who influenced William Pitt to set up the first Board of Agriculture, with himself as President.

Skene

According to tradition, the Skenes are an exceptionally early sept of Clan *Donnchaidh*, long before it adopted the name of Robertson. One of the most widespread of legends (compare those of the Armstrongs, Campbells and Turnbulls) tells how a younger son of the chief saved the life of the king by killing a wolf with his knife. The event is placed in the 11th century. It is scarcely likely to relate to Malcolm Canmore, for the men of Atholl would probably have knifed him rather than the wolf. The two previous sovereigns were Macbeth and his stepson Lulach, the last truly Celtic kings ruling in the old Scotland beyond the Forth. This was before the introduction of heraldry: which throws a confusing light on the legend. For the Gaelic for a knife is *Sgian*, which is said to be the original form of Skene, while its coat-of-arms shows three wolves' heads impaled on dirks such as the one

Skene

said to have saved the king's life. On the other hand, the Robertson arms contain three wolves' heads without the dirks, as though the wolf was already the pre-heraldic emblem of Clan *Donnchaidh*.

The Skenes were said to have been rewarded with the lands in Aberdeenshire named after them, rather than the other way round. Here, at any rate, southern governments found them when John and Patrick of Skene submitted to Edward I of England in 1296, among the other prominent men of the kingdom. After that, Skenes appear on all the right battlefields. Adam of Skene was killed at nearby Harlaw in 1411, Alexander at Flodden in 1513, and his grandson Alexander at Pinkie in 1547. James Skene of Skene suffered in Charles I's cause.

The most outstanding literary figure of this name was William Forbes Skene, appointed Historiographer Royal for Scotland in 1881.

Smith

Between the 1715 and 1745 rebellions, an English official called Burt wrote from the Highlands, describing the process which so greatly increased the number of Smiths there. He referred to Glengarry. 'Some few years ago, a company of Liverpool merchants contracted with the chieftain of this tribe, at a great advantage to him, for the use of his woods and other conveniences for the smelting of iron; and soon after, they put their project in execution, by building of furnaces, sending ore from Lancashire, etc.' The decimation of English forests for this most wasteful of purposes had been forbidden, and so the Highlands were stripped instead, and the scanty soil of their hills exposed to galloping erosion. Burt described the strife between competitive Smiths, resulting in a murder followed by a public hanging of the culprit.

Of course, the profession is as ancient as the skill of the Celtic iron-workers who swept across Europe and colonised Britain before Caesar's invasion. Margaret Fay Shaw recorded a Gaelic ballad of the Smiths in her *Folksongs and Folklore of South Uist*. With its fusion of Ossianic and old Norse themes, it remained one of the most popular in the entertainer's repertoire. One name for a smith is *Ceàrd*, and to this day people refer to vagrants as 'Ceàrdan', after the travelling tin-smiths, often descendants of broken clans, who used to travel the Highlands, mending pots and pans. But the Smithy Ballad *(Duan na Ceàrdaich)* also calls the smith *Gobhainn*, and with his long tradition of hereditary professions the Gaelic Smith signs himself *Mac a'Ghobhainn*.

The island of Lewis, that last bastion of Scottish Gaelic culture, has naturally produced distinguished Sons of Smiths to this day. John Angus Smith, wartime naval commander, distinguished educationalist, Vice-Principal of Jordanhill College since 1956, belongs to Lochs, although he was born in North Uist and reared in Mull. Iain Mac a'Ghobhainn, the most distinguished poet and author of this name in Scottish history, was born at Bayble in Lewis. In 1965 his collection of Gaelic poetry *Biobuill is Sanasan-Reice* was published, while he has issued three volumes of short stories, *An Dubh is an Gorm, Burn is Aran* and *Maighstearan is Ministearan*. Amongst his English poetry, 'Deer on the High Hill' was received with particular acclaim. Under the English form of his name, Iain Crichton Smith, he has also published several novels and short stories.

He has himself published a translation of the Gaelic poem in which he expresses the stresses of his bilingual heritage. 'In the dress of the fool, the two colours that have tormented me—English and Gaelic, black and red, the court of injustice, the reason for my anger, and that fine rain from the mountains and these grievous storms from my mind streaming the two colours together so that I will go with poor sight in the one colour that is so odd that the King himself will not understand my conversation.' The poem does not use the word *Breacan*: the colours of the tartan have run.

Another poet of this name presents a rare example of quite different origins. In contrast to those Scots who have earned distinction after emigrating abroad, Sydney Goodsir Smith was born in Wellington, New Zealand, and came to Scotland to become a leading poet using the Lowland Scots tongue. His *Skail Wind* was published in 1941, *Figs and Thistles* in 1959, and *Carotid Cornucopius* in 1964.

Stewart (Royal)

Royal Stewart

The 16th-century Scottish historian, Boece, gave the Stewart kings a mythical ancestor of the ancient house of Kenneth Mac Alpin called Banquo, whom Shakespeare was careful to include in 'Macbeth' for the satisfaction of the first Stewart king to occupy the English throne, James VI. Today those who attach a sentimental importance to a Celtic origin for the Stewarts have the equal satisfaction of knowing that they came from just beyond the borders of Normandy, and descended from a Breton named Flaald. Their town of Dol, with its beautiful Norman Cathedral, still commemorates the illustrious and ill-fated dynasty to which it gave birth.

But Flaald apart, the ancestors of the Stewarts moved towards their goal like any other Anglo-Norman family, acquiring estates in England after the Conquest, and moving to Scotland with David I. Here they received the hereditary court appointment of High Steward, and Walter the 6th High Steward married the daughter of King Robert Bruce. When his only son David II died childless, his grandson Robert Stewart succeeded as Robert II. This king left at least twenty-one children, of whom his grandson James I wiped out the most senior representatives as soon as he had the opportunity. The curious result was that for a long period of Scottish history there was no near heir to the Stewart king (who was frequently a minor) while there was an ever-increasing number of collatoral descendants of royal Stewart blood. In the circumstances it is noteworthy that the Scottish

(*Above*) Dress Stewart; (*below*) Hunting Stewart

Stewart of Atholl

crown never passed from its rightful owner to be tossed amongst them, as in the English Wars of the Roses or the Tudor usurpation. In fact it was not until the English had been given a dominant interest by the Union of Crowns that the Stewart succession was first interrupted, then destroyed.

Almost every Stewart sovereign remains to this day a subject of lively controversy. What ought to be beyond dispute is their failure to integrate the Gaelic half of their kingdom with the Lowland half from where they ruled it. For the most part they treated its peoples with an incompetence and a savagery that does little credit to their supposed Celtic origins. Only when the Stewarts had been rejected by their English-speaking subjects did they fall back on the Gaels for support—and thus complete the ruin of both.

Stewart of Atholl

The province of Atholl became one of the most prolific areas of Stewart settlement. In 1822 that devoted Athollman, General David Stewart of Garth, explained how this had occurred. 'James Stewart, son of Alexander Stewart, Earl of Buchan and Badenoch, commonly called the Wolf of Badenoch, second son of Robert II, first of the Stewarts, is said to have built the Castle of Garth, and settled there some time after the year 1390. There are now living in the district of Atholl, within its ancient boundary, 1937 persons of the name of Stewart, descendants of this man in the male line, besides numbers in other parts of the kingdom. The descendants in the female line are considerably more numerous, as few women leave the country, in proportion to the number of men who enter the army and resort to different parts of the world. We have thus upwards of 4000 persons now living in one district, descended of this individual.'

After the murder of James I in 1437, his widow remarried the Black Knight of Lorne, who descended from the 4th High Steward, before his family had inherited the crown. The widowed Queen gave birth to Sir John Stewart of Balveny, and his half-brother, James II, bestowed on him the earldom of Atholl, which had previously been held by several royal Stewarts. Early in the 17th century the earldom passed with an heiress to the Murrays, but by this time several other dynasties had been planted there, beside that of Garth. There were the Steuarts of Cardney, descendants of another illegitimate son of Robert II, and those of Ballechin, founded by a natural son of James II. The seat of the principal chief was Blair Castle, the last in Britain to be subjected to a siege, and still intact with its treasures. But the centre of jurisdiction at nearby Logierait was dismantled after the abolition of the feudal jurisdictions in the aftermath of Culloden, as Stewart of Garth recorded. 'The hall in which the feudal Parliament assembled (a noble chamber of better proportions than the British House of Commons) has been pulled down, and one of the most conspicuous vestiges of the almost regal influences of this powerful family has thus been destroyed.' As Stewart went on to describe, it was the clansmen themselves who were the next to be swept away, through-out much of the Highlands.

Stewart of Appin

One of the branches of the Stewarts that became most completely integrated in the affairs of the Gaelic west was that of Appin. They obtained their footing there in the first place by marriage. Sir John Stewart of Bonkyl was the younger son of the 4th High Steward from whom the Black Knight of Lorne descended. Sir John had a younger son Sir James who was killed at Halidon Hill in 1333, and who in turn left a younger son Sir Robert. It was Sir Robert's son who married the heiress of the Lord of Lorne, and their son who consequently succeeded as the first Stewart Lord of Lorne. The next heir was understandably murdered by the dispossessed MacDougalls in 1463, and it was the son of the murdered man, Dugald, who became the first Stewart of Appin.

This junior cadet branch of the royal house was soon plunged into Highland affairs when Duncan, 2nd Stewart of Appin, was appointed Chamberlain of the Isles by James IV. It was he who built Castle Stalker on the Cormorant's Rock in Loch Linnhe, whence the

Stewart of Appin

rallying cry of the Stewarts of Appin, *Creag an Sgairbh* – Cormorant's Rock. We know that James IV was twice in the western Highlands during 1493, and three times during the next couple of years, and it may well have been at this very castle that he forfeited the Lordship of the Isles. In Gaelic it means Hunter's Castle, and traditionally it was built as a seat for royal hunting and fowling expeditions. Seen from Appin, with the mountains of Mull and Morvern in the background, this castle in the Loch is one of Scotland's finest sights, and fortunately it is at present being most faithfully restored.

The Stewarts of Appin and Ardsheal fought under Montrose at Inverlochy in 1645; and at Sheriffmuir in 1715. They remained Jacobite in 1745, and it was in the aftermath that the famous Appin murder occurred, immortalised by Robert Louis Stevenson in *Kidnapped*. Colin Campbell of Glenure was one of the factors administering the forfeited estate when he was shot near Ballachulish in Appin in 1752. Allan Breck Stewart, the suspect, made his escape. But James Stewart, a half-brother of the chief, was carried before an all-Campbell jury at Inveraray presided over by Argyll himself, convicted and hanged. A cairn still marks the place of his execution. The wheel had turned full circle for the clan which had supplanted the MacDougalls of Lorne.

Sutherland

By the opening of the 10th century the Norsemen had conquered all the offshore islands of Scotland. The Orkney earls married into the Scottish royal house, and by the 11th century Earl Thorfinn the Mighty ruled territories that included the Caithness peninsula and an extensive coastal area to its south which was called Sudurland, or Southland. It extended into Ross-shire, whose county town is called Dingwall, the name the Scandinavians gave to their legislative assembly places. It was somewhere near here that Thorfinn defeated his cousin King Duncan, and chased him south into Macbeth's realm of Moray, where Duncan was murdered.

Early in the 13th century Sutherland was erected into a Scottish earldom, and granted to a nobleman of Moray whose family was probably of Flemish origin, though it had married into the royal house of Moray. A Sutherland clan evolved, with a Chief powerful enough to protect the most northerly cathedral on the mainland, at Dornoch. Only a very small portion of its mediaeval structure survives in the 19th-century church which stands on the same site; and the earldom itself fared little better. For the 14th and 15th centuries were a period of baronial anarchy in Scotland, with the crown in eclipse under weak kings or during the reigns of minors. The Gordons were invested with vice-regal powers in the north, and used these to seize the Sutherland earldom. The Earl of Huntly's second son, Adam Gordon, obtained in 1494 a 'brieve of idiocy' against Earl John of Sutherland, although he had possessed the wit to maintain himself in this office through troubled times for nearly forty years. Adam Gordon married the Earl's daughter in about 1500. He brought a further charge of idiocy against Earl John's elder son, and a false charge of bastardy against his younger son. The death of King James IV at Flodden in 1513, with the flower of Scotland's nobility, made it easier for the Gordons to consummate their crimes. Adam Gordon called himself Earl of Sutherland without ever obtaining a title from the crown, murdered one of Earl John's sons, and terrorised the Sutherland heirs so that they did not dare to advance their claims. In 1601 Adam Gordon's descendant obtained a remarkable grant from James VI which provided that the earldom should never be lost to the Gordons through an heiress. If the line of Adam Gordon should fail, it would pass to the Gordons of Huntly who had no claim to it by descent.

This stipulation led to a legal battle for the earldom when the Earl died in 1766, leaving an only daughter. The nearest Gordon heir claimed that he was the true Earl according to the charter of 1601. But the House of Lords, sitting as supreme court of appeal, was shewn that there had been an heir male in 1515 when Adam Gordon usurped the earldom, and his Sutherland descendant was there to enquire how many centuries were required to legalise Gordon crimes. Their lordships responded by bestowing the earldom on the late Earl's daughter, who carried it to her husband, a member of the fabulously wealthy English family of Leveson-Gower, who was created 1st Duke of Sutherland.

Meanwhile the Sutherlands of Forse continue to represent the disinherited line of the old Sutherland chiefs. They descend in the direct male line from Kenneth, second son of the 6th Earl. Another interesting branch of this stock were the descendants of Nicholas, second son of the 4th Earl. He settled at Duffus in Moray under a charter of David II in 1365, and although the castles of his descendants at Spynie and Duffus were battered by the Gordons, they survived into Jacobite times. But Kenneth Sutherland, Lord Duffus, joined the 1715 rising and his estates were forfeited. He fled abroad, became an Admiral in the Russian navy, and married a Swedish noblewoman. Although the Duffus estates were restored to his grandson, his line is now extinct. But he enjoys an accidental immortality because his portrait in the Scottish National Portrait Gallery is one of the earliest and most interesting of a nobleman wearing the kilt.

Thomson

The Sons of Thomas use a wide range of surnames, all of them corruptions of the Gaelic original *Mac Thómais*. They include Mac-Thomas, MacCombie, MacCombe and MacComie. In the Council of Scottish Chiefs there sits the Chief of a Clan MacThomas.

A branch of this name belonged to the Clan Chattan confederation of which Mackintosh was the principal. Living in Glenshee and Glenisla, sufficiently close to the frontiers of the Gaelic-speaking world, it is perhaps not surprising that their name should have suffered corruption, like Gow, another Clan Chattan name. But Thomsons who moved into a wholly Gaelic milieu have naturally used this correct English form in an English context, and the proper Gaelic form in a Gaelic context: just as a Smith in similar circumstances would not use Gow, but either *Mac a'Ghobhainn* or its English equivalent.

A distinguished instance of this is that of James Thomson, who went to the island of Lewis shortly before the Forty-Five, and who was described as a schoolmaster when he acted as witness to a document in 1749, written by the minister of Barvas. His namesake James Thomson was also a schoolmaster in Lewis in the present century; and he is the first notable poet of this name, and the father of the poet *Ruaraidh MacThómais*. The published collections of the latter include *An Dealbh Briste* (1951), *Eadar Samhradh is Foghar* (1967), and *An Rathad Cian* (1970). In English, their author is Derick S

Thomson, Professor of Celtic at the University of Glasgow, and editor of the Gaelic quarterly, *Gairm*. His massive services to scholarship have included collaboration with Dr John Lorne Campbell in editing the Lhuyd manuscripts.

In 1964 Sir Roy Thomson, the proprietor of newspapers throughout the world, was created 1st Lord Thomson of Fleet. One of the supporters to his coat-of-arms is described as a shepherd 'wearing a kilt of the usual tartan proper to Thomson of that Ilk and his dependers.' While there are examples of family tartan being included in a heraldic blazon in this way, it does not lie within the jurisdiction of the Lord Lyon of Scotland to bestow a tartan upon a family, neither has this ever been connected with heraldry in the historical past.

Turnbull

One of the valleys that runs north out of the Cheviots into Teviotdale carries Rule water to its parent river. It is one of those pockets in which the most ancient stock of any country might survive, taking in the new blood of successive immigrants or conquerors, yet retaining an original identity. Bedrule lies in the recesses of hills that had once divided the Welsh-speaking kingdom of Gododdin from English Northumbria, and later formed the debateable land between Scotland and England. It is the original cradle of a tribe called the Turnbulls.

The earliest record of them appears in the time of the Anglo-Norman Kings of Scots. A Richard de Rullos is named there in 1130: a Gilbertus de Behulle in 1248. The district itself is called Terra de Rul in 1266. But it seems unlikely that its inhabitants descend from one of the Anglo-Norman families whom the Scottish Kings brought from England or France. The name Turnbull, and its legendary origin, suggest quite different affinities. Hector Boece related this legend as historical fact in 1526, in his account of the manner in which a man named Roull saved the life of King Robert Bruce in the forest of Callander, from a wild boar or bull. 'After the beast felt himself sore wounded, he rushed upon the King who, having no weapon in his hand, had surely perished if help had not come. Howbeit, one came running unto him who overthrew the bull by plain force, and held him down until the hunters came who killed him outright. For this valiant act the King endowed the aforesaid party with great possessions, and his lineage to this day is called of the Turnbull.'

Had this been historical fact, it would provide supporting evidence that Robert I had planted a Turnbull in Bedrule in the same way as he planted a Burnett at Banchory, for services rendered. But in addition to the negative evidence, there is the positive presence of a William 'dicto Turnbull' in records earlier than Bruce's reign. In any case, the heroic progenitor of the tribe who slays a dangerous wild beast belongs to the stock-in-trade of Celtic legend. The MacLeods have a version of it, and the oldest one of all in Scotland was brought among the

Ossianic tales from Ireland. In this one, Diarmaid, legendary progenitor of Clan Campbell, kills the wild boar in Gaelic ballad and folk tale. The principal difference between the Campbell and MacLeod versions on the one hand and the Turnbull one on the other is that of language. The Welsh of the Gododdin epic—Scotland's earliest poem—had given way to English over a thousand years before the poet of the Turnbull country, John Leyden, wrote in 1801:

> His arms robust the hardy hunter flung
> Around his bending horns, and upward wrung,
> With writhing force his neck retorted round,
> And rolled the panting monster to the ground,
> Crushed, with enormous strength, his bony skull;
> And courtiers hailed the man who *turned the bull*.

Leyden has identified the beast as a bison a few lines earlier. But it is a bull's head that is incorporated into the coat-of-arms of Turnbull, as of MacLeod, while the Campbell heraldry contains a boar's head. But heraldry was a form of military identification introduced into Scotland from about the 12th century, with all the other kit of the Norman feudal system. It made use of the emblems of an older society, as well as introducing those of the newcomers. The three bulls' heads of Turnbull (variously adorned in later matriculations) appear to belong to a pre-heraldic, Celtic past like the legend that accounts for them. But they were displayed in many a Border battle, and notably at the defeat of Halidon Hill in 1333, when a Turnbull knight challenged any one of the enemy to single combat.

By the time of John Leyden the poet (1775—1811), the Turnbull country stood on the threshold of the industrial revolution. He was born in the village of Denholm near the junction of Rule water and the Teviot, and joined Sir Walter Scott in collecting their *Minstrelsy of the Scottish Border*, that monument to a vanishing way of life and its traditions. The greater part of Denholm was owned at this time by John Turnbull (1735—1816), whose wife was Jane Leyden; and the lives of their descendants illustrate the great dispersal that was about to take place in the rural Scotland of the clans. Their son Joshua (1785—1828) became a lawyer in Glasgow, where he died leaving an only son Thomas, aged four. Thomas Turnbull (1824—1908) qualified as an architect, married a Scottish wife, and then emigrated. He settled first in San Francisco in the turbulent days that Stevenson depicted in *The Wreckers*. There he built a number of churches and other public buildings before moving on to New Zealand in the latter days of the Maori wars. His earthquake-resistant buildings in Wellington all withstood the 1942 earthquakes there. But he was not the only Scot of his name among the immigrants there, and his own descendants have multiplied until the name is probably commoner in the antipodes today than in Bedrule.

When Thomas Turnbull died, a monument of Aberdeen granite was brought all the way from Scotland to commemorate him, while another of his name founded New Zealand's Alexander Turnbull Library in Wellington.

Urquhart

Like the neighbouring name Munro, Urquhart is considered to be of Gaelic origin, and various topographical derivations have been attempted for it. The locality called Urquhart lies on the north side of the Great Glen, where woods descend steeply to a promontory that dominates the eastern end of Loch Ness. It was the obvious place to build a fortress guarding old Pictland from the Gaelic west. The great mediaeval stone castle of Urquhart that was erected on this promontory has one of the most spectacular settings in Scotland.

It stood within the vast sphere of influence of the Comyn family. When Robert Bruce won the crown and destroyed the Comyn power in the north it was natural that he should have built up the authority of his supporters there. William of Urquhart became during his reign Sheriff of Cromarty, the fertile peninsula beyond Inverness which is called the Black Isle because the snow will not lie there when the hills beyond are white. In 1357 David II granted the hereditary sheriffdom of Cromarty to Adam of Urquhart, William's son, and so this dynasty was established. In 1470 William Urquhart of Cromarty built there a castle of the characteristically Scottish tower form.

His successor, Sir Thomas Urquhart (1582–1642), became something of a favourite of James VI, sharing with him a love of learned pursuits. Sir Thomas was also a spendthrift, though his son explained piously: 'too strict adherance to the austerest principles of veracity proved oftentimes damageable to him in his negotiations with many cunning sharks, who knew with what profitable odds they could screw themselves in upon the windings of so good a nature.' This son inherited his father's name and erudition. He attended Aberdeen University during its golden age, and also fell under the spell of his great-uncle John, of whom he wrote: 'he was over all Britain renowned for his deep reach of natural wit, and great dexterity in acquiring of many lands and great possessions, with all men's applause.'

Such was the background of Sir Thomas Urquhart (1611–1660), surely the most eccentric genius in Scottish history. From university he went on the grand tour of Europe, where he collected a library of books for his ancestral tower. He supported Charles I in the Civil War, and fought for Charles II when he was routed by Cromwell at Worcester in 1651. Unfortunately he had brought all his writings with him in four trunks filled with manuscripts. While Urquhart was taken prisoner English soldiers ransacked his lodgings, where his papers were discovered. 'The soldiers merely scattered them over the floor; but reflecting after they had left the chamber on the many uses to which they might be applied, they returned and bore them out into the street.' While the greater part of his work on a universal language and on the genealogy of the Urquharts was used to light soldiers' pipes, and for an even less savoury purpose, Sir Thomas was carried a prisoner to the Tower of London. Here in 1653 he published the first book of Rabelais, one of the world's supreme masterpieces of translation. In 1660 he died, not yet fifty years old: according to tradition, what killed him was a fit of Rabelaisian laughter when he was informed of the Restoration of the King. His last draft of Rabelais was published after his death.

His line was extinguished, the Cromarty properties sold, the ancestral tower demolished. But the chiefship of Urquhart was kept alive by the descendants of Sir Thomas's ingenious great-uncle John. In 1766 George Urquhart (c. 1733–1799) went to Florida, and his son David settled in New Orleans. His descendant Kenneth Urquhart of Urquhart (b. 1932), a historian, lives still in Louisiana.

Wallace

The term 'Welsh' appeared in the earlier English form of Weallise and the mediaeval form Wallensis, and was applied to the British peoples from Strathclyde in Scotland to Brittany in France who spoke that branch of the Celtic family of languages now represented by Breton and Welsh. In the 12th century the Kings of Scots were still addressing their subjects as distinct ethnic groups: French and English, Scots and Welsh. Hence the surnames Inglis, Scott and Wallace. The ancient capital of Strathclyde is still remembered as Dumbarton, the Fortress of the Britons.

In the second half of the 12th century a man called Richard, defined as a Wallace, obtained lands in Ayrshire, which belongs to the former kingdom of Strathclyde. His property was called Richardston, now Riccarton; and his great-grandson, Sir Malcolm Wallace, received the lands of Elderslie in Renfrewshire. Such was the background of Malcolm's son William, who was to evoke a national spirit which united so many disparate peoples and to earn his place as Scotland's greatest patriot.

Sir William Wallace of Elderslie was born between 1274 and 1276. In 1286 Alexander III, King of Scots died, leaving his grand-daughter the Maid of Norway as his sole descendant. When the Maid died in 1290 the direct line of the kings of Scots was extinct, and the crown was in dispute between collatoral claimants, all of whom were subjects of Edward I of England. He was invited to adjudicate between them and at once revived the claim of his predecessors to be Lord Paramount of the kingdom of Scotland. He then selected the rightful heir, John Balliol; but treated him with such ignominy as a vassal king that King John was finally provoked into resistance. Thereupon Edward invaded Scotland, carried John Balliol off to the Tower of London, and subjugated his kingdom.

It was now that Wallace emerged as a guerilla leader of indomitable courage and skill. One of the English captains reported in 1297 that Wallace was 'lying with a large company in the forest of Selkirk'. A force moved north to destroy him, and the same summer Wallace routed it at Stirling Bridge. Stirling Castle, the key to the kingdom, surrendered to him and in a few weeks the Scots were invading England itself. Wallace and his associate Sir Andrew of Moray were able to write to foreign countries on behalf of 'the community of the realm', to inform them that they could now resume trade 'because the Kingdom of Scotland, thanks be to God, has been recovered by war from the power of the English.'

In fact the war of independence continued for many years longer before it was won. In 1304 Wallace himself was betrayed to the English and executed in London with extreme cruelty. But he had sown the seeds of patriotism as none of his nation had done before him, and those who have garnered the harvest have raised him to the place of highest honour.

Although he left no known descendants, there are many fortunate enough to bear his name who can trace their descent from the same house of Riccarton from which he sprang.

Wemyss

This name is a corruption of the Gaelic *Uamh*, meaning a cave. Below the ruins known as Macduff's Castle, on the coast of Fife, are caves containing Pictish drawings; and these in all probability gave rise to the local place-name Wemyss. It became the surname of a cadet branch of the royal house of Duff, descendants of Gillemichael, who was Earl of Fife early in the 12th century. When senior male lines failed, that of Wemyss became Chief of Scotland's senior clan, although it never reverted to the patronymic of MacDuff.

Sir Michael of Wemyss ensured the family's future prosperity by

Wemyss

supporting the cause of Robert Bruce. Thereafter the name multiplied in many branches. Its senior line rose to the peerage in the reign of Charles I, and again survived the hazards of the century of revolution and counter-revolution to emerge in the 18th century as the senior representatives of the ancient earldom of Fife. But they held the earldom of Wemyss, and after the Forty-Five even the surname of the Chiefs of Clan MacDuff was changed again. The Earl's eldest son Lord Elcho supported Prince Charles Edward, and after his attainder his younger brother was invested with his titles. But this earl adopted the name of Charteris when he fell heir to the fortune of his maternal grandfather.

While Charteris remains the name of the earls of Wemyss to this day, despite their descent in the male line from the house of Duff, the chiefship of Clan MacDuff passed to the descendants of a younger son of the 5th Earl who have not changed their name. It is they who live in the Castle of Wemyss which was built early in the 15th century to replace the older stronghold, and enjoy with the chiefship the title of Wemyss of Wemyss.

The 12th Earl of Wemyss and 8th Earl of March (b. 1912) is Chief of the name of Charteris. He is President of the National Trust for Scotland, while his brother Lord Charteris is Chairman of the National Heritage Memorial Fund.

Index

Acknowledgments

The tartans illustrated in this book were photographed from samples supplied by Captain D.W.S. Buchan of Auchmacoy; Sir Iain Moncreiffe of that Ilk; the Strathmore Woollen Company Ltd, Forfar, Angus; Lochcarron Handloom Weavers, Lochcarron, Ross-shire; Lochcarron Products Ltd, Galashiels, Selkirk; and The Scotch House, Knightsbridge, London.

The clan symbols reproduced on the endpapers of the hardback edition were drawn by Rosemary Grimble.